AGAINST THE SPECTER

OF A DRAGON

Contributions in Military History

1. The River and the Rock: The History of Fortress West Point, 1775-1873
   Dave Richard Palmer

2. Dear Miss Em: General Eichelberger's War in the Pacific, 1942-1945
   Jay Luvaas, Editor

3. Schoolbooks and Krags: The United States Army in the Philippines, 1898-1902
   John Morgan Gates

4. American Gunboat Diplomacy and the Old Navy, 1877-1889
   Kenneth J. Hagan

5. The Image of the Army Officer in America: Background for Current Views
   C. Robert Kemble

6. The Memoirs of Henry Heth
   James L. Morrison, Jr., Editor

Against the Specter of a Dragon

The Campaign for American

Military Preparedness, 1914–1917

John Patrick Finnegan

Contributions in Military History, Number 7

Greenwood Press
Westport, Connecticut • London, England

Library of Congress Cataloging in Publication Data

Finnegan, John Patrick.
   Against the specter of a dragon.

   (Contributions in military history, no. 7)
   Bibliography: p.
   1.   European War, 1914-1918—United States.
2.   United States—Military policy.   I.   Title.
II.   Series.
D619.F45   355.2′12′0973   74-288
ISBN 0-8371-7376-0

Library of Congress Catalog Card Number: 74-288
ISBN: 0-8371-7376-0

First published in 1974

Greenwood Press, a division of Williamhouse-Regency Inc.
51 Riverside Avenue, Westport, Connecticut 06880

Manufactured in the United States of America

To My Mother and Father

Contents

Preface   ix

Introduction   3

1   The Most Unfit Army   5

2   The Politics of Defense   22

3   The General Staff Proposes. . . .   42

4   The Private War of General Wood   57

5   A Cold Day for the Army   73

6   War in Time of Peace   91

7   The Large Regiment   106

8   Pacifists and Jeffersonians   121

9   Congress Disposes. . . .   139

10   Summer Maneuvers   158

11   A Certain Tide To Be Reckoned With   173

12   A Pause Between Two Breaths   184

13   Conclusion   189

     Notes   197

     Bibliographical Essay   235

     Index   247

Preface

Napoleon once wrote that a constitution ought to be brief and obscure. A preface should only imitate a constitution's brevity. Many people have helped me in the preparation of this book. I would like to extend my special thanks to E. David Cronon of the University of Wisconsin, who supervised the dissertation from which the present work stemmed, and to David A. Shannon of the University of Virginia, who encouraged me to start work on this project. My former colleague at Ohio University, George C. Herring, Jr., shared with me his knowledge of the source materials. Edward M. Coffman of the University of Wisconsin generously read through the manuscript and helped speed its way to publication. I have been well served by my editors, Jay Luvaas of Allegheny College, and Colonel Tom Griess of the United States Military Academy, as well as by the staff of Greenwood Press. Of course, the book could not have been written at all without the help of the librarians and archivists at the Library of Congress, the National Archives, the Cleveland Public Library, the Wisconsin State Historical Society, and the libraries of Columbia University, Harvard University, Ohio University, Princeton University, Swarthmore College, the University of Virginia, the University of Wisconsin, and Yale University. Finally, I must acknowledge an intellectual debt to Walter Millis, whose writings first interested me in the study of American national security policy.

AGAINST THE SPECTER

OF A DRAGON

Introduction

The preparedness movement, Walter Millis has written, was "one of the most remarkable episodes in our long and generally aberrant military history." This is an apt description. The military preparedness movement (it had a naval twin) began as an outgrowth of the Progressive Era, when a little group of dedicated officers and civilian administrators attempted to reform America's small and obsolescent military establishment and bring the armed services closer to the center of American life. In the Edwardian years of peace and domestic reform, this effort had limited success. But the onset of World War I in Europe, shattering the confidence of a generation, gave the proponents of defense a chance. From modest beginnings, preparedness flowered into a huge and exotic blossom.[1]

Now the military gained the civilian allies which it needed. Panicked by the European convulsion, a good many opinion-makers of the American upper and middle classes decided that war could, after all, happen here. Out of power, elements of the Republican party, along with Theodore Roosevelt, picked up the issue of America's defenselessness. The *Lusitania* crisis in the spring of 1915 spurred the Wilson Administration into embracing the cause for both diplomatic and political reasons. By the fall of 1915, preparedness had become a popular fad and a craze, riding the progressive currents of national efficiency and individual duty. Many voices called for an American renewal through a mobilized patriotism. In some ways, preparedness had changed from a movement to reform the Army into a device to make over American society.

3

The preparedness forces were not allowed free play. Congress was under rural domination and skeptical. The Wilson Administration, while draping itself in the flag, never embraced the extremes of the movement. The Defense Act of 1916 gave the military all that it had wanted before the war, but in the supercharged atmosphere of the times, its provisions no longer seemed nearly enough. The Army and its friends demanded a total preparedness. By the end of 1916, the military preparedness movement, now evolved into a drive for a universal military training which had previously been unthinkable, had gained renewed impetus.

The striking aspect about the movement was its lack of relation to foreign policy. Preparedness did not get the United States ready to intervene in World War I—but then it was never designed to. Preparedness was almost purely defensive. Its thrust was isolationist, not interventionist, despite the personal attitudes of many supporters. In a collapsing world, America was arming against nameless dangers which would follow the end of the European War. This approach partially resulted from the origins of the movement. Without rethinking its own premises, the Army General Staff cheerfully used a war-generated hysteria to help pass the program it had designed in peacetime. Partially, it was a result of human confusion: it is sometimes easier to get people to act than to think.

Not everyone was swept up by the preparedness movement. Large segments of a more tradition-minded America remained unaffected by the military fever. At the Republican Convention of 1916, a delegate derided the campaign. There might be talk of guns and drums, the delegate said, but the United States would not long stand in fear and trembling before the "specter of a dragon."[2] This approach was not a wholly useful one. Not only were there many Americans trembling at just such specters, but the nation did stand in need of a coherent national security policy. The pity was, that in preparing to meet the nightmares of the future, the preparedness forces did not ready themselves to meet the demanding realities of the world in which they actually lived.

1

The Most
Unfit Army

The fault is not so much with our army as it is with ourselves as a nation.

—Henry L. Stimson

On the evening of April 22, 1914, a distinguished-looking man in civilian clothes limped down the granite steps of the ornate State, War, and Navy Building beside the White House. The man was Major General Leonard Wood, the retiring chief of staff of the United States Army. The day before, marines and sailors had stormed the Mexican city of Vera Cruz at the orders of President Wilson. Wood's next duty assignment would be to organize a field army to fight, if need be, in Mexico. The forces at Wood's disposal could defeat Mexico. But the general was grimly convinced, as he stepped down after four years as Army chief of staff, that they could not defend the country against attack by a first-class opponent. The United States Army, in the minds of many of its officers, was an instrument inadequate to America's needs as a world power. Wood was in the forefront of a movement to reform it.[1]

The Army in 1914 was both absolutely and relatively small, and was cut off from the life of the nation. Leonard Wood commanded a little less

5

than 100,000 men, spread thinly from Tientsin, China, to Puerto Rico and the Panama Canal Zone. This force was not inexpensive; Congress appropriated around $100 million for the Army each year, a sizable sum in 1914. But it was almost a constabulary rather than a fighting force. Two years before, a magazine article had called it, hyperbolically, "the most unfit army the United States has had since the Revolution." The entire Army, at home and abroad, consisted of thirty regiments of infantry, fifteen cavalry regiments, six field artillery regiments, and one hundred seventy companies of coast artillery, along with supporting troops. All of the regiments except those on foreign service were maintained at a peace strength which was less than half of their war complement; they were only the frameworks of fighting units. Recently passed legislation setting up an enlisted reserve had so far produced less than two squads of men. The Organized Militia was under state control. The Army did man a series of formidable coast defenses at the principal seaports, with disappearing twelve-inch guns and huge mortars. But the mobile army to back up these static defenses was diminutive. The General Staff which directed the Army was small and overworked. Under normal conditions, it had no official contact with the Navy. President Wilson had recently dissolved the only coordinating agency, the Joint Army-Navy Board, in a fit of anger at what he thought was its intrusion into foreign policy. The Army's war plans were defensive ones, geared to protecting the nation from invasion. Only against Mexico was there a contingency plan (Plan Green) for offensive action.[2]

The United States Army was dwarfed by the forces of most other major powers. In this respect, it differed from its sister service, the United States Navy. Of course, the Navy had complaints of its own: it was undermanned and lacked a proper staff organization. Most of its thirty-one battleships had been rendered obsolete by the introduction of the all big-gun ship into the world's navies in 1906, and Congress was slow in providing replacements. However, the Navy was still the third or fourth strongest in the world. The Army was smaller than that of some Balkan powers.

There were understandable reasons for this seeming neglect of the Army. Americans, the secretary of war had stated in his department's 1913 *Annual Report*, were "a peaceful and unmilitary people." At least, Americans liked to think so. Certainly, there was an element of antimilitarism running through the whole Anglo-Saxon tradition; large standing armies smacked of tyranny, of Oliver Cromwell, and James II. This distrust of centralized military power had rooted itself even more deeply in American soil. The American Revolution had created a legend of armed farmers defeating professional hirelings. George Washington had known better, but the nation had chosen to remember only his favorable comments on citizen-soldiers, not his cautionary qualifications. A state-controlled citizens militia had been written into the Constitution. The regular military had started out as a small peacetime custodial force for guard duty and Indian police. And so it had remained. Jeffersonian economy, Jacksonian democracy, and the business values of the Gilded Age had all successively, in one way or another, worked against the growth of a sizable military establishment. Ideological distrust had been reinforced by the conditions of American life.[3]

It was not that Americans were uniquely peaceful. But ever since 1815, the United States had enjoyed security from attack behind vast ocean moats. Its neighbors on the North American continent were militarily feeble. Americans had been free to turn their peaceful energies into the vast task of national development, and to fight their serious wars with *ad hoc* hordes of volunteers who sprang to arms and then disbanded once the fighting was finished. This process had appeared to be eminently successful to the average American. The highly informal American military system had even managed to survive the ultimate test of the Civil War. After that conflict, the United States had been able to develop into a free, unplanned, and *laissez-faire* society. There was no credible foreign enemy in sight for a generation. Under these circumstances, Congress and the public could, and did, ignore whatever claims the professional military might put forth.

Even America's entry into the arena of world power at the turn of the century had not changed things to any degree. If the size of the American Army increased to meet new imperial responsibilities, its importance in American life did not. By 1900, the major nations of Continental Europe, along with Japan, had fashioned great conscript armies after the iron model of the Prussian military machine. The United States never thought of following this example. It retained an army that was still a relatively small professional force of paid volunteers—the only major volunteer army left in the world besides that of Great Britain. Instead, the country concentrated its martial energies on building up the Navy, which was obviously useful as a first line of defense, and which had been popularized by the writings of Captain Alfred Thayer Mahan.[4]

By the time of the Wilson Administration, the Army still occupied one of the lower places in the scale of national priorities. Many Americans now discounted the likelihood of a major armed conflict. The twentieth-century world had seen the beginnings of the Hague Court and the Carnegie Endowment for International Peace. The Taft and Wilson Administrations had both invested a good deal of diplomatic energy in concluding arbitration treaties with foreign nations. It seemed that an era of international peace was at hand. War was an atavism which Christianity, trade, and education would stamp out. In such a milieu the United States Army remained, in 1914, a thing set apart, a small disciplined force trained for war in a large undisciplined country which hoped for peace.

The Army was not without its strengths. It possessed a high degree of professionalism. Almost half of the small officer corps was composed of West Point graduates. Many officers had seen field service in the Philippines or along the Mexican border. The enlisted men were hard-bitten, well-drilled, and competent. The basic weapons, the Springfield rifle and the three-inch field gun, were technically excellent. But, by its very nature, the United States Army labored under built-in handicaps.

A volunteer army was an expensive army, especially in the United States. Troops had to be recruited on the open market, and maintained at an American standard of living. High personnel costs, coupled with the heavy transportation costs involved in moving troops across enormous distances on land and sea, made the United States Army much more expensive to operate, on a man-for-man basis, than a Continental conscript force. At the same time, the government's compensation was hardly generous; Army privates received $15 a month. The combination of low pay and stern discipline meant that the Army rank and file was recruited from the unskilled and the unemployed, plus a leaven of adventurous youths. The private soldier was proof of many of the inequalities in American life which reformers in the twentieth century were trying to ameliorate. The disparity in background between officers and men reinforced the caste nature of the service. There was a rigid social barrier separating officers and enlisted men, to the extent that all conversation between them was supposed to be in the third person. Public esteem for the soldier was even lower than the pay. In 1912, the Democratic party platform had urged the states to pass civil rights legislation to protect uniformed soldiers from discrimination.[5]

When not despised, soldiers were ignored; as the Army's presence in the country was almost invisible, it was easy to forget its existence. Part of the Army was overseas. The long-troubling Mexican situation had forced the deployment of two-thirds of the remaining mobile forces along the desolate border. Under ordinary conditions, most of the Army was dispersed in lonely western outposts left over from the Indian wars—out of sight and out of mind. The Army was an artificial society, a small closed world, psychologically and physically remote. In the words of Colonel Hunter Liggett, it was "an alien army . . . alien in the practically complete separation from the lives of the people from which it [was] drawn."[6]

Some in the Army accepted its weakness and isolation as inevitable. Wood and his forward-looking colleagues in the officer corps did not; instead, they were committed to institutional reform. They wanted to build an army that was at once internally efficient, close to the American people, and fit to fight. The times were congenial to this effort. The early twentieth century witnessed a general wave of reform in the United States which historians have called the Progressive Movement. At the turn of the century, many people viewed America as a country gone awry. Its politics were corrupt, its economy dominated by expanding trusts, its cities, polyglot slums in which bewildered countrymen mingled with a growing mass of illiterate immigrants. In reaction, the American middle class, joining forces with other groups, attempted to regenerate the nation. The thrust of the Progressive Movement was to rationalize and democratize American life. Progressives hoped to reform the political parties, curb the power of monopoly, and humanize the cities. The campaign for army reform by concerned officers and their civilian allies must be examined in this wider context.

The military reformers by no means shared all of the wider political, social, and economic goals of many civilian Progressives. The Progressive Movement was not all of a piece. Army officers had little in common with social workers, concerned labor leaders, or the spokesmen of disgruntled farmers. Most Progressives in civilian life felt that an era of international peace was at hand; military men generally tended to take a grimmer view of the world. There was one further difficulty. Most of the reforms of the Progressive Era touched intimately on the life of the average middle-class American. Progressive Army officers were hard put to explain why there was such a need to renovate America's land forces when no enemy was at hand.[7]

Nonetheless, there were certain elements common both to the military reform movement and the wider Progressive Movement. Progressivism was more than an abstract, idealistic movement; it had a hard side to it, and citizen Progressives were as much interested in efficiency as their military counterparts. Like Progressives in civilian life, the military Progressives appealed to values higher than the pocketbook. Both groups shared a similar belief in the capacity of an aroused and informed electorate to make correct decisions.

In this progressive era, the optimism and will necessary for a sustained reform effort were not lacking. The military reformers were convinced that change could be brought about. Behind their conviction was their knowledge that some change had already taken place. Progressive officers knew that the United States Army in 1914 was a force engaged in a continuing evolutionary process.

*   *   *

The Spanish-American War had produced a considerable body of military reform. The United States had entered that conflict with a tiny Regular Army of 25,000 men. By the end of 1899, the country had found itself with 100,000 regulars and volunteers holding down an empire. The progress made during the war was consolidated by the astute New York lawyer, Elihu Root, the greatest secretary of war in a generation. It was Root, serving first under William McKinley, then under Theodore Roosevelt, who did the most to pull the Army into the twentieth century. The secretary of war secured congressional authorization for a permanent regular establishment of 100,000 men. He set up an elaborate structure of service schools crowned by a Staff School and the Army War College. The secretary encouraged the passage of the Dick Act of 1903, which gave federal recognition and support to the Organized Militia of the states. Most significantly, Root tried to rectify the grave deficiencies in the Army's organization.[8]

Root abolished the old and disfunctional post of commanding general of the Army. Instead, he substituted a chief of staff at the head of an Army General Staff. The Army now had a clear command structure and a central planning body. The chief of staff, as the secretary of war's deputy, would curb the baronial powers of the permanent bureau chiefs who ran the administration and supply services. The new staff system was designed to eliminate the cleavage between the Army in the field and the Army stationed behind desks in Washington. Staff officers would now be appointed on a detail system, ensuring constant rotation between the staff and the line.

But Root had only half-reformed the Army, for Congress and public opinion would only go so far. Moreover, not all of the new steps were completely effective. The General Staff system never quite took hold. Successive chiefs of staff were old Indian-fighting generals ill at ease with the problems of higher administration; the General Staff itself found that, while it planned for the Army of the future, the bureau chiefs continued to run the Army of the present. The secretaries of war who followed Root were Republican politicians whose main interests lay elsewhere and who lacked Root's dynamism and broad vision. For a time, the Army settled back into a new kind of routine. The next major reform impulse came during the Taft Administration, when Wood and Henry L. Stimson took the Army in hand.[9]

Leonard Wood became chief of staff in July 1910. Wood was a distinctively different sort of general. A Harvard Medical School graduate and one-time Army contract surgeon, he had used the occasion of the Spanish-American War to shift his occupation from White House physician to colonel of the Rough Riders. From there he had moved into the Regular Army and launched a brilliant career. An amateur touched by genius, schooled in the belligerent nationalism of his friend Theodore Roosevelt, Wood believed in the necessity of fashioning the Army into a fighting machine that could deal with the inevitable conflicts of the future. He threw himself into his new job with tremendous energy and zest, showing a talent for propaganda as well as for administration. And yet, by leading the fight for progress, Wood hurt as well as helped the

Army, for he was surrounded by glamor and by enemies, a stormy petrel of reform. Politicians suspected him of being a militarist, and fellow-soldiers accused him of being a politician.[10]

Wood's reform efforts soon received valuable reinforcement when Henry L. Stimson joined the Taft Administration as secretary of war. Stimson, a law partner of Elihu Root, owed his appointment to his legal acumen, not his military experience; the secretary of war had to deal with the problems of the newly acquired overseas territories and the rivers and harbors program as well as with the Army. But he was to prove an excellent collaborator for Wood. The patrician New York lawyer was interested in the military and was an activist willing to fight for reform. He shared Wood's belief that military service represented one of the highest expressions of national ideals. Together, the two men launched a renewed assault on the limitations of the Army.[11]

The Army's new civilian and military chiefs confronted a whole agenda of problems which the Root reforms had been unable to solve. One of them was the simple question of control. The old bureau chiefs with their excellent congressional connections had not been touched by the earlier legislation. They still ringed the chief of staff, hampering effective action. The chief of staff faced the necessity of establishing the supremacy of his own position. There was also a need to reorganize the General Staff into usefulness.[12]

Another task was to reform the system of officer promotion. Although generals were selected on the basis of merit, promotion to the grade of colonel was on a strict basis of seniority in branch. This system had two bad effects. First, it led to vicious infighting as branches lobbied for favorable treatment by Congress. (This was particularly disturbing to the reformers because the Washington-based bureaus had an advantage in this political competition over the combat arms in the field.) Second, it thwarted the advancement of promising young officers. Field officers were reaching their commands ten years too late. "The army is like a tree with a vigorous root and a dead top," Wood fretted. A uniform promotion list and a merit system of promotion would solve this problem.[13]

Yet another deficiency in the Army was its organization and positioning. The Regular Army was still deployed just as it had been in the Indian wars, in small forts mostly located in the empty country between the Missouri River and the West Coast plain. The nation's mobile forces were strewn over forty-nine Army posts in twenty-nine states. This dispersal of the Army into penny-packets created a host of problems. It increased the separateness of the Army from civilian life, created psychological strains on the troops, and imposed heavy transportation costs. It also impaired military efficiency. The wholesale dispersal of the Army in the wilderness destroyed any attempt to give tactical cohesion to large units. As one officer put it, the Army was playing "a sort of military solitaire." There was no tactical organization anyway; the Army was divided into geographic areas. When the Mexican Revolution first exploded in 1911, it was necessary to send troops to the border. It took six weeks of painstaking effort to assemble a Maneuver Division out of scattered, half-strength regiments and concentrate it on the Texas border under the command of inexperienced general officers. It seemed clear to the military Progressives that the Army needed both tactical organization and strategic concentration.[14]

The main problem which the reformers faced, however, was that the Army was simply too small to fight a serious war. The Regular Army was only large enough to serve as the nucleus of the nation's forces in a major conflict. And worse, it was a core without an apple. Behind it there were only the Organized Militia set up under the Dick Act and whatever hastily assembled volunteer forces could be called into being. The first-line reserve, the Organized Militia, although aided by Regular Army instructors and a $2 million a year subsidy from the federal government, was a ramshackle congery of state guards, dubiously led and only 120,000 strong. The volunteer armies, of course, did not exist. What all of this meant, as the War Department itself confessed, was that the real defense of the nation would depend on "volunteer forces composed of entirely untrained citizens commanded in great part by equally untrained officers." The organization, equipment, and supply of these hordes would be arranged only when war broke out. The Regular Army nucleus would itself be disorganized by an influx of untrained recruits, since its peace-strength units would have to be filled out to fight properly. In short, the country was unprepared.[15]

Stimson and Wood rejected the traditional military pessimism which held that, because of its very nature, the American democracy would probably never be ready for war. Instead, the military Progressives sought to adopt European methods to the American scene. This approach meant creating a reserve system. Instead of remaining a static force in being, the Regular Army should become a military school. It would take in, train, and discharge soldiers as rapidly as possible, thus creating a pool of trained manpower. In the event of war, these reservists would become the fillers for the enlarged Regular Army, and would also serve as replacements. The same thing could be done with the militia.

The secretary of war and his chief of staff were convinced that with this approach, it would be possible to shorten training time. A more desirable type of man might be attracted to the colors. The Army would no longer be a mercenary force, but, rather, the embodiment of the armed nation. This idea had major drawbacks, however. It would turn the Regular Army into reverse. The Army had traditionally been a professional organization of career officers and long-service soldiers. Previous chiefs of staff had deliberately encouraged veteran soldiers to reenlist. The policy saved the expenses of recruiting, and old soldiers could be farmed out as noncommissioned officers if and when volunteer armies had to be raised. If the Army wanted to change its policy and process as many reservists as possible, it would have to discourage reenlistment and shorten the term of service. This idea was unpopular in many quarters of the Army. It would throw a heavy burden on the adjutant general's recruiting service, since the new service would be a revolving door, sending reservists out as it brought recruits in. Many officers questioned the feasibility of giving short-service troops adequate training. (Wood and Stimson favored releasing trained men after as little as one year.) There was one final problem: the scheme was a pale imitation of the huge armies of Continental Europe. However, while Continental governments were able to rely on conscription to fill the ranks, this was unthinkable in the *laissez-faire* America of William Howard Taft. The United States Army would have to rely on a combination of patriotism and pay to attract recruits. There was a serious question as to whether a short-service army with a high turnover rate could be kept up to strength.

Wood and Stimson faced formidable obstacles in carrying through their reform program. Within the Army itself, there were strong conservative forces. The bureau chiefs in particular had a vested interest in preserving established routines and the autonomy of their own domains. The Commander-in-Chief, William Howard Taft, lacked any real commitment to military reform, and was presiding over a floundering administration. The Republican party which controlled the Senate had a stake in maintaining the existing distribution of Army posts; the Democrats who had newly organized the House of Representatives were economy-minded and antimilitary. Public opinion was marvelously apathetic. By 1912, the whole campaign had produced as much conflict as progress.

*   *   *

The first major struggle in the reform campaign was the "Battle of the Doctors" between Wood and Major General Fred C. Ainsworth. As adjutant general, Ainsworth was the most powerful bureau chief in the Army. Like the chief of staff, he had originally entered the military as an Army doctor. An impressive figure with bushy eyebrows, piercing eyes, and a dramatic cavalry mustache, Ainsworth looked every inch the soldier, even in the civilian clothes all desk officers wore in Washington. Actually, Ainsworth was a super bureaucrat, whose main services to the nation had been in straightening out the Records and Pensions Office under the Harrison Administration. From there he had mounted to power on a pyramid of fifty million index cards. Congress, pleased by the speedy service he provided in handling veterans' pension claims, had created a series of positions expressly for him. Ainsworth had become a major general, then military secretary of the Army, and finally adjutant general.[16]

Ainsworth was intelligent and competent, but he had a prickly personality (he was not on speaking terms with the assistant secretary of war and many of the bureau chiefs) and was something of a monomaniac. As *The Nation* put it, "when a man of ability has devoted his life to a single thing like a card-catalogue system, he is very apt to confuse the means and the end." While the chief of staff visualized the Army as a fighting machine controlled by the General Staff, Ainsworth tended to see its role as keeping tidy records for the adjutant general's office. Although Ainsworth and Wood started out on good terms, both personal and institutional reasons made a collision almost inevitable. The final clash came over Wood's attempt to eliminate red tape by doing away with the cumbersome bimonthly muster roll. This intrusion onto his preserve stung Ainsworth into colorful insubordination. The adjutant general was forced out of the Army under threat of court martial.[17]

Ainsworth had immensely solid congressional connections which transcended party lines. He had already done much to shape the 1912 Army Appropriations Bill in ways that ran counter to the demands of the reformers. His dismissal simply shifted the reform battle from the State, War and Navy Building to the Capitol. When the military Progressives approached Congress with their plans for rationalizing the Army, they found themselves caught between two fires. The Old Guard Republicans in the Senate insisted on preserving the existing and politically profitable arrangement of Army posts. The Democrats of the House showed a fierce desire for retrenchment of the whole Army. Both Houses wanted to attach riders to the Appropriations Bill depriving Wood of his post as chief of staff. The House Military Affairs Committee, chaired by Representative James Hay, an able but antimilitarist southerner, proved to be especially obstructive.[18]

The result was a lengthy and confused political struggle. Stimson summoned up allies in the Senate, and pressed Taft to veto undesirable Army legislation. Not until August was a reasonably satisfactory bill passed, embodying some reform demands. The 1912 Army Appropriations Act created an enlisted reserve for the first time, although not along the lines the reformers had requested. Under the new law, troops would enlist for a seven-year hitch, serving four years with the colors and three in an unpaid reserve. The law also consolidated the Army's supply services and created a new Army Service Corps to take over duties previously performed by civilians and detached soldiers. On the other hand, there were what Stimson called "very crude and very drastic" provisions. The 1912 Act slightly reduced the General Staff. The enlistment period had actually been lengthened. So-called Manchu laws now placed stringent and hampering limitations on the detached service of officers. The useless Army posts were still there. Essentially, the War Department had won only a defensive victory; it had fought Congress to a deadlock. And the protracted battle had left scars. General Wood, the embodiment of Army reform, had clearly become a political liability to his own cause.[19]

Reform, the military Progressives now realized, would take a long time. A chastened Secretary Stimson wrote to a friend: "My own experience during the past year has been that even in the moderate reforms we have been working at we have been too radical and have bitten off rather more than we can chew in the present state of public opinion." The American people and the political system were just not interested; public attention was on other matters. In 1912, the Progressive Movement was at its crest. The surging forces of the age broke the Republican party in two. The Old Guard stayed grimly with Taft, as did Stimson and some other moderates. But many Progressives followed the bolt of Theodore Roosevelt into a new Progressive party. To the horror of business circles, Roosevelt and his supporters now demanded a Newer Nationalism which embraced a wide spectrum of political, economic, and social reforms, and which even seemed to favor state socialism. The splintering of the Republican party ensured the victory of the Progressive-oriented Democratic candidate Woodrow Wilson. The Democrats also gained control of both Houses of Congress. Defense was not even an issue in the campaign. The world was at peace, and the energies of the nation were devoted to consideration of domestic reform. Making the Army fit to fight was not a concern that affected the lives of most Americans. In the context of 1912, the military reformers were marginal men.[20]

In the meantime, Stimson and Wood continued their efforts in a lower key. With the legislative route blocked, the reformers turned to an educational campaign and some administrative action, while Stimson mended fences with key congressmen. One thing, at least, could be done immediately. Some congressmen had criticized Stimson's reform proposals on the grounds that the Army had no set master plan for development and that the recommendations of successive secretaries of war simply canceled each other out. In the summer of 1912, the Stimson-Wood team ordered Captain John M. Palmer of the General Staff to draw up a plan for organizing all land forces of the United States. Aided by three other officers, Palmer produced a draft report, copies of which were furnished to the bureau chiefs and the divisions of the General Staff. The secretary of war presided in person over the ensuing debates in a series of public conferences to which congressmen were invited. The final report was not approved until every general officer in the continental United States had had a chance to state his opinion. Stimson and Wood intended that the document would embody the general consensus of the whole

Army, thus making it impossible for Congress to dismiss their views as individual expressions of opinion.[21]

The 1912 Report on the Organization of the Land Forces contained little that was new. It was a comprehensive restatement, in sixty pages, of the views of the military Progressives. The model it offered for the United States was that of the British military system, with its small Regular Army backed up by reserves and organized territorials. The report recommended a short-service Regular Army backed by an organized reserve. This force would be concentrated strategically and be given a tactical organization. Finally, the Regular Army would be expanded. There were already enough troops in the United States to make up three incomplete infantry divisions. These units would be brought up to full peace-strength over a period of years in five increments. After that, a fourth division would be added. Such a mobile force of four complete infantry divisions was "the goal toward which all effort should be directed."[22]

The report gave special emphasis to the idea that the Army must be organized for war. The Regular Army was important only as "the peace nucleus of the greater war army." It would have to be supplemented by an efficient militia. Although some officers considered the Organized Militia to be an unreliable military asset, it was the only backup force available and so could hardly be disregarded. (Secretary of War Stimson, in fact, had come around to supporting federal drill pay for militia units that met federal standards.) The militia should be upgraded, organized into tactical divisions, and made subject to draft into the armed forces of the United States, thus freeing it for service outside the country. Volunteer forces would provide the third line of defense. Here the most urgent need would be for trained officers. The report suggested that the government provide a cadre for the citizen forces by granting reserve commissions to graduates of military colleges. Somehow, in the event of war with a first-class power, the United States would have to field 460,000 mobile troops and 42,000 static coast defense troops. Finally, the report called for a Council of National Defense to coordinate the Army and the Navy with the nation's foreign and financial policies.[23]

The 1912 Report on the Organization of the Land Forces seemed at the time to be a benchmark in the Army's history. As Wood wrote approvingly, it provided "the first statement of a national military policy for which any Administration has stood." The document crystallized the thinking of the Army and set up a base for a renewed educational campaign directed at the public. Furthermore, some of the recommendations could be carried out by administrative decree. In January 1913, the secretary of war again convened the generals, showed them the report, and announced that he planned to immediately impose a tactical organization on the Army by grouping it into divisions. After some predictable spluttering by elderly brigadiers, the conference generally assented, and the plan went into effect in mid-February. It was put to immediate use. Mexico bubbled over again as President Francisco Madero was overthrown, and troops were urgently needed once more to screen the border against raiders. This time it took only one telegram from Washington to send the brand-new Second Division to Texas.[24]

* * *

The return of the Democratic party to power in 1913 broke up the productive Wood-Stimson relationship, as the secretary of war returned to private life. But the change in government was not too traumatic for the Army. Despite all of his enemies, Wood retained his post as chief of staff. The new secretary of war was Lindley M. Garrison, a leading New Jersey equity lawyer and the former vice-chancellor of the state. Garrison had no military experience, and had haphazardly been selected for his job at the last minute. But he was a good government man with a forceful personality who soon won the admiration of many of his generals. As for the new Commander-in-Chief, Woodrow Wilson was a man of peace with an indifference, and even an aversion, to things military. Nevertheless, he was rigidly determined to keep the Army free from partisan politics, as his retention of Wood proved. The change in administrations did produce some inevitable discontinuity. Stimson's plan for giving federal drill pay to the militia was scrapped, and nothing further was done to implement the proposals of the 1912 Report on the Organization of the Land Forces. But the momentum for reform was not lost.[25]

Wood continued to conduct a propaganda campaign that showed imagination and a willingness to go beyond strictly military channels. The Army, he was convinced, must take its case to the public. One step the chief of staff took in early 1913 was to encourage the formation of an

Army League to act as a civilian lobby for defense. Private citizens could agitate in ways that would be indiscreet for generals. The Navy already had such an organization of boosters, with many prominent names on the masthead, if little money in the treasury. Wood's principal helper in this effort was Frederick L. Huidekoper, a well-bred Washington lawyer and dillettantish military historian who had been demonstrating the nation's unpreparedness for war ever since 1906. Huidekoper was fertile with ideas, but this particular project never scored even the limited success of the Navy League.[26]

Other devices showed more promise. In the summer of 1913, Wood sponsored two camps that gave military training to college students. The Army could give young men military training and a chance to work off their patriotic enthusiasm. It would also be able to expose America's future governing class to correct military ideas. Only a few hundred students attended the first two camps. But the camp alumni formed a permanent organization, and Wood secured the services of an advisory board of college presidents. Four student-training camps were scheduled for 1914. The Army was building a bridge to the colleges and their large pools of potential volunteer officers. This movement would grow.[27]

*   *   *

As Wood stepped down from his post as chief of staff in 1914, the United States Army was not yet fit to fight a major war. But Wood and his fellow military Progressives had some reason to be satisfied. Constructive changes had been made, and would continue. For a time, the chief of staff had worried about the selection of his successor. He saw deep reactionary forces still at large in the Army, and feared he might be replaced by a member of "the standpat group who [sic] object to learning foreign languages, and who believe that nothing can be learned from any foreign army and that a small army is all-sufficient, and that reserves are unnecessary." Instead, Wood was succeeded by Major General W. W. Wotherspoon, an officer of his own choosing. When no war with Mexico resulted from the Vera Cruz occupation, in July 1914 Wood took charge of the Eastern Department, the most important military command in the United States. The Department's headquarters was conveniently located on Governor's Island in New York harbor. There, Wood would be·

surrounded by influential friends who might push the coming of a modern army. He did not intend to be idle.[28]

Military reform was still largely a preoccupation of forward-looking Army officers and the small band of politicians and publicists who shared their views. But they believed that progress was inevitable. They felt that the necessity of the reforms which they advocated was self-evident; sooner or later, an enlightened and informed public opinion would force Congress into making the necessary preparations for national defense. Meanwhile, the short-term prospects for new Army legislation were favorable. The new fortifications for the Panama Canal, the Hawaiian Islands, and the Philippines were on the verge of completion. As soon as these had been garrisoned, so few regular soldiers would be left in the continental United States that there would be a strong case for enlarging the Army.[29]

On June 28, 1914, the heir-apparent to the throne of Austria-Hungary, Archduke Franz Ferdinand, was assassinated in Bosnia. By August, the great military machines of Europe had been set in motion in a general war. The guns of August were to lend a new urgency to the drive for reforming the American military establishment.

2

The Politics of Defense

Six months ago I should have been a mighty poor politician if I had preached about our lack of national defense. Today I should be a mighty poor politician if I were to drop the subject.

—Representative A. P. Gardner

The outbreak of World War I in Europe caused an immediate revulsion against war and armaments in the United States. To most Americans, the European convulsion seemed to confirm the American tradition of pacific isolationism. The only saving grace of the bloody mess would be that it would teach anew the folly of military preparations. As Nicholas Murray Butler, the president of Columbia University and Taft's running mate in 1912, put it,

a final end has now been put to the contention, always stupid and often insincere, that huge armaments are an insurance policy against war and an aid in maintaining peace. . . . The time may not be so very far distant when to be the first moral power in the world will be a considerably greater distinction than to be the first military power. . . .

The New York Times weightily rebuked a congressman who brought up the threat of the Yellow Peril with the calm statement, "The United States is in no position to adjust its policies to any belief in future wars. We are not a warlike people, and we have no desire to imitate the warmakers of Europe." A West Coast paper hopefully observed that "the last fortnight has been worth as much to the peace movement as a century of peace congresses." The pacifist-leaning *Nation* magazine predicted that "next winter there will be a strong demand that we begin to retrench in our naval armaments."[1]

This period of self-congratulatory international innocence did not last very long. Important elements of American society began to reevaluate the European War and its lessons for the United States. To many Americans, the war looked more and more like a Prussian attempt at world domination, instead of a tragedy arising out of the mistaken militarism of Continental Europe. The opinion-leaders of the country had strong cultural ties to Germany's opponents and a high-minded commitment to the formalities of international law so dramatically violated by Germany in the interests of military efficiency. Helped along by a skillful campaign of Allied propaganda, these men increasingly came to see the war as a struggle between good and evil, with evil having the advantage of greater military preparation. Belgium had been peaceful, neutral, and feebly armed; Belgium was now a battlefield trampled by invaders, a country of gutted cathedrals and murdered hostages. Might not the same thing happen to America, once the fighting in Europe ended? The Germans were obviously ruthless and aggressive, and even if they did not triumph in Europe, they might still lash out across the seas. Other nations, too, might suddenly emerge as enemies in the postwar world. A year before, a world war was unthinkable, but now here it was, stark and real. America had better get ready for whatever the future might hold. "For the first time since the Spanish War, there is a general sense of physical uneasiness in this country and a disposition, at least, to listen to prophets of military evil," the editor of *The Atlantic Monthly* noted. *The New York Times*, shaken from its brief complacency, editorialized that "there is a growing feeling that the European War is getting nearer to us."[2]

So America, threatened by vague fears of a disoriented world, began to look to its defenses. The early agitation for defense reforms had come from generals and admirals, aided by a few civilian allies. But their efforts had not really captured the public imagination. Now the European War provided the favorable climate for the growing preparedness campaign. In the fall of 1914, the cry for greater defense was taken up by politicians and by citizen groups hitherto uninterested in the subject. Despite all the zeal of the service reformers, the Army and Navy had been comparatively neglected; the fat volumes of annual reports relating their deficiencies had quietly collected dust on library shelves. Now came the awakening.

The first move in the campaign for increased defense came in mid-October, both feeding on and helping to shape the growing mood of national unease. Representative A. P. Gardner of Massachusetts introduced a resolution in the House calling for an investigation of the state of the nation's defenses by a national security commission. Gardner, the son-in-law of Henry Cabot Lodge, was a vaguely progressive Republican (he had supported the insurgents in their fight to curb the powers of Speaker Joseph Cannon) who had never before attracted much public attention. He had recently returned from Europe, where he had witnessed the initial triumph of the German military machine. Explaining the purpose of his resolution, Gardner declared that he had sat like a coward in the House for twelve years while the nation had remained defenseless, but now he felt he had to speak out. His proposed commission of three senators, three representatives, and three presidential appointees would throw a "public searchlight" on America's weakness. This was a new and hostile world, and "42-centimeter guns and super-dreadnaughts present[ed] stronger arguments than past victories and present treaties." Germany might menace the Monroe Doctrine after the war ended; Japan was our enemy because of America's Oriental exclusion policy. The defense of the republic was entrusted to an undermanned fleet that had slipped to third in world ranking, to a tiny Regular Army, and to a scarcely larger militia, 60 percent of which could not use the Army rifle.[3]

Other voices were swift to join in the demand for reform. Loudest among them was that of former President Theodore Roosevelt. Roosevelt had always been an advocate of a strong, armed America, and he viewed the international scene as a Darwinian struggle in which the unfit would be eliminated. By the end of October, Roosevelt was assuring the students of Princeton that he had personally seen the plans of two of the warring empires to seize great coastal cities of the United States and hold them for ransom. By November, Roosevelt was advocating universal military training for all young men. As the Progressive party he had led was abandoned by the people in the November elections, Roosevelt began to turn from peacetime reforms to sterner stuff. Defending one's country could be morally exhilarating, too, evoking the "virile strength of manliness which accepts as the ideal the stern, unflinching performance of duty." The new reform combination would be "righteousness with force," and on an international scope.[4]

The Wilson Administration initially reacted to the clamor for defense with derision. Wilson called the defense discussion "good mental exercise"; it was a scare tactic, he recalled, that had been going on ever since he was a boy of ten. Neither Wilson nor his administration was disposed to show much concern for the needs of the armed forces. Wilson himself was a liberal idealist, ready to fight for a vision, but better at preaching than acting the Commander-in-Chief, and certainly uninterested in the technical details of war. He was flanked by a pacifist secretary of state and a Navy secretary more interested in moral power than seapower. Other Cabinet members, in the eyes of one defense advocate, were "a set of men insular and provincial, uneducated in a historical sense, lacking in historical perspective and grasp of the relation of America to the great world forces now so active." Southern Democrats, traditionally frugal and antimilitarist, dominated Congress.[5]

Moreover, there were positive reasons for ignoring the agitation. The Wilson Administration was not rattled by vague threats of impending disaster. Instead, Wilson saw the war as a chance for America to exercise her moral leadership and mediate the crisis as the last great impartial neutral. This role of peacemaker would become untenable, it seemed to the President, if the United States too began arming itself. In addition, Gardner's proposed investigation into defense inadequacies under a Democratic administration could easily turn into a partisan weapon. The initial demand for preparedness seemed to have been launched by Republicans of the most blatantly partisan and imperialist stripe: Henry Cabot Lodge and his allies, joined together with Colonel Roosevelt. Wilson rejected the ideology of these men and suspected their principles. He was confident that the agitation was simply a surface storm, and that the vast mass of the American people wished only for peace, neutrality, and the continued de-emphasis of the country's military machinery.[6]

The Wilson Administration was not monolithic, however. It contained people who were very much interested in promoting a stronger Army and Navy. The enigmatic Colonel Edward M. House was the President's chief unofficial adviser and his *alter ego*. A devout believer in the balance of power and in the need for America to play a world role, House had established close contacts with General Leonard Wood and had urged the necessity of military preparations on the President whenever he had a chance. Lindley Garrison and his assistant secretary of war, the Kentuckian Henry S. Breckinridge, backed military reforms. Within the Navy Department, the assistant secretary, Franklin D. Roosevelt, was an agitating force. He looked upon his chief, Josephus Daniels, with condescension; the North Carolina newspaper editor, Roosevelt wrote after the outbreak of the war in Europe, was "bewildered by it all, very sweet, but very sad." Daniels was a Cabinet ally of William Jennings Bryan, while Franklin Roosevelt shared views on armed might amazingly similar to those of his cousin Theodore, and had worked with Congressman Gardner in formulating his congressional resolution. Within the armed services themselves there was of course Wood, still at his work of military education, while in the Navy Rear Admiral Bradley A. Fiske, a bantam fighting-cock, bombarded Secretary Daniels with memoranda claiming that "the navy could not stand inspection, because it had been kept so divided up for a year and a half," and that the Navy lacked men, departmental organization, and training. Fiske was more explicit on what America had to fear than the politicians were; he noted at the end of October that he could not "get any one to bet 2 to 1 that we will not be in war in two years." While his colleagues were thinking in terms of long-range building programs, Fiske believed the Navy needed an immediate increase in fighting personnel and war plans for "Black and Orange"—Germany and Japan.[7]

The campaign for defense continued. Gardner gained editorial support from the prestigious *New York Times*, as well as from Republican-controlled papers. Soon a new group of defense advocates prepared to move into the field. S. Stanwood Menken was a New York lawyer who had sat in the galleries of the British House of Commons as England decided to enter the war. In November, Menken sent out letters to a hundred and fifty New Yorkers active in public affairs, asking them to cooperate with him in appealing for a congressional investigation of

America's defenses. The response was overwhelmingly satisfactory. With a world war going on across the grey Atlantic, New York was unnerved by the thought of its possible helplessness before armed attack. In December, a committee of fifty met at the Hotel Belmont and formed the National Security League, spurred on by the warnings of the aged Anglophilic publisher, George Haven Putnam. What would happen, asked Putnam, if the victorious Germans demanded the right to invade Canada through the Port of New York? The committee elected Menken president of the League and swiftly decided to back the Gardner inquiry. This was mildly embarrassing to the Wilson Administration, since the League, while containing many Republicans, was ostensibly nonpartisan and Menken himself was a Democrat. The League was composed of rather substantial citizens, many of whom were active in the better clubs and were listed in the Social Register. Nicholas Murray Butler might try to impugn the motives of the League's founders, but as *The New York Times* pointed out, one had only to look at the names to realize that they were not wild-eyed jingoists or profiteering patriots, but "sober-minded citizens, many of them peace advocates, though not of the extravagant kind, merchants, financiers, professional men of all shades of political opinion."[8]

Other organizations quickly followed the Security League's lead. The National Civic Federation, dominated by enlightened business leaders, unanimously pledged support to a Council of National Defense. Urban business and professional men, steeped every day in war news from their papers, were ready converts to the defense cause. The European War raged on, civilization seemed turned upside down, and the newspapers were worrying about what would happen when the war ended: "in what direction will the victors turn for spoils, with their millions of armed men tugging like bloodhounds at the leash?" The voices of fear increased, and the fact of the war continued to hang like a dark cloud over the country. When Congress met in December, the galleries at the opening session were crowded with society women engaging in the latest fad—knitting for the troops in Europe.[9]

Wilson refused to be swayed by the clamor. He finally met Gardner and told him that he was opposed to an inquiry into defense, for it could create very unfavorable international impressions. The President felt secure in the midst of the turbulence. He believed that even if Germany won the war, she would triumph as an exhausted nation, unable to be a serious challenge to America for many years. In his annual message to Congress, Wilson answered the defense question with high rhetoric. America's defenses should be based not upon a standing Army nor a Reserve Army, but upon a "citizenry trained and accustomed to arms"—a phrase which could mean anything or nothing. It would be silly to build up the Navy unduly until the lessons of the war had been learned. "We shall not alter our attitude . . . because some among us are nervous and excited," the President said. "More than this, proposed at this time," Wilson went on sonorously, armament

> would mean merely that we have been thrown off our balance by a war with which we have nothing to do, whose causes cannot touch us, whose very existence offers us opportunities of friendship and disinterested service which should make us ashamed of any thought of hostility or fearful preparation for trouble.[10]

It was a fine and noble speech, but, as it turned out, utterly mistaken. Wilson was satisfied with the effort. He wrote House, "Well, the broadside has been fired off and I hope sincerely that it will have the desired effect in quieting those who are seriously in danger of making trouble for the country." House, who had been insisting that the country had to arm itself immediately, as usual found it politic to agree with his President. When the war ended, he replied, there would be a different feeling about militarism over the whole world. "Public opinion in this country will applaud you for not being carried away by the excitement of the moment." Gardner had predicted that the President would try to lay the cold hand of death upon the preparedness movement, and he had been right.[11]

*   *   *

But the agitation for defense did not die. It was obviously too good an issue for the Republicans to drop. As *The New Republic* pointed out, "it offers the opportunity which every party seeks of converting patriotic feeling into partisan capital." Ex-President Taft, in retirement from active politics at Yale Law School, commented unsympathetically, "of course the motive for the agitation is political. . . . the danger of invasion or war is less by reason of the European war than it would otherwise be." Among other uses, the preparedness issue provided a ready-made bridge between elements of the foundering Progressive party and the Republicans. Defense was a cause in which Roosevelt and his followers could join hands with the Old Guard. But the defense agitation was principled as well as partisan; Lodge, Roosevelt, and their allies were simply reiterating and emphasizing beliefs about the role of force in international affairs that they had held since the 1890s. The underlying fact, as the conservative Taft and the radical *New Republic* agreed, was that the Army and Navy had been shabbily neglected by Congress in peacetime and needed to be made adequate to their responsibilities.[12]

Meanwhile, reformers fought on within the Wilson Administration. If Josephus Daniels persistently squelched the more extreme demands and warnings of his admirals, Lindley Garrison proved a major solace to his generals. Garrison was the strong-minded maverick of the Cabinet, boldly independent of the Wilson line, a man with his own opinions who won the admiration of subordinates and even earned the respect of some antimilitarists. Curt with importuning politicians, capable of an almost Rooseveltian rhetoric, Garrison seemed to embody the progressive ideal of an administrator who ran his department without fear and without favor. The secretary of war was decidedly unhappy with the chalk and water of Wilson's defense policies, and determined to take a strong stand in his own department's 1914 annual report. On the eve of retirement, Major General Wotherspoon, who had turned out to be an unspectacular chief of staff, was gingered into a show of activity by Assistant Secretary of War Breckinridge. The two civilians and Wotherspoon produced a radical report showing the feebleness of the Army, over the scandalized objections of a couple of bureau generals who feared that any attempt at agitation by the Army would only boomerang. The chief of staff asked that the Army be doubled to a strength of 205,000 men; the secretary of war, in his own terse fourteen-page report, made a more modest request, which still managed to conflict with the President's views. Garrison requested that the formations of the mobile army be recruited to war strength. This would involve an Army increase of 1,000 officers and 25,000 men. The secretary also spoke out for more artillery and an enlarged flying corps.[13]

The secretary's stand meant walking a political tightrope. Garrison got much support, but from the wrong quarters. Lodge felt the report was "a most courageous thing for him to do." Wilson, who had been sent the report before delivering his own annual message to Congress, remained silent. Oswald Garrison Villard, an influential newspaper editor at that time close to the administration, confirmed the belief of Wilson's private secretary that the report had been used against the President's policies. So, while crusading for defense, Garrison was forced to guard his own rear. As a Cabinet member, he had to attempt to deny the Republicans any political ammunition. The secretary of war was in an ambiguous position, and the situation was further complicated by the fact that General Wood, the most active Army reformer in uniform, was an intimate of Theodore Roosevelt and an object of suspicion to Wilson. Wood was a highly articulate general, as zealous a publicist as he was a soldier. Garrison urged the general to drop into the background, a most uncongenial role. It was bad, Garrison said, for generals to get involved in a propaganda campaign for increasing the Army. "Better let the momentum come from without," he advised. The secretary was not at all averse to taking the needs of the Army to the public, but he intended that the War Department would speak with one voice, his own.[14]

Garrison found it necessary to point out both that the country was defenseless and that it would be highly unpatriotic of the Republicans to mention the fact. On the one hand, the secretary of war pleaded for an Army increase of 25,000 men, which would double the size of the mobile forces available in the United States. At that time, Garrison warned, any first-class military power that got beyond the fleet could "pulverize our small regular army and punish us to a humiliating degree." An increase in the Regular Army would at least give the country "a head to our spear," and a trained reserve could then be built up behind it. On the other hand, the secretary warned the Republicans, not too cryptically, "to continue in the vein of the abstract, if party A makes a political issue out of a nation's alleged unpreparedness for war, it will probably over-state the gravity of the situation and drive party B, in self-defense, to rush to the other extreme and assure the people that everything is lovely."[15]

*   *   *

By January 1915, it might have appeared that the demand for greater defense measures was sweeping the country. Informed opinion seemed convinced that the United States was, as *The New York Times* expressed it, a "great, helpless, unprepared nation" in a world of war. Most large-circulation magazines were editorially committed to preparedness, and most of the large daily newspapers supported a bigger army and navy, especially the latter. Sentiment for defense among the press was especially strong on both coasts; opinion was more evenly divided in the Mississippi Valley region, where the editorial opponents of army and navy increases seemed, for a change, to be more vehement than the supporters. Educators and statesmen identified themselves with the cause. Polls showed that two-thirds of America's college presidents favored military training for their students, while most governors wanted a stronger citizen soldiery.[16]

The business classes, too, were quick to rally to the preparedness movement. Some Progressives charged that this was because the War Trust wished to promote a grandiose program of armaments; actually, business motivation seems to have been less dramatic. Businessmen, large and small, read the same newspapers and shared the same sentiments as the other urban Americans who were swept up by the cry for defense. They had a material interest, too. As one magnate put it, "this is simply a business proposition, to be considered without any excitement or hysteria." If the country were attacked while unprepared, he said, "then I think the securities of my corporations would shrink from a present market value of about $37,000,000 to approximately $10,000,000 in less than thirty days . . . we should have the most frightful panic in New York and Chicago that the world has ever seen." Bernard Baruch would later charge that the unpreparedness of the country was holding back the stock market. Unpreparedness was bad business, but there was no evidence that the preparedness movement was the creature of munitions manufacturers, despite a number of scattershot charges.[17]

The agitation was also developing an organizational framework. The National Security League now had a permanent headquarters on New York's Pine Street, an impressive roster of honorary directors from the major parties, including Theodore Roosevelt and one-time Democratic presidential candidate Alton B. Parker, and a committee organization. The major committees were headed by civilian experts long identified with the cause of Army and Navy reform; Henry L. Stimson chaired the League's Army Committee and J. Bernard Walker of *The Scientific American*, the Navy Committee. This arrangement incidentally ensured that the League would commit itself to the plans of the military professionals and not strike out on new paths of its own in quest of defense. The League began to lay plans for an educational campaign and for expansion beyond New York City; hopefully, a branch could be established in every state. The Navy League continued its activities with renewed hope. W. C. Church, the editor of the *Army and Navy Journal*, decided to do a little independent work on his own. He established a private Information Bureau in Washington to advance the cause of the military, funded by money put up by himself, Bernard Baruch, and Standard Oil partner H. H. Rogers.[18]

The civilian preparedness advocates thus had leadership, organization, some money, and the highly effective backdrop of the European War to dramatize their cause. Yet, despite their success in winning over many newspapers, the business and professional classes, and the eastern social elite, the preparedness campaign which they espoused did not convince the Wilson Administration or the American people as a whole. Most of the clergy, organized labor, farmers, and townspeople remained apathetic or hostile to increasing the Army and Navy. Preparedness was an urban movement in a still rural America, deriving most of its support from a minority wing of the Republican party. A majority of people in each of the major parties, the vast mass of the American voters, remained unconvinced, and this could be clearly seen in the mirror of Congress. The best people might back defense, but the voters did not.[19]

The practical effect of this state of affairs was that the reforming efforts of Garrison and Gardner made almost no impact on the 1914-1915 lame-duck session of Congress. Garrison submitted a series of seven bills to Congress in December 1914, calling for an Army increase of 25,000 men along with a number of peripheral reforms. But his program quickly bogged down. Congress and the administration were thinking in terms of retrenchment, the legislative docket was congested with legislation because of the prolonged battle over Wilson's ill-fated Ship Purchase Bill, and the leaders of both the House and the Senate Military Committees regarded the bills with disfavor for quite opposite reasons.[20]

*   *   *

Ironically, it was the European War itself which helped kill any chance for an Army increase. In early January, there was a conference at Garrison's house, attended by the secretary of war, the secretary of the Navy, and the heads of the congressional committees that dealt with defense measures. The secretaries presented their programs. Daniels wished simply to continue the accustomed naval program of laying down two battleships a year; Garrison stated the case for a 25-percent increase in the size of the Army. Congressman Oscar Underwood of Alabama, the Democratic floor leader in the House, then pointed out that any ambitious program of Army increase was impracticable; the European War had reduced trade to such an extent that governmental revenues, largely derived from import duties, had fallen off, and strict economies would have to be observed. By the end of the month, the Wilson Administration was actually thinking of reducing the Army and Navy to meet the problem.[21]

Continuing on this line, the House Military Affairs Committee rejected the Garrison program in toto. Chairman James Hay announced that "I am utterly opposed to adding a single man to the standing Army as it now exists." A troop increase of the size Garrison had proposed would cost the country $27 million a year. Nor was Hay interested in piling up a reserve of materiel. He felt that this would only leave the government with a mound of obsolescent equipment. All the House would do was pass a regular Army Appropriations Bill, although for once most of the Army's ordinary requests were accepted without a fight, perhaps because the requests were so modest. The final bill, "the unregenerate action of a group of unrepentant sinners," as *The New Republic* put it, went through the House after a spiritless debate which few Republicans bothered to attend. It was not just Democratic congressmen who were unsympathetic to the reform and enlargement of the Army. Representative James Mann, the Republican floor leader, made his own contribution to obstruction by knocking out a small appropriation providing for military observers in

Europe. Out of a concern for neutrality, the Wilson Administration had already declined to let any high-ranking officers visit the warring armies; Mann's action meant that the United States Army would be forced to make its plans with only a second-hand knowledge of European military developments.[22]

In the Senate, the situation was different. Here, Garrison ran into the formidable personality of the new chairman of the Military Affairs Committee, Senator George Chamberlain of Oregon. Chamberlain, a progressive Democrat, was a big-army man concerned with the possible menace of Japan. The chairman informed the secretary of war that he disapproved of the Army legislation which the War Department had submitted, even though he had been willing to sponsor the bills. Although Garrison's proposals were perhaps individually good, the senator observed, all of them had not been given General Staff approval, and they represented at most only a "continuation of what may be called the system of piecemeal legislation." Chamberlain demanded that the War Department submit a general reorganization bill based on the disregarded 1912 Report on the Organization of the Land Forces. He proposed an end to all the patchwork legislation tacked on to the appropriation bills as riders. "I do not think that Congress should be asked for what the War Department thinks it can get, but for what the country actually needs," Chamberlain told the secretary. Meanwhile, nothing could be done until the next session of Congress.[23]

By the beginning of February Garrison was ready to resign. He was discouraged and worn out by the fight, he had a poor personal relationship with the President, and he felt isolated in the Cabinet. The secretary of war did not quit, however. The President persuaded him to stay on, for a Cabinet resignation on a policy issue would be a blow to the administration and the Democratic party.[24]

Representative Gardner got equally rough treatment from Congress as he pressed his battle for defense with colorful persistence. Gardner showed a real flair for propaganda; he had a staff member send every Chamber of Commerce in the country petitions for an investigation of the defense situation which could then be mailed to their congressmen. Public response seemed encouraging, but congressional reaction was less so. He requested a hearing from the House Rules Committee on his resolution calling for an investigation. Five ex-secretaries of war, he announced, were ready to testify in support of the resolution. The Rules Committee refused to hear his witnesses and rejected his resolution. The normal committee structure of Congress could adequately supervise the nation's defenses, he was informed. Gardner then decided to sit in on the defense committee hearings. The House Military Affairs Committee hearings had already closed, and the Naval Affairs Committee at first refused to let Gardner question the witnesses. Gardner adroitly circumvented this rule by asking his questions through the intermediary of a friendly Republican member of the Committee. Gardner made the newspapers, but did not win over the Naval Committee.[25]

Gardner's first real victory came when the House adopted his resolution calling upon the secretary of war to report on the state of the coast defenses. Congress had a special interest in the Coast Artillery Corps, since it was a strictly defensive and necessary part of the military. More importantly, Gardner had been making lurid charges that battleships with fifteen-inch guns could anchor out of range of our shore batteries and demolish lower Manhattan. The coastal guns would run out of ammunition after two hours of firing anyway, he charged. But the secretary of war's report to Congress was reassuring. The twelve-inch guns mounted on disappearing carriages that were the mainstay of the continental defenses did have a limited range, but this could be increased, and the ammunition supply was 73 percent of that considered necessary. The War Department and the General Staff were not interested in spending money on coastal defense; they wanted to concentrate on building up the mobile forces instead. Gardner's subsequent move to amend the Fortifications Bill by appropriating $1 million for coast-defense gun ammunition was crushed by a vote of 219 to 38. Congress had emphatically not been stampeded. As the bill's astute manager, Kentucky Congressman Swagar Shirley, pointed out patiently, "It is not practicable at any one time in any one year to do everything that anyone may suggest as being necessary or desirable to prepare us fully for an emergency if it should happen tomorrow. Men properly consider the probability of such emergency."[26]

Gardner was undismayed. His next move was to assemble the entire Army's enlisted reserve in a dining room of the Willard Hotel, in order to dramatize the nation's weakness. This was quite feasible, since the reserve consisted of only sixteen men. Gardner's action struck some people as a bit frivolous. In his energetic campaign, "Gussie" Gardner had accomplished practically nothing and had irritated Congress. To his colleagues, the flamboyant congressman riding his hobbyhorse of defense had become a figure of fun. A piece of doggerel quoted on the floor of the House perhaps expressed the general sentiment:

> With teeth a champing in its gums
> and ears that beat like muffled drums
> The horrid gussiegardner comes
> A-gussying all day.[27]

*   *   *

As the winter and spring wore on, the preparedness drive continued, gaining fresh momentum from events abroad. In February, the Germans declared a submarine warfare zone around the British Isles in which belligerent merchant vessels would be sunk at sight; since American citizens calmly continued to travel in Allied ships across the Atlantic, this was an ominous move. The war darkened the front pages of the nation's newspapers, a seemingly permanent thundercloud. The magazine *Current Opinion* reported in April that "nothing has become plainer during the past few weeks than the growth during the progress of the European war of a widespread belief that we of the United States must get ready to fight somebody." That same month, the ambassador to Italy, Thomas Nelson Page, privately warned the administration that there would be more than one country in Europe when the war ended that might think of recouping its losses by a trans-Atlantic adventure. After the war, the United States might have to "if not show our teeth, at least make it known that we still have them."[28]

The Wilson Administration maintained its serene course. The President showe no outward disposition to change his policies. In early May, Secretary of the Interior Franklin K. Lane wrote House that he and Garrison were the only Cabinet members who supported larger military expenditures. There was, of course, activity at lower levels of the administration. General Wood continued to conduct a discreet propaganda on his own initiative from Governor's Island, and the Army General Staff, at Garrison's direction, began working on the sort of comprehensive bill Senator Chamberlain had requested. The Navy General Board, having obtained a rudimentary staff organization from Congress with the help of its best friend, Richmond P. Hobson, now turned to a little intrigue. With the connivance of Franklin Roosevelt, the Board laid plans to turn the spring maneuvers into a war game in which the defending fleet would be annihilated by a superior attacking force, an educational project strongly resisted by Josephus Daniels.[29]

The turning point for the preparedness movement came on May 7, 1915. That afternoon the German submarine raider U20 torpedoed the great Cunard liner *Lusitania* off the Irish coast. The *Lusitania* went down with eleven hundred civilians, over a hundred of them American citizens. It was an outrage against the structure of international law Americans had pledged to support. The European War, "with which," Wilson had once declared, "we have nothing to do, whose causes cannot touch us," had made its fatal entrance into American life. The impact of the *Lusitania* crisis was in a sense paradoxical. The pro-Allied realists who had been claiming that America was totally unprepared to fight now demanded that the nation instantly declare war. The rest of the country, and the Wilson Administration, began to think in terms of defense.[30]

Wilson decided to vindicate American rights by the pen and not by the sword. Except for increasing the guard at a few depots, he ordered that no preparations be made for any military emergency while relations between Germany and the United States were the subject of diplomatic negotiation. But negotiations proved a long-drawn-out process; the Germans were committed to their submarine campaign and their first diplomatic reply was unsatisfactory. The second American note was stronger, so strong, in fact, that Secretary of State William Jennings Bryan resigned rather than approve it, thus profoundly affecting the balance of Wilson's Cabinet. But the awkward thing was that the ultimatum had nothing behind it. Everyone knew that America had no force to intervene with, and was in no way prepared to affect the outcome of the war. The American ambassador to Germany told Wilson bluntly, "the Germans fear only *war* with us—but state frankly that they do not believe we dare to declare it, call us cowardly bluffers and say our notes are worse than waste paper." On the other hand, a last-minute attempt to launch a crash program of military preparedness could make it impossible to settle the *Lusitania* crisis peacefully because of its effect on the diplomatic climate.

The Wilson Administration was in deep need of a sword in hand as well as an olive branch. To use the vocabulary of a later age, it lacked a "credible deterrent."[31]

The international crisis gave a tremendous boost to the preparedness agitation, as Americans looked to their arms in a burst of spontaneous patriotism. Theodore Roosevelt made plans to lead a division of volunteers to the front, officered by the cream of the Regular Army, a sort of super Rough Riders. The Navy League, somewhat irrelevantly, demanded that Congress be called into session to pass a $500 million bond issue for a long-range naval building program. The ranks of organizations like the Navy League and the National Security League swelled; the Navy League alone gained 11,000 new members that summer, and spawned a Woman's Section. In June, the National Security League held a Conference on Peace and Preparedness, mostly emphasizing preparedness. Three hundred delegates from twenty-five states gathered at New York's Hotel Astor, whose lobby had been decorated for the occasion with a torpedo and fourteen-inch shells. The same month a Conference Committee on National Preparedness was organized to coordinate the work of nine different groups that were now involved in the movement, including the Security and Navy Leagues.[32]

While many voices were now united in crying for preparedness, there was less unanimity on how preparedness should be achieved or exactly what we should be prepared for. There was a notable dearth of hard proposals for raising an expeditionary force able to fight abroad against Germany. Instead, patriotic fervor channeled itself into demands for defensive measures. Since it was clear that neither Germany nor anyone else was going to attack the United States, at least until the war in Europe was over, preparedness had to be aimed at a peculiarly vague target in the future. It became the exaggerated response of a generation brutally shaken out of a calm faith in peace and progress into the belief that "the events of any 24 hours are liable to change the history of the world." The *Lusitania* incident seemed to have proven that anything was possible. Thus, thoughts on the aftermath of the war evoked horrendous potentialities. The preparedness advocates envisioned a nightmarish future of worldwide struggles for commercial dominance. As the new chief of naval operations, Admiral William S. Benson, warned, "When the war in Europe is ended there will be tremendous indemnities to be paid. Our national wealth will remain undiminished. Already the eyes of avarice have been turned upon us. What the result will be God only knows.'' *The New Republic* offered a shrewd analysis of the preparedness drive. Behind the movement, it reported, there was ''a limited amount of justifiable apprehension, a real need for a better army and navy, some genuine patriotic aspiration, a new expression of the instinctive fighting spirit of the early American . . .'' But there was also ''too much incoherent panic and muddled thinking.''[33]

Both prudence and political necessity now impelled the Wilson Administration to throw its support behind the preparedness drive. The United States, armored mostly in moral righteousness, was now involved in a chilling and unexpected confrontation with the strongest and most ruthless military power on earth. House, Wilson's closest adviser, was glumly convinced that the President had never realized the gravity of the country's unprepared position. If war came with Germany, he confided to his diary, ''it will be because we are totally unprepared and Germany feels we are impotent. The trouble with the President is that he does not move at times with sufficient celerity.'' Colonel House confided some of his thoughts to Wilson, who was then taking a well-earned summer vacation in Cornish, New Hampshire. ''I wonder,'' House wrote in early July, ''whether the time has not come for us to put our country in a position of security. I wonder too whether we did not make a mistake in not preparing actively when this war first broke loose.'' At least America could be ready for the *next* crisis.[34]

Political considerations also had to be taken into account. The public mood was such that House privately felt Wilson would be lost unless he got aboard the preparedness bandwagon. In August, Wilson's private secretary, Joseph Tumulty, would explicitly raise the point with the President. The Republicans would only have two possible issues in 1916, Tumulty wrote—the tariff and national defense. The latter issue could be defused, Tumulty went on, if Wilson could devise a ''sane, reasonable and workable programme'' acceptable to Cabinet, Congress, the Army and Navy, and the people. Tumulty shrewdly beckoned the President to the task by pointing out its difficulty; the job ''will tax your leadership in the party to the last degree.'' Speed, however, was essential, since ''in the carrying out of this programme we cannot afford to hesitate or to blunder, because as election day approaches trivial mistakes will be magnified and exaggerated by the opposition."[35]

Wilson, who was no political fool, had doubtless speculated along these lines himself. The preparedness current was irresistible. Wilson's Cabinet had already begun to shift ground. Robert Lansing, the new secretary of state, was a hard-line lawyer convinced that America would have to fight Germany sooner or later. Even Josephus Daniels, it was noted, under a particularly heavy barrage of criticism as an intellectual twin of Bryan, had begun to show a "newly developed zeal" that summer, and demanded that the Navy General Board produce a five-year building program at the end of June. In mid-July there was a Cabinet meeting devoted exclusively to preparedness. Gradually Wilson swung around and embraced the movement. Armaments might be a useful counterweight to diplomacy in these times, and the defense movement offered ample scope for Wilson to demonstrate his visionary leadership. Preparedness, after all, might become as much a moral crusade as unpreparedness. By taking charge of this popular cause, Wilson could at once guide it away from excess into useful channels and convert it into a triumph for the Democratic party.[36]

On July 21, Wilson wrote to his secretaries of war and the Navy, asking them to draw up defense programs that he could submit to Congress in his next annual message. He did not promise that he would present Congress with the complete programs, but "the important thing now is to know and know fully what we need." Wilson added the pious but foredoomed hope that the programs recommended would "be of such a character as to commend [themselves] to every patriotic and practical mind." On the same day the third *Lusitania* note went out, declaring that the German replies had been "very unsatisfactory," and that America intended to maintain freedom of the seas "without compromise and at any cost."[37]

The connection between these two news items was only apparent. Although Germany might have interpreted the call for reports on defense as a diplomatic signal that America was not, after all, a Quaker nation, for all practical purposes the compartment between American foreign policy and American defense policy was watertight. The crisis with Germany was at hand, while Congress would not even consider the defense measures until December. Preparedness was therefore a long-run policy, to be pursued "without regard to present day controversies," as Wilson accurately informed the press. In effect, defense policy would be made in a vacuum. *The New Republic* had cautioned, "preparedness consists more in knowing what we have to do and why we want to do it, than in a feverish haste to make ready to do it in some particular way." But this point was lost on the men to whom the preparedness issue had now been entrusted.[38]

3

The General Staff
Proposes. . . .

*It cannot be assumed that all the intelligence of the
army is embodied in the General Staff. It would be a
small package to contain such a large amount of goods.*

—Major General Tasker Bliss

When Wilson made his call for a defense program in late July of 1915,
the War Department was ready. On its own initiative, the Department had
been busily at work preparing its plan ever since March. The European
War had provided an opportunity to advance the Army that was just too
good to be missed.

A number of reasons had led Secretary of War Garrison to formulate a
comprehensive plan for Army development in the late winter of 1915.
The next session of Congress, scheduled to meet in December, would be
the long session, and would have ample time to consider thoroughgoing
reform proposals. The powerful Senator George Chamberlain had explicitly requested that new Army legislation be submitted in line with
some general plan of development, such as that presented in the 1912
Report on the Organization of the Land Forces. Finally, it was necessary
to rally the Army behind one constructive plan in order to get any

concrete results. For the Army, as usual, was a nest of intrigue, divided into a set of factions each of which had its own legislative connections.[1]

Garrison had had many chances to find this out. He had already exiled one General Staff colonel to New York for attempting to influence Senator Chamberlain behind the War Department's back. The secretary of war's own set of proposals to Congress had been sniped at from the rear by the General Staff, on the grounds that the secretary had ignored the 1912 report. "You can readily see how quickly men such as our antagonists in Congress will take up the charge . . . that the Army itself has no policy," General Leonard Wood grumbled. The General Staff had particularly objected to the proposed enlargement of the Coast Artillery Corps. After the defeat of this proposal, the Corps, miffed at its neglect, showed signs of wanting to attach itself to the Navy, with the same status as the Marine Corps. This pleased the other generals even less. The Army would lose most of its stake in America's overseas empire if this proposal went through. As General W. W. Wotherspoon warned, "these combined influences, using the magic word defense, which appeals to the yellow streak, would receive the major portion of the country's consideration, and little would be left for the mobile army."[2]

Clearly then, the Army as a whole had to be unified behind some military policy, or the opportunity presented by the war to obtain defense measures might be lost. Garrison moved decisively. His first step was to muzzle the Army, a move previously suggested by the President himself for other reasons. On February 23, 1915, the secretary issued General Order No. 10, commanding officers of the Army to "refrain, until further orders, from giving out for publication any interview, statement, discussion or article on the military situation in the United States or abroad." The Army could no longer afford the luxury of publicly divided counsels, nor the irritation of congressmen at loquacious officers. To get positive legislation, the Army would have to pull in one direction and speak with one voice. That voice would be Garrison's. Many Army officers agreed with this action. "I think the Secretary has made a great advance in placing the gag on the Army," one wrote Wood, who did not particularly care to be gagged. Anybody who put his head up to confuse the issue, the officer went on, should be crushed with the "heel of oppression."[3]

The secretary of war's next move was to obtain a long-range plan of Army reorganization. Garrison ordered the War College Division, the planning unit of the General Staff, to set about this task on March 11. The secretary had a clear idea of what he wanted. He had in mind, he wrote, something like the 1886 report of the Endicott Board on coastal fortifications. Although Congress had never formally adopted the report, the nation's sea-coast defenses had been gradually built up over the years in accordance with its recommendations. Hopefully, the new plan would do the same thing for the Army as a whole, laying down authoritative guidelines for Congress. The plan would not be adopted immediately. "It cannot be expected that Congress will ever by formal resolution approve and accept a broad military policy, translate it in terms of a comprehensive bill, and pass the bill with all the necessary appropriations of money to carry it out." It would not even be wise to ask for this, the secretary went on philosophically, since it might only throw the defense question into the political arena, "tying it to the temporary fortunes of one party." Better a slow movement to the inevitable goal.[4]

Getting down to particulars, Garrison asked the War College Division to produce a revision of the 1912 Report, bringing it up to date and eliminating everything unnecessary. There were four main points to be decided: the recommended strength of the Regular Army and Organized Militia; the question of reserves; the problem of organizing supplementary volunteer forces; and the amount of reserve material and supplies the Army should lay in store. Once more the General Staff should solicit the views of department commanders and bureau chiefs on these points.[5]

The secretary of war was enthusiastic about this project. As the work began, he spurred the General Staff on to exert its best efforts in producing a monument of military planning that would last for years. "This country has never had a well-thought out, wrought out, and agreed-upon military policy. This is the first opportunity within the life-time of those now active to have this done," Garrison exhorted. But of course this was not true. The Army had come up with just such a plan in 1912. The problem was that master-plans had short lifetimes, and the Army was just too diverse a body ever to agree on anything.[6]

The actual staff-work on the project proceeded on two parallel lines. The committees of Brigadier General Montgomery M. Macomb's War College Division, after fusing their own work with the views of the department commanders and bureau chiefs, were ordered to come up with a draft proposal by June 15. General Macomb or a member of the coordinating committee stopped in at the office of the chief of staff every two or three days and kept him informed. At the same time, Garrison convened a series of meetings of the top echelon of the War Department in private dining rooms at the Shoreham or the Army and Navy Club, beginning in late April. There Garrison and Assistant Secretary Henry S. Breckinridge, not even bothering to change into the customary evening clothes, dined with three senior generals and talked into the midnight hours. The War College Division would initiate the proposals, but it was this group that would actually decide.[7]

Two of the three senior generals were relatively new arrivals to the high-ceilinged offices of the War Department. The new Army chief of staff, succeeding Wotherspoon, was Brigadier General (later Major General) Hugh L. Scott, a fine old cavalryman with a walrus mustache and bullet-mangled hands who had campaigned on the western plains and in Cuba and the Philippines. Scott possessed a variety of unexpected talents: he was a leading authority on sign-languages, an expert on the care of horses, and a talented conciliator. He was also loyal, conscientious, and had a rock-like solidity of character. "You would almost as soon expect to see the Washington Monument walk off its base as to see the General flustered," *The Nation*'s correspondent wrote admiringly. Yet, Scott fitted rather awkwardly into his new job. He was a better outdoorsman than desk soldier, and special quasidiplomatic missions to the Piute Indians and Pancho Villa cut sorely into his time. While solid, he was not very imaginative; he tended to echo the conventional wisdom of the General Staff. Ex-President William Howard Taft was not always the best judge of human character, but when he wrote of Scott, "as Chief of Staff he is wood to the middle of his head," he may have had a point.[8]

Fortunately, Scott was backed up in his duties by the new assistant chief of staff, Brigadier General (later Major General) Tasker H. Bliss, his friend and West Point classmate. Bliss was a very unusual general indeed. A massive figure with a dome-like forehead and a face that resembled Bismarck's, Bliss was something of an Army intellectual. A professor's son, he had attended West Point to save his family the expense of providing for his education; with his ever-present pad and pencil and ash-covered suits, he still retained a suggestion of the scholar about him. The assistant chief of staff had one of the keenest minds in the Army. He was neither an agitator for reform nor an ideologue, but he possessed brilliance combined with common sense, and his mind was not cluttered with the smug assumptions of many of his military colleagues. As one of his former subordinates later put it, he was "quite the best type of what is known as the 'old army.' "[9]

The third member of the military triumvirate taken into Garrison's counsel was the judge advocate general, Major General Enoch Crowder. A hard-working bachelor who had become the first general of his West Point class, Crowder was a skillful Army lawyer who did not always agree with the General Staff. In an Army narrowly confined by legalistic interpretations of detailed congressional statutes, Crowder was the most powerful bureau chief since Fred C. Ainsworth; he could also be almost as obstructive as Ainsworth, although he went along with the Garrison program. As judge advocate general, Crowder would draw up any actual military legislation the War Department might submit. Consequently, he was included in the little departmental dinners.[10]

*   *   *

Thus, by May, the planning machinery was already in gear. The *Lusitania* incident, which rocked the nation, had curiously little effect on the process. In case of war, Scott suggested to the secretary of war, the National Guard should be mobilized and sent to the Mexican border to relieve the Regular Army, and there should be a call for volunteers, after the proper authorization by Congress. This was almost the extent of the Army's staff-work for a possible war with Germany. The only senior officer with a sense of reality was Bliss, who began working out, more or less on his own, a plan for sending twenty-two divisions to Europe if America had to intervene. Otherwise the Army, floating in a foreign policy vacuum, preferred to plan for the possibilities of the future rather than the needs of the present. Such contingency plans as the War College Division possessed dealt only with occupying Mexico or repelling a hypothetical invasion. The War Department made no official plans for raising a force that might intervene in Europe. Wilson had never requested it to do this, and the Department was wholly ignorant of the President's intentions, "a bit hung up in the air, like Mahomet's coffin," as Scott put it. The War Department's planning for the Army serenely ignored the possibility of immediate use.[11]

Instead, the War Department concentrated its efforts on framing long-range plans. Unfortunately, it did not labor very smoothly. In action, the War College Division seemed disorganized and slow, while showing disturbing tendencies to delve into extraneous minutia hardly appropriate in framing a general plan. The Division was small, quartered miles away from the War Department itself, and as it turned out, rather indifferently staffed. As Wood confessed, "when Hay forced through the unconditional Manchu Act, we either had to leave the General Staff half full or put in some men who to say the least were not all that can be desired from the standpoint of General Staff work." General Macomb himself seemed "very unsatisfactory and weak" as an administrator to some of his subordinates. By mid-June, Garrison was impatiently demanding the promised results. So far the Division had produced only a statement on the Regular Army. But what concerned the secretary of war most was what the Division would recommend in the way of reserves. This was the heart of the matter. Since a modern army was simply a training machine, the size of the machine should be determined by the need for trained reserves, not vice versa. General Macomb could only reply apologetically that much of the work had already been done, and that the committee was still assimilating reports from War College students and general officers. The mass of data so far piled up was "all that the committee can handle," but Macomb assured the secretary of war that doubtless the essence of the nation's future military policy was hidden somewhere in it. The General Staff itself was at loggerheads over many points, especially over the question of reserves, and General Macomb was unable to say when an agreement on this question would be reached. "Infinite patience is required to overcome the new difficulties which every discussion brings out," he added helpfully.[12]

At length all was finished, and the War College Division was able to submit the results of its labors in the form of an Epitome of Military Policy in July. The Epitome was much more ambitious than the 1912 Report on the Organization of the Land Forces. In 1912, the General Staff had visualized slowly increasing the Army by yearly increments in order to obtain three complete infantry divisions at peace strength in the continental United States; afterwards, the Army would attempt to persuade Congress to begin building up a fourth division. The Epitome boldly demanded the four divisions and their auxiliaries immediately. The Regular Army should consist of sixty-five infantry regiments, twenty-five cavalry regiments, twenty-one field artillery regiments, and support troops. All units would be maintained at war strength, providing a regular force of 281,000 men. The mobile forces in the continental United States alone would amount to 121,000 men, a larger force than the entire existing Army. The big mobile army would be backed by a large reserve. Troops would enlist for two years of active duty and six years in the reserve, which meant, according to the calculations of the General Staff, that there would be a force of 500,000 fully trained men, regulars and reserves, available in the United States in eight years. Since the Regular Army units would be at full strength, the reserves would be used not as fillers, but in new units brigaded side by side with the existing mobile army.[13]

This was not all. The Epitome envisioned a second-line force, ultimately amounting to half a million men, that would back up the Regular Army and its reserves. The 1912 Report had assumed that the Army would be reinforced in time of war by the militia and newly mobilized civilian volunteers. The Epitome discarded this idea as inadequate. The National Guard was dismissed as untrustworthy. Since the War College Division felt that it took a year to train a soldier adequately, the volunteers would have to be given some military instruction before war actually broke out. Therefore, the framers of the Epitome, vastly elaborating on a suggestion from Garrison, came up with a proposal for a federally controlled peacetime training force, manned by part-time volunteers. Under this plan, citizen-soldiers would train three months a year for three years. If war came, they would need only three more months of training to be ready for combat. The force would be known as the Continental Army, a name that the Staff thought "appropriate, distinctive, and possessing grand historical associations." After all the steps advocated by the General Staff in the Epitome had been taken, and the necessary stockpiles of war material laid in, the United States would be able to field a million fully trained and equipped men in ninety days.[14]

This plan had two drawbacks. One was the fact that the plan bore almost no relation to the diplomatic crisis in which the United States was involved at the time. The War College Division was planning for the future; the sizable armies which it deemed necessary would take years to develop. A second was the plan's curious obsolescence. While the greatest war of attrition in history went on in Europe, the United States General Staff was still committed to the belief, as it had been in 1912, that what counted in war was the force in being at the very beginning of the conflict. The Staff believed that "during the first weeks of war in this country the military situation will probably be critical." But this could be true only on one assumption. The Army planned by the General Staff was structured, quite simply, to repel a full-scale invasion of the United States; any other purpose would be secondary.[15]

The Atlantic and Pacific oceans were broad and America's ports well fortified, but the imagination of the General Staff's committees over-leaped all of this and conjured up a threat credible enough to justify an army as large as they had proposed. The method of the War College Division was simplicity itself as it calculated the possibility of trans-oceanic attack. Captain Dennis Nolan of the General Staff succinctly stated the Army's assumptions: "The number of troops in the first and succeeding expeditions . . . is a function of a.) the size of the enemy's army, and b.) the number, size and speed of the vessels of the enemy's merchant marine that can be used as transports." To simplify matters, the American staff officers eliminated the complicating factor of the European War and used the army and merchant fleet strengths of foreign powers as of August 1, 1914. To further simplify matters, the staff officers assumed the American fleet would not be able to offer any effective opposition. The logistics of a possible invasion were calculated by using the U.S. Army Field Service Regulations, which optimistically stated that a 6,000-ton merchant vessel could carry 2,000 troops with ammunition, wagons, and supplies for three months. Using these methods of figuring, the War College Division could come up with some alarming results which made the threat of invasion plausible. In fact, even Austria-Hungary appeared to have dangerous potentialities.[16]

Perhaps the most meaningful appraisal made by the War College Division concerned the capabilities of Imperial Germany, the most formidable military power in Europe. Germany could theoretically land 435,000 men and 91,457 animals on the East Coast in 15.8 days. In three months, using only 50 percent of her shipping capacity of 3,000 tons and up, Germany could deploy 1,161,000 troops and 243,000 animals. (The United States Navy, doubtless hiding from destruction in its fortified bases, would be impotent to prevent the troop-carrying armadas from shuttling across the Atlantic with the regularity of the Staten Island Ferry, the estimate assumed.) With just three waves of troops, Germany could land enough men to entrench from Baltimore and Washington to Erie, Pennsylvania; after that, reinforcements could be sent to mop up New York, Pennsylvania, and New England, thus gaining control over 35 million Americans and the steel factories and gun plants. "The accomplishment of the plan outlined above for the invading forces instead of being a noteworthy military achievement," the Staff report went on, "would be a commonplace military operation ridiculously easy of accomplishment." The report used Germany only as an example, however. The General Staff was careful to be impartially suspicious. There was, after all, the British-Japanese alliance to be considered, which practically placed "a powerful army on our northern frontier." And "England or any other nation will do what she thinks her vital national interests demand."[17]

The groundwork for a hundred Sunday supplement scare stories had been laid—and laid by the Army General Staff. It was all nonsense, of course: the Army knew nothing about amphibious operations and was in no position to learn anything, since it had been denied the opportunity of sending adequate military observers abroad. The War College Division's calculations were exercises in arithmetic, not war. They took no account of the capabilities of the Navy or the difficulties of landing armies on open beaches against opposition. Strangely enough, neither the Army nor the Navy had ever given any consideration to the techniques of defense against amphibious assault, which was the whole theoretical menace to the nation. They ignored the logistical problems of supplying an army across an ocean, and of course they ignored the political obstacles that prevented a full-scale incursion into the Western Hemisphere by any power. If Captain Nolan felt that a German invasion would be "ridiculously easy of accomplishment," the German General Staff felt "America cannot be attacked by us" and despaired of even assaulting Britain without the invention of totally new weapons. Germany was the most logical enemy, and the German Navy, as it turned out, did not have the bunker capacity to cross the Atlantic and fight, since it was designed to be used in the North Sea. But the Army was not deliberately trying to bamboozle the country. It was itself a captive of its own rigid ideas. Politically ignorant, relatively uncoordinated with the Navy, the Army demanded maximum insurance against the worst that could conceivably happen to the United States.[18]

The assumption of the likelihood of future invasion attempts inherent in the General Staff's Epitome was not challenged when the plan was submitted to the secretary of the war and the rest of the Army. But other features were criticized. For it turned out that the Epitome was a pretty vulnerable document. General Wood was not impressed when the plan came to his desk; he noted in his diary, "Saw Gen Staff Mil. Policy; looks like promotion scheme and rather weak." Lieutenant Colonel W. H. Johnston, a General Staff officer marked down by Wotherspoon as an "habitual trouble maker," was even more cutting. He circulated a memorandum among his colleagues cataloguing the internal inconsistencies of the plan.[19]

Johnston pointed out that the General Staff had nowhere tried to answer the question of just where the men for its proposed army would be obtained. In the past fiscal year, the Army had been able to recruit only 35,941 men. (The Army had accepted only 24 percent of applicants, and had later rejected some of these.) To meet the troop requirements projected by the Epitome, 320,000 recruits a year would be necessary for the Regular Army and the Continental force. The Continental Army would fail anyway; Americans could scarcely be expected to sacrifice their jobs periodically "simply to receive 50 cents a day, while losing higher pay or losing positions entirely." The whole scheme, as Johnston had earlier noted, seemed to assume that the volunteer force would somehow be composed exclusively of college students, a silk-stocking army for the rich. The only way to get the necessary manpower for such an army was conscription, and although almost all the officers in the War College Division privately favored this method, the General Staff had not bothered to mention the subject in the Epitome. This was just as well. Conscription might be a nice way of raising an army, but in the United States of 1915, peacetime conscription seemed as politically possible as monarchy.[20]

Garrison was equally taken aback by the General Staff plan. It would obviously be fabulously expensive to implement; Garrison felt that it

would cost $500 million the first year, although the General Staff pre-
ferred to figure the cost a little differently. Any such amount would
"chill, if not effectively destroy" the drive for Army reform, the secretary of war told the President. This would quintuple the Army's present
budget, and would be too much of a shock for a Democratic Congress.
The secretary had asked the General Staff to formulate a long-range plan,
but this was not quite what he had in mind. There was a need for a more
gradual approach to the defense problem, and so the secretary of war,
with the concurrence of his senior advisers, asked the General Staff to
come up with a more modest proposal that Congress might actually pass.
The General Staff could ask for more units, but they would be maintained
at peace strength, not war strength. A Regular Army of 140,000 or so
men was all that was practicable; no larger force could be housed in
existing military installations. (General Crowder doubted that a larger
force could even be recruited.) The planned reserves would fill up the
Regular Army to fighting strength, and the Continental Army would have
to be relied upon for the rest.[21]

*   *   *

The General Staff finally moved down out of the clouds and cranked
out a plan that might be mildly feasible and that at least satisfied Garrison
and the chief of staff. The Regular Army would be increased in two
increments to a strength of a little over 140,000 men. This would allow
the creation of ten new infantry regiments and four field artillery regiments, along with fifty-two companies of coast artillery and various
auxiliary units. Ironically, this enlargement of the Army would mean
scrapping another long-cherished reform of the military Progressives.
Now every Army post would have to be retained to accommodate the new
troops. In addition to the regular force, there would be a Continental
Army of 400,000 men, to be raised in yearly increments of 133,000. The
proposed terms of service for both regulars and volunteers were made less
stringent and more appealing; regulars would have only a four-year
reserve obligation after their two years on active duty, and the men of the
Continental Army would have to train for a total of only six months or so,
spaced out over three years.[22]

*   *   *

In its final form, the Continental Army marked a new departure in the military thinking of the General Staff. Up to this point, it had been assumed that the only way to get effective reserves was to pass men through the Regular Army itself. Now the reserve training force was to be a thing apart. But the Continental Army was also the Achilles heel of the whole plan. Garrison had originally envisaged merely some sort of sketchily trained federal volunteer force, a home guard familiarized with arms by a month in camp and a little refresher training. The General Staff, always theoretical-minded, felt that this was totally inadequate. Six months' training was the minimum amount that would give satisfactory results, and this training could not be given all at once or it would disrupt the training schedules of the Regular Army. So the training periods of the proposed Continental Army would be strung out over three years, causing maximum inconvenience to most prospective volunteers. The exact length of the proposed training was never quite decided upon, although six months was the period used for figuring out the costs. Garrison himself accurately expressed the difficulty: "With respect to the period of intensive training which may be finally determined upon, there will be two points of view. One will be that whatever period may be finally fixed is not long enough, and the other will be that it is too long."[23]

There was an even worse drawback. By coming out for the Continental Army, the War Department was forced to scrap the Organized Militia as a first-line reserve. This was a fateful decision, deliberately made by the secretary of war and his senior advisers. It would irretrievably alienate the National Guard lobby and states' rights congressmen. But the secretary of war was convinced that the existing Organized Militia was a broken reed, which could never be made into a dependable federal reserve. Assistant Secretary Breckinridge, who had served seven years in the Kentucky National Guard, had an even lower opinion of the usefulness of the state troops. The judge advocate general, at first an advocate of a federalized militia, now had changed his mind. Under the Constitution, he concluded, the United States government might be able to set standards for the militia's personnel, but it could not adequately supervise its training, and any law Congress passed federalizing the militia might be unconstitutional. Obviously, the defense of the United States could not be staked on a disputed piece of legislation.

The problem was that the War Department basically did not trust the militia system. The Army still remembered with horror the performance of the militia in the War of 1812. The Army wanted any reserve formally under its own control, and from this point of view the existing National Guard appeared to be not a military asset but an obstruction to an effective defense policy. The War Department's solution was to push the militia aside, bribe it with an increase in federal appropriations, and relegate it purely to the role of a state force. There was another possibility, however. The plans for the Continental Army were still vague. Individual National Guardsmen, or even whole units, if their states consented, might join up with the federal force in some way—no one had really thought this through very well. But in any event, the Continental Army meant downgrading the traditional militia system, a move which could prove explosive. Even as he advocated the policy, Crowder warned, "It will not do to under-estimate the opposition which the proposition of the continental army will encounter."[24]

On September 17, Garrison submitted his recommendations on military policy to Wilson. It was a moderate program. The cost would be substantial, some $183 million the first year and more later, but this figure was unavailable. The Regular Army would be increased 40 percent, but the real innovation would be the federally controlled reserve of the Continental Army. The new plan bore a resemblance to an old one; it committed the War Department "in principle," as Crowder noted, to the proposals General Emory Upton had made in 1880. Upton had been a noted Army reformer of the nineteenth century who had shot himself while ill and in despair over the difficulties of implementing any of his ideas. Garrison's program was to prove almost equally frustrating to its author.[25]

The difficulty was that it was a compromise measure, and that it could be criticized as such. The key to the whole program was the Continental Army, which satisfied nobody, not even its creators. Because of the need for strict economy, the Continental force could not be given adequate equipment; moreover, there was the open question of whether it could be recruited at all. The secretary of war himself declined to say that the scheme would work, although he felt that "this [did] not in any way alter the course which we should pursue." If the Continental Army failed, it would prove "the inability of any volunteer system to produce results." Presumably the country would then have to turn to some form of compulsory service. There were many civilians who felt that if the failure of the Continental Army might mean conscription, it would be best if the scheme were not even tried.[26]

At the same time that Garrison submitted his own proposals, he also submitted to the President the swollen plan of the War College Division, now prestigiously entitled "A Statement of a Proper Military Policy for the United States." The Statement was in effect the production of a committee of the War College Division, but it bore the imprimatur of the General Staff. When this fact came to the attention of the public, it would inevitably tend to undercut Garrison's own recommendations. Garrison had tried to unite the Army behind one plan; he had succeeded only in apparently creating a cleavage between the "political" recommendations of the War Department and the military recommendations of the General Staff "experts." As Garrison told Wilson, his own plan had been approved by Scott and Bliss, and since the General Staff as a whole was composed of junior officers, not experienced generals, its recommendations could not be taken uncritically. The General Staff, Garrison put it cuttingly, lacked the "wisdom, experience, accumulated theoretical information, and knowledge of practical matters" to frame a military policy. But these deficiencies would not be appreciated by the public at large, and the gap between the recommendations of the secretary of war and those in the Statement of a Proper Military Policy would provide a tempting opportunity for preparedness enthusiasts to exploit. The monumental study Garrison had commissioned the War College Division to undertake had turned into a millstone around the neck of the department. The debate on military defense policy had not been ended. It had only just begun.[27]

There was one more difficulty. Neither Garrison's plan nor the General Staff's bore a proper relation to American foreign policy. What the United States needed was a strong armed force in hand while the European War raged; what it got was competing long-range blueprints. In his report, Garrison completely sidestepped the issue: "From some sources will come criticism based upon the assumption that there is an emergency to be met and that the proposed plan fails to meet it. The obvious answer is that no plan of permanent military policy can be devised which would at the start be adequate to meet emergent conditions.'' The War Department, Navy Department, and State Department all shared the same building, the gambrel-roofed Victorian monstrosity which bulked beside the White House, but they moved in different worlds.[28]

It was just as well. Wilson would certainly not have brooked any planning that tried directly to relate the military establishment to the war in Europe. In August 1915, as the War Department had been formulating its final recommendations, the President had called in Henry Breckinridge, and had shown him a copy of the *Baltimore Sun* which stated that the General Staff was preparing a plan in the event of war with Germany. ''Trembling and white with passion,'' Wilson ordered Breckinridge to investigate the report; if it were true, every officer of the General Staff would be relieved at once and ordered out of Washington. Breckinridge conveyed the order to Bliss, who was presiding over the Army in the absence of General Scott. Bliss had privately devised just such a plan; he diplomatically and very properly pointed out to the assistant secretary that making war plans was the Staff's duty, and such action as the President had demanded would be silly and would just kick up a political row. After this incident, the military planning of the War College Division was camouflaged. But the *Sun*'s story had been in error anyway. Bliss's memorandum to the secretary of war had been confidential, and the War College Division had in fact been completely innocent of the crime of planning to fight Germany abroad. As General Macomb reassured the chief of staff, as for the ''idea of sending an army to Europe . . . no such plans have ever been prepared, nor even contemplated by the General Staff.'' In 1914, an Army officer had written that an attempt by the United States to fight an offensive war against the military powers of Europe would be more futile than the ''Children's Crusade of 1212.'' The next war would be a ''defensive war on our own soil.'' With remarkable persistence and irrelevance, this is what the War Department was still preparing for in the summer of 1915.[29]

4

The Private War
of General Wood

*The most aggressive, the most persistent, officer who
was ever Chief of Staff, in my memory, was General
Leonard Wood. Whatever may be his merits or de-
merits, he was a man who had the courage of his
convictions and who never lost an opportunity to express those views.*

—Representative Swagar Shirley

*I am out for national preparedness, and I am going to
get it.*

—Major General Leonard Wood

The General Staff and the War Department were not the only military
factions pressing for preparedness. General Leonard Wood continued to
wage a private campaign of his own. Wood was no longer chief of staff,
but he was still senior major general in the Army, commander of the
important Eastern Department, and the most magnetic and charismatic

figure around. He still retained the strongest loyalties of many young activist officers. With the energy of a dervish and an unconventional willingness to operate outside the normal chain of command, Wood was not disposed to play a quiet, subordinate role. "The old element of hustle still follows my headquarters," he noted with pride. If the War Department in 1915 thought primarily in terms of presenting a defense program acceptable to Congress, Wood, a born military politician and propagandist, sought to mobilize a public constituency which would compel Congress to prepare the country. Increasingly, Wood called for a more total preparedness than the War Department requested, nothing less than universal military training, the nation in arms.

This was a sensitive business, on the very borders of legitimate activity. Wood's efforts were not accepted with good grace by his superiors. The senior general in the Army was too imaginative, too unorthodox, and all too political. A Democratic administration could never overlook the fact that Wood was a close friend of Theodore Roosevelt, who showed increasing signs of wishing to rejoin the Republican party and lead it on a crusade for preparedness. Wood was a fine soldier, but a bad subordinate, a "talking general," as the pacifist Oswald Garrison Villard put it, and in the march for defense he seemed to be following a different drummer.[1]

Although he was a highly competent military administrator, Wood was not a man to tie himself to a desk. From the start of his assignment to Governor's Island, he found ample opportunity to cover the country. The Eastern Department sprawled from Maine to the Gulf Coast (in addition to taking in Puerto Rico and Panama), and Wood's frequent inspection trips gave him an official pretext to travel spreading the gospel of preparedness. Wood was one of the few high-ranking officers capable of making an effective speech, and he covered his department thoroughly, speaking in civilian clothes to students, clubmen, and business associations whenever the opportunity arose. Often, he delivered several such talks a week. Back at his headquarters, the general dictated thirty letters a day, wrote introductions to books on preparedness, maintained close contact with magazine editors like Lawrence Abbott, George Harvey, and William C. Church, and artfully used every available means to bring the Army to the attention of the public. He paraded troops in New York City whenever possible. The Army had been an almost unnoticed phenomenon, tucked away in the back spaces of the country and the back pages of the newspapers. Wood wanted publicity and he got it. "Your propaganda is certainly having effect in all parts of the country," General Scott had written.[2]

Not all of the attention that the general attracted was favorable. Wood's speech to the New York Merchant's Association in December 1914, thoroughly at variance with Wilson's policy of calming the nation on defense, had decidedly annoyed the President. The general's relations with the secretary of war also deteriorated. Lindley Garrison was sympathetic to defense, but he liked to run a taut organization. Garrison demanded that all propaganda activities emanate from his own office, so that the Army would speak with one voice. This irked Wood; if the preparedness agitation were to be confined to the secretary's own talks, he fretted, "I am afraid that he will not be able to cover the ground as it should be covered." There was a growing tension between the War Department and its field commander in New York, partially due to political differences, partially to the clash of two powerful personalities, each convinced of the rectitude of his course. When the Army was muzzled in February 1915, Wood did not stop his propaganda. He went underground, speaking to audiences where no reporters were present and privately advising authors who wished to write on preparedness. But this quiet undercutting of official policy was, of course, fraught with "considerable risk," as Wood admitted to Brigadier General James Parker. The general's continuing attempts to have the Army take the initiative and work through civilian organizations not recognized by law sometimes backfired and placed Wood in an exposed position.[3]

In early 1915, there had been the case of the American Legion, a proposed volunteer civilian reserve that had been the brainchild of the editor of *Adventure Magazine*, Arthur S. Hoffman. Hoffman and his associate, a former volunteer officer named Dr. J. E. Hausmann, planned to compile a list of specially qualified men who would pledge to volunteer their services in time of war. Wood readily agreed to cooperate with the Legion. Not only was he happy to help patriotic civilians, but the card index of available personnel with skills or military training the Legion proposed to provide was something the War Department did not have and would surely need in the event of a general mobilization. One of Wood's aides, Captain Gordon Johnston, advised the pair on what information the Army would like to have, and Johnston was present at the terminal of the Governor's Island Ferry where the promoters held their first press conference. All in all, it seemed to Wood to be a useful exercise in military-civilian cooperation.[4]

The secretary of war, unfortunately, did not see it that way when he encountered a clipping from the *New York Sun* entitled "Volunteer Legions Will Drill to Meet War Call." To the War Department, the American Legion seemed either a gimmick which would actually impede any attempt to set up a real Army reserve, or a political maneuver of Theodore Roosevelt. At any rate, Garrison felt that the Army should ignore the organization. As the chief of staff informed Wood, "he says that he thinks a very sharp line should be drawn between all these things; either they ought to be all civilian or all army. . . . if the thing is a good idea he wants a function in it himself." Wood hastily disassociated himself from the Legion, to the accompaniment of a barrage of newspaper criticism, which seemed to fear the creation of a private army. In the end, the American Legion went on without government encouragement or support, acquired an impressive advisory board of former Republican secretaries of war, and enrolled some 14,000 members qualified for service by the end of the year. The War Department showed no further interest in accumulating a card file of skilled civilians.[5]

The problem against which Wood chafed was that if civilians did not do something, it seemed nobody would. In the event of war, the general felt, the Army would need all sorts of support from the civilian society, and yet the Army seemed naggingly indifferent, content to wait on the slow pace of congressional legislation. The American Legion fiasco threatened to chill other promising ideas. Barclay Parsons of the American Society of Civil Engineers wanted to organize members of his society into an Engineer Reserve in case of emergency, he told Wood, but the War Department's indifference to the American Legion seemed to put this proposal in danger. Despite rebuffs, General Wood continued to take initiatives outside of the War Department, and continued to build bridges between the Army and the Society it served. In the fight over the American Legion, the peace-minded Episcopal Bishop David Greer had indignantly accused Wood of "organizing civilians and trying to influence public opinion." The details of the Bishop's charges in that instance may have been erroneous, but, in essence, that was exactly what Leonard Wood was trying to do.[6]

One of Wood's persistent interests was in promoting military training in the colleges and universities. This would provide a nucleus of trained reserve officers, and it would also help educate the American upper classes to an awareness of the country's defense needs. There were military colleges in existence in the United States, but, with the exception of the Virginia Military Institute and Norwich College in Vermont, their training was inadequate. Military training of some sort was compulsory in sixty-eight land-grant colleges, but it was largely a matter of bored undergraduates executing the rudiments of parade-ground drill. Wood wanted to introduce advanced military training courses, combining lectures with practice, into the nation's top colleges. He felt that military science, properly taught, could attract students. Training could be given at no expense to the government (always an important consideration) by volunteer officers on detached assignment for recruiting duty. As always, Wood was trying to operate outside the normal Army framework, using voluntary enthusiasm rather than government funds to achieve results.[7]

By the fall of 1915, the movement was showing some success. Harvard was contemplating a lecture course, and the students, on their own initiative, were in the process of forming a drill battalion, while President Lowell himself became interested in the proposition. There was a serious attempt to introduce training at Princeton, and Yale University, though not attempting a lecture course, did set up four batteries of field artillery in the Connecticut National Guard. In fact, all this activity threatened to outstrip the capacities of the War Department. "I do not see where the officers are coming from to meet the demands," the chief of staff complained. Even more successful was the student military instruction camp movement that Wood fostered.[8]

Wood had set up the student training camps in 1913 when he had been chief of staff. The Army allowed high school and college students to take military training at their own expense for five weeks. The beginnings had been modest. In the first year, 222 students attended one of the two summer encampments. By General Wood's shrewd design, the main camp was held at Gettysburg, on the site of that year's Blue and Grey reunion. At the end of the final sixty-five-mile hike at Gettysburg, the trainees organized the Society of the National Reserve Corps of the United States, electing President Henry S. Drinker of Lehigh University as its president. In the fall, an Advisory Board of University Presidents for the camps was organized, with Drinker as secretary and the equally martial-minded head of Princeton University, J. G. Hibben, as president. Wood had not only given some students a little military training, but he had also helped create a potentially influential civilian lobby for the Army, with which he kept in close touch. The student camps program was one of the general's less controversial ideas. Giving college students a taste of outdoor life through the military seemed unobjectionable to almost everyone; even Wilson endorsed it. The movement retained a certain useful immunity from suspicions of militarism.[9]

There were four such camps in the summer of 1914, with three times as many college students in attendance as before. The camp at Burlington, Vermont, was especially noted for its size and efficiency, and for the fact that it was attended by a considerable number of students from prestigious eastern colleges. The seed had been planted, and Wood sought to nurture it by every means possible. This was the way to win over the future leadership of the nation to a program of national preparedness, for it was the Ivy League which would increasingly dominate the student camps, for better or for worse. Unpaid soldiering was an upper-class avocation. Since poorer students generally had to work during the summer, only a small number of trainees came from the state universities.[10]

As commander of the Eastern Department, Wood continued to press vigorously for the continuance of the college camps, maintaining close liaison with President Drinker. But the War Department seemed indifferent to the program, which it dismissed as a publicity maneuver rather than a serious attempt to create a reserve. Congress had neglected to provide appropriations for the camps; while they were conducted openly, they existed in the chinks of the Army's machinery, and the Army, bound by red tape, did not take too favorable an attitude toward anything not specifically authorized by law. Although the college students paid for their room and board at the camps, there were collateral expenses, and when the controller of the treasury disapproved an expenditure of $5,000 that had been used for maintenance at the 1914 camps, the future of the student training movement hung in doubt. Even after the *Lusitania* crisis, which surely seemed to indicate the desirability of some kind of military training, it was uncertain if the four camps slated for 1915 would be held.[11]

General Wood did not intend to let this promising movement die simply because of the inactivity of Congress. Nearly a thousand students had already enrolled for the 1915 summer camps, more than half of them for the Plattsburg, New York, camp in Wood's own department. If Congress and the controller were unsympathetic, the general would raise the money himself. Wood was well connected, his headquarters was right across the water from Manhattan Island, and the financial community of New York in the summer of 1915 seemed both pro-Ally and possessed of a patriotism quickened by the fear of shells raining down upon Wall Street. It was a good time for the defense program. Theodore Roosevelt asked if he could help raise money, a partner in the important banking firm of Kuhn, Loeb offered to make himself responsible for the cost of continuing the eastern camps, and Bernard Baruch promised Wood a donation of $10,000, if necessary. Colonel J. J. Slocum of New York offered $5,000 to the secretary of war to support the camps.[12]

In the end, all of these monetary pledges were not necessary. The controller and Judge Advocate General Crowder finally came to an amicable agreement on a legal fiction; if student camps could not be held without congressional authorization and funding, young men might still attend camps of instruction for the regular forces at no expense to the government. Since regular troops had to be in camp to train the students anyway, this seemed to get around the problem nicely. The controller really did not want to be obstructive after all. But the money Wood now had available could still be useful. Since some students were unable to pay their own way to camp, the private funds were used to provide military scholarships for them, thus giving the camps a somewhat more democratic aspect.[13]

The sinking of the *Lusitania* provided the opportunity for the further extension of Wood's campaign to win over the civilian community to defense. The shock of the crisis acted as a trigger to mobilize the latent patriotism of the upper and middle classes. The milieu of the Progressive Era had left elements of the elite classes vaguely dissatisfied with their society and eager to assume personal responsibility for promoting the public good. The impact of World War I focused the attention of this group on national defense. Leonard Wood's training camp movement

provided a specific and highly visible framework for mobilizing the
energies of this more mature group.

*   *   *

The outbreak of the war in Europe had already interested some business and professional men in military training. One of them was Grenville Clark, a young, aristocratic, and well-connected New York lawyer.
Clark was a Harvard man, big, earnest, cheerful, and tenacious. In
November 1914, he had written Theodore Roosevelt that he hoped to
organize ''a small military reserve corps composed of young business
men, lawyers, etc., who would go through a very light sort of training to
fit themselves to be of some use in any real emergency.'' Perhaps, Clark
suggested, it would be possible to organize a small private cavalry unit.
This would help the men to be ''of some, though of course, not of much
use'' if there should be a crisis. Perhaps more importantly, Clark felt, it
would at least be a concrete gesture setting a positive example. The young
lawyer admitted that the response to the idea in his circle was mixed. A
short time later, an officer at the Presidio in San Francisco wrote General
Hugh Scott that some older men had expressed an interest in taking
military training at the proposed West Coast student camp. The chief of
staff wrote back that Congress had not sanctioned adult camps and that no
money was available.[14]

It was the *Lusitania* crisis which brought this movement to a head.
Right after the sinking, Clark, his law partner Elihu Root, Jr., and
Theodore Roosevelt, Jr., invited a dozen friends to lunch at Delmonico's
to consider what could be done. As *The New York Times* described the
group, they were ''young professional men, the sons of leaders in
political, social and professional life . . . mostly Harvard graduates, all
under 35 years of age, who have been closely associated both socially and
professionally for a number of years.'' The fifteen fired off a telegram to
Wilson on May 10 demanding strong measures against Germany, and
then decided to back words with deeds. A Committee of One Hundred
was formed, centering around the Harvard Club, and delegates from this
group approached General Wood and his staff, asking to be included in
the student training camps. Here was a golden chance to link the amateur
zeal of the nation's elite with the professional requirements of the Army,

and Wood was not the man to miss it, however apathetic the War Department might be. The general promised to hold a camp for businessmen at Plattsburg, after the student camp ended, if the Committee could produce twenty-five adult volunteers, and then assigned the group a couple of aides. To be sure, the general looked on the idea as a temporary expedient. As he wrote President Drinker, "the real work has got to be done in the colleges," since the business classes would doubtless lose interest in defense if the nation wriggled out of its present difficulties. But the business camps were more successful than perhaps even Wood had expected.[15]

By June, the drive to enlist the business community was well under way. The initial efforts had been made by distinguished Harvard alumni, and the movement retained a high social tone. The offices of the recruiting bureau were set up on Wall Street, membership lists of New York clubs were used to send out 15,000 application forms, and the rally at which General Wood endorsed the whole idea (tactfully quoting President Wilson's praise for a citizenry trained and accustomed to arms) took place at the Harvard Club itself. At first, the Committee had obtained only a handful of volunteers, but this became a multitude after Wood's speech on June 14. Additional recruiting committees sprang up in Boston, Philadelphia, and Baltimore. The movement was a success, and it spread all over the country. The New York group had direct contacts in Chicago and California, and the example alone was enough to encourage emulation. By the end of the summer, business groups in the Midwest and West had forced the creation of adult camps at Fort Sheridan, Illinois, the Presidio, California, and American Lake, Washington. But it was the Plattsburg camp, under Wood's jurisdiction in upstate New York, which held the attention of the nation in the summer of 1915.[16]

When the Business Men's Camp Special pulled out of Grand Central Station on August 9, the passenger list ensured that the Plattsburg camp would at least be a success in terms of public relations. The trainees were a select group, surely the most socially distinguished assemblage ever to have volunteered for military service as private soldiers. The thirteen hundred businessmen who assembled at the camp the next day included the mayor and the police commissioner of New York City, a Morgan partner, the football coach of Harvard, the Episcopal bishop of Rhode Island, three sons and a cousin of Theodore Roosevelt, and Richard

Harding Davis, the noted and romantically famous war correspondent. *The Scientific American* reported that "fully twenty per cent of the privates are men of national and international note, and over thirty-five per cent of them are successful businessmen who are well known throughout the country." Most of the men were in their thirties and forties, but there was a sprinkling of older men. Overwhelmingly, the group came from the Middle Atlantic States and New England. And overwhelmingly, the group was from the upper classes, recruited from the colleges and clubs of the East Coast. Attendance at camp cost the average enrollee $100, although some impecunious volunteers had been aided by private funds. There had even been some attempts made to blackball applicants of insufficient social standing, which Wood had vigorously resisted. In short, the businessmen's training regiment was not only much larger than the college group which had preceded it, but much more impressive.[17]

The Plattsburg training camp consisted of sixteen rows of brown pyramid tents set on a sloping hill next to the waters of Lake Champlain. All around were the Adirondacks and the Green Mountains. In this Spartan but not unattractive environment, the olive drab-clad trainees drilled, marched, and maneuvered for five weeks, assisted by a regular Army cadre of forty West Pointers and some two hundred enlisted men. The businessmen cheerfully adapted to dirt-floored tents and squad drill, and showed rapid progress in learning the rudiments of soldiering. They were terribly in earnest. General Wood himself, in chain spurs and clutching his familiar dog-headed riding crop, personally supervised the training. Sometimes sightseers drove into camp to watch too, and gawked from their touring cars at the drilling troops. In the evening, the men attended lectures or campfire talks by General Wood in a natural amphitheater down by the lake. By the end of the five-week session, the trainees had been divided up by aptitude or physical condition into infantry, cavalry, artillery, and signal troops, and mock battles were going on all over the Adirondack countryside. The professional officers were highly pleased with the way the training had come along.[18]

Plattsburg was not just a military training camp; it was, in a way, a kind of secular retreat for a generation. There, amid simple martial surroundings, the upper-class elite underwent a conversion experience of patriotism, individual responsibility, and collective action. As a professor enthusiastically reported, the most striking aspect of Plattsburg was the moral change it produced: "From a well meaning miscellaneous lot, unaccustomed to taking orders, we had become a most odd psychological unit." Plattsburg was a way for the elite to assume personal responsibility for achieving a noble goal, to prove that America was not effete or too proud to fight, to set an example of real democracy, with diverse men working shoulder to shoulder for a common end. It filled some deep yearning of the American upper classes; in an America that seemed flaccid and divided, these people wanted orders and psychological solidarity. Episcopal Bishop C. H. Brent of Rhode Island, temporarily turned Army private, enthused about "the democratic influence created by the close contact in the simple conditions of tent life." At last, the bishop went on, Americans had realized that there was "something in the nation worth protecting by corporate action." He told Wood, "I know of no truer means of visualizing the nation in its ideal character than along the lines that you are promoting." For at least some of the nation's elite, the army camp had somehow become a paradigm for the good life in America.[19]

The international situation helped account for Plattsburg, of course; most of the trainees were ardently pro-Ally, if not interventionist. (As John O'Hara once wrote, "Nobody went to Plattsburg with the thought that he might one day take the place of a wounded Uhlan.") But the Plattsburg spirit looked within as much as abroad. In Grenville Clark's words, the camp "was not conceived merely as a means of obtaining security against external enemies, but of strengthening the nation internally against internal forces making for weakness and lack of national unity." In 1912, Theodore Roosevelt had asked for a New Nationalism of social reform through corporate action. Now, amid the shock of the European War, many American voices seemed to call for a Newer Nationalism of olive drab. *The New Republic* saw military preparedness as an essential ingredient for social regeneration. It asked editorially, "Is there anything which would do the average American more good than participation in a well-ordered community life?"[20]

There was some military value in the training camps, yet, as Greenville Clark put it, "the most valuable lesson that we have learned is that of our own incompetence." The important fact about the training camps is that they were the entering wedge for a system of universal military training.

Some of the most influential men in the country were learning first hand
the complexities of soldiering, the efficiency of West Pointers, and the
failure of American military policy. Armies could obviously not be put
together overnight; it was necessary for civilians to prepare themselves
for defense and to subordinate their judgment to that of military experts in
these matters. There seemed to be other lessons. Soldiering could be
uplifting (at least for five weeks), and the squad tent, where all were
equally deprived, could be a rude school of democracy. Universal military training could regenerate and homogenize America as well as defend
it. It seemed to the Plattsburgers that the camps embodied the best values
of a democratic America, and it was natural to wish to extend this
experience to the whole nation by law.[21]

Implicit in much of this thinking was that Plattsburg and the other
camps were cross-sections of democratic society. Wood could write the
president of the American Federation of Labor, with apparent sincerity,
that the Plattsburg regiment was "a very typical American group." Yet,
of course, the Plattsburgers were a most unrepresentative group of
privates. The value of the camps to the Army was precisely the fact that
they provided a means for indoctrinating America's elite, leaders of
opinion in peace as well as potential leaders of men in war. As General
Wood put it later, "if you look at the occupations of these men you will
begin to appreciate what the influence of a movement of this sort is." The
Army declined to run the camps as a social fraternity, and a fund was
available to pay some of the expenses of the poorer trainees. Later, there
would be a search for some token representation from the labor movement at the camps. This was as far as democracy would go—until
universal military training was adopted, and then the Plattsburgers would
be part of the officer caste.[22]

The camp contained not only the seeds of a movement for universal
military training but the germs of political controversy as well. General
Wood, the military godfather of the operation, was known to be a
Republican and was suspected of having views on military and foreign
policy more congenial to Theodore Roosevelt's than to President
Wilson's. The very existence of the camp might be viewed as a subtle
political thrust against a none too defense-minded Wilson Administration. Wood had to be on his guard against political implications being
read into his evening lectures. Meanwhile, administration supporters

among the camp members maneuvered to prevent the preparedness issue from being used as a weapon against the Democratic party. Dudley Field Malone, the collector of the Port of New York, wrote Wilson, "I thought if men like myself, closely identified with you and your administration, and the Democratic Party, should go to this camp at Plattsburg, it would be at least one of many steps to kill any idea that the opposition party and its returning prodigal, Mr. Roosevelt, alone are vitally interested in this great problem." General Wood had invited Wilson, Taft, and Roosevelt, as present or past Commanders-in-Chief, to address the men at a regimental parade on August 25, and Malone particularly urged Wilson to come. The President politely declined, on the grounds that it was not "the timely or all-wise thing to do"; anything he wanted to say about preparedness he would say to Congress. Taft also declined. Theodore Roosevelt, however, accepted—and his speech seemed to plunge both Wood and the Plattsburg camp into the thick of partisan politics.[23]

Roosevelt made his appearance at camp dressed, with some dramatic effect, in a wide-brimmed hat, riding jacket, and leather leggings. He enthusiastically watched a sham-battle, and commented "Bully" as the business trainees drove the opposing Regular Army force into the Saranac River with a bayonet charge. That evening, the colonel spoke in the natural amphitheater to the trainees, cadre, and local civilians. His speech was emphatic, and the interview he gave reporters as he left was even more pointed. Just what he said where became a matter of some dispute. At any rate, newspapers the next morning carried the story that the ex-President had used Plattsburg as a platform from which to flay the Wilson Administration in unusually colorful terms. His statement, "to treat elocution as a substitute for action, to rely upon high sounding words unbacked by deeds, is proof of a mind that dwells only in the realm of shadow and shame," was particularly striking.[24]

Wilson was furious at the reports, and President Drinker bitterly assailed Roosevelt for hurting the camp movement by partisanship; even the sturdily Progressive Republican *Chicago Tribune* felt that the former president had provided "a lesson in insubordination." *The New York Times* treated the incident sympathetically, however, and it seems that the Plattsburgers were delighted by whatever Roosevelt did say. As one observed later, while Roosevelt had been indiscreet, if he had been discreet his hearers would have been astonished and disappointed.

Neither Roosevelt nor the defense movement was hurt by the incident, but Wood had been compromised. Wilson blamed the general for connivance in a partisan attack on him on a military installation, and ordered the secretary of war to reprimand him. Thus, Wood sank deeper into the bad graces of the administration. Wood did not deserve the rebuke, for he had not deliberately tried to embarrass the President. But the administration's antagonism was a natural one; it was deeply sensitive to the political implications of preparedness and was determined to keep the issue under control.[25]

*   *   *

The first Plattsburg camp ended on September 4, the start of the Labor Day weekend, as the volunteers snake-danced through the camp and the band played "Hail! Hail! The gang's all here!" But the movement had only begun. A second, smaller camp began on the same site two days later, with six hundred businessmen enrolled. And the "veterans" began to organize in a permanent fashion, as Grenville Clark had suggested on one of the last nights of encampment. The men selected as their chairman Robert Bacon, a man who seemed to exemplify the Plattsburg spirit and who would be a linchpin of the whole civilian preparedness movement. A Morgan partner, former ambassador to France, and one-time secretary of state, Bacon was an austere figure, totally committed to the Allied cause and gripped by compulsions to duty, a "Late George Apley"-like character. Under Bacon, there was a committee of elected delegates from the companies, which was ultimately expanded to get better geographical representation. By December, the organization had its own newsletter, *The Bulletin of the First Training Regiment*, and was stretching out hands to the students of the National Reserve Corps and to the businessmen who had graduated from other camps. By the beginning of 1916, all of these groups, together with the advisory board of college presidents, had coalesced in a consolidated organization, the Military Training Camp Association. Drinker was chairman of the new group's Governing Committee, the omnipresent Grenville Clark was secretary, while two of Clark's closest associates, Lloyd Derby and DeLancey Jay, served respectively as executive secretary and treasurer. Meanwhile, the Plattsburg graduates had begun to lobby for a permanent place in the War

Department's structure, a bit against the advice of General Wood, who felt a more cautious approach was desirable. Wood had helped to create a powerful pressure group for preparedness, but it would be an autonomous organization with a will of its own.[26]

In their approach to the War Department, the Plattsburgers consciously played a double game. The Plattsburg graduates wanted universal military training; Grenville Clark, the secretary of the Executive Committee, assured Roosevelt that they did not intend to "lie down on the universal service idea." On the other hand, this goal could only be achieved by educating as many people as possible to its need, and the best education was the training camp experience itself. So, while agreeing with Roosevelt's goals, the Military Training Camp Association cheerfully dealt with the Wilson Administration, promising their support for the proposed Continental Army in return for federal funds for the training camps and reserve commissions for their graduates. The Association volunteered to help the Continental force "both by having such of its own members as are qualified serving in it and by recruiting others for it." Clark pointed out to the War Department the strategic position of the members of the MTCA. While widely scattered, they had a unity of purpose, they were prominent, they were connected with large employers of men, and they could point to their own example.[27]

Garrison and Assistant Secretary Henry Breckinridge were interested by the proposition. In response to the requests of the MTCA delegation, the secretary of war appointed a three-man board of General Staff officers to confer with a delegation of Plattsburgers headed by the noted Philadelphia lawyer George Wharton Pepper. Wood had feared taking any proposals to the General Staff on the grounds that they might be turned down, but the Army board proved sympathetic. In 1916, it came out with a recommendation that the student and businessmen's camps be continued as distinct entities (with an age limit of twenty-four as the dividing line between them), and turned into three-year officer training programs. Ultimately, as more and more students were trained, the business camps could be phased out. Congress would still have to pass on all of this, but the important thing was that the initiative for a federal reserve force was now coming from an interested citizen lobby, not just professional soldiers.[28]

As a "talking general," Wood had scored a real measure of success.

Perhaps his very lack of a West Point background had helped him in approaching the public. With effort and persistence, he had outflanked Congress, propagandized the upper classes, and helped generate a new constituency of military-oriented civilians to support preparedness and Army reform. He had inspired imitators; impressed with Wood's success, the activist-minded assistant secretary of the Navy, Franklin Roosevelt, proposed a Navy program similar to Plattsburg. While the general had not influenced as many citizens as he fondly believed, he had reached some of the "best" people. The universal military training which he now endorsed was gaining the support of a substantial portion of the citizenry. Of course, the vanguard of the preparedness movement was a dangerous place for a maverick department commander to be. Wood was too zealous, too visible (between November 1915 and June 1916, he would go on to speak 156 times before 138,000 people and write countless introductions), and too independent. The displeasure of the Wilson Administration with this "not-very-subordinate" subordinate grew. But Wood was not intimidated. As he wrote his friend and patron Theodore Roosevelt, he had "played the game squarely and openly and shall continue to do so. I am out for national preparedness and I am going to get it."[29]

5

A Cold Day for
the Army

*For some reason there is not the same controversy
about the navy that there is about the army. The navy is
obvious and easily understood. The army apparently is
very difficult to understand.*

—Woodrow Wilson

*The Democratic Party is at the mercy of its own Con-
gress, which has taken as its inspiration and its exem-
plar the obstinate and stupid little beast universally
employed to represent it in the symbolism of caricature.*

—The New York Times

The passage of a preparedness program, presidential private secretary
Joseph P. Tumulty wrote Wilson in early August 1915, would be "the
ultimate test of our party's power to govern the nation." The Democratic
party would be dealing with this great and pressing issue on the very eve
of the 1916 campaign, and would stand or fall by the results. The fight

would tax the President's leadership to the utmost. A defense program had to be devised which would be acceptable to the Cabinet, the Congress, the armed services, and the people. Above all, Wilson's politically minded secretary went on, the program must "have Democratic harmony written all over it."[1]

This was sensible advice, but the task presented certain difficulties. For as Wilson began to frame his preparedness program, there were signs that the Democratic party was not united on the issue of defense. William Jennings Bryan, the Christian pacifist who had just resigned as secretary of state, could be counted on to oppose any military initiatives by the administration, and Bryan cast a long shadow over one wing of the party. To the opinion-makers of urban America, however, Bryan was rather a comic figure, and Wilson's more defense-minded advisers tended to discount the threat. Colonel House felt his opposition could be disregarded, and Tumulty, that perhaps it should even be invited. The attitude of that more obscure figure, James Hay, presented a different kind of stumbling block to any plans for military reform. Hay, the chairman of the House Military Affairs Committee, occupied a critical position in the legislative machinery and was a small-army man notoriously unsympathetic to the desires of the General Staff. As the War Department hammered out its program, the shrewd Virginia congressman indicated that he had some ideas of his own on defense. He wrote Wilson's postmaster general, Albert S. Burleson, who handled congressional liaison, that he had seen newspaper reports that the General Staff wanted a regular army of 500,000 men. This, he told Burleson, would be impossible. In Hay's opinion, "it would be wise to increase the regular army to the extent of providing that its organization be kept to war strength in time of peace and that we should increase our filed [sic] artillery. Something must also be done for the organized militia." Burleson assured Wilson that the congressman was "anxious to cooperate" on defense; actually, Hay was willing to cooperate only on his own terms.[2]

The difference of approach to the problems of the military between Hay and Secretary of War Garrison was complicated by a personal animosity, of which the President was well aware. Wilson told Garrison's enthusiastic assistant secretary, Henry Breckinridge, that Garrison's brusque manner and judicial aloofness had alienated the chairmen of the military committees, as well as some of the secretary's own Cabinet colleagues. Hay had practically sent the President word that he would not support any scheme of national defense favored by the secretary of war. Only if Wilson himself assumed responsibility of authorship would he back it. In return, Breckinridge shot back the opinion that Hay was a "narrow minded venomous man" with an antipathy to the Army, mostly interested in increasing the appropriations for the Front Royal Remount Station in his home district and in evening old scores. As for the other Democratic members of the House Committee, Breckinridge went on, they were not as bad as Hay, but were "just ignorant of military affairs." Yoking the Democratic secretary of war with the Democratic congressional power structure was a challenge indeed for Wilson's powers of leadership.[3]

Nor were Wilson and Garrison always in agreement; the President preferred to work with Josephus Daniels, the secretary of the Navy. When the outline of the revised General Staff plan, which called for a regular force of 140,000 backed by a Continental Army, became available in August, the secretary of war sent it on to the President, suggesting that it be floated as a trial balloon. "Whatever of value is to be accomplished will be in response to public opinion," the secretary urged. Wilson did not agree. He did not want any plan leaked out that the White House had not made up its mind to support. Anyway, he replied to Garrison, "I think the detail of the policy the country is willing to leave to us." Garrison persisted in his desire to mount a propaganda campaign to prepare the public to accept the War Department's proposals, but Wilson was equally firm in sticking to his point. The President was unwilling to be prematurely committed to any one plan by his department head, and both men showed themselves to be stubborn. The President was clearly more interested in dealing with Congress than in playing with public opinion.[4]

This lack of Democratic harmony on detail did not seem very important in the fall of 1915. What was important was that the President, by adroitly reversing himself, had assumed the leadership of the preparedness movement. "The demand for reasonable preparedness is clear enough, and our own judgments go with it. We are not being driven, but going of our own accord," Wilson had written the secretary of war. Now the President moved deliberately to translate the wishes of the people once again into action and to seize a broad, middle-of-the-road position isolating both the pacifists and the militarists. When the steamship *Arabic* was attacked by a German submarine on August 20, there was a renewed flareup of international tensions, but Germany bowed to Wilson's demands and abandoned unrestricted submarine warfare against passenger ships. By September, *The New York Times* was authoritatively stating that the President felt free to develop national defense plans because there now could be no suspicion that they were directed against any particular nation. Already the President was refusing to heed the appeals of liberal pacifists like Oswald Garrison Villard and declining to see a delegate from the American League to Limit Armaments. The civilian preparedness organizations, seeing the conversion of the administration, largely swung into line behind it. Congress, out of session, seemed favorably disposed; the *Chicago Evening Post* reported that congressional sentiment was ten to one in favor of defense increases. The nation appeared ready to follow the President's lead. As Senator William E. Chilton of West Virginia wrote Tumulty brightly, "I do not know what the President's policy will be, but I am sure that it will be the right one." Riding what he felt was the deliberate groundswell of public opinion, Wilson assured the sensational novelist Thomas Dixon that there was no need to stir the public up in favor of national defense.[5]

Gradually, the details of the administration's proposed defense program seeped out to the public, perhaps against Wilson's desires. In mid-October, *The New York Times* carried front-page stories that the defense estimates had been made, and that the administration planned to ask Congress for $400 million for defense. The Wilson program was a moderate approach to the issue, the paper reported, much along the lines of that recommended by former President Taft. Wilson had accepted Garrison's proposals, and an even more innovative naval program. The President privately felt that the Navy was more important than the Army, and he and Daniels had concurred on a five-year building program which would lay down ten dreadnaughts and six battle cruisers by 1921. This seemed to settle the defense issue. The administration had seized the high ground; preparedness, as the peace-loving *Nation* unhappily put it, "has been removed, for the time being, from the hands of the fanatics, and taken charge of by the politicians."[6]

The hard-liners on preparedness were not satisfied by Wilson's program. The administration, they grumbled, had refused to come out for universal military training or a really big army, and it had declined to build all the battleships that the Navy General Board demanded. (The admirals wanted a fleet equal to Britain's.) But they were dismayed by the President's political astuteness. W. H. Cowles, publisher of the Spokane *Spokesman-Review* and a leading advocate of universal training, wrote Theodore Roosevelt gloomily, "It seems to me that this plan involves the very danger which we discussed; namely, it is a plan which is liable to satisfy a great many people," even though it would be ineffective. The *Washington Post* summed up a general opinion: "The President has the country with him in this policy of preparedness, with him cordially and enthusiastically, and by a sentiment so nearly unanimous that the new dissentients, however noisy, will produce no change in the views of the people."[7]

The President had moved to secure the support of key congressmen for defense legislation as soon as he had decided to embark on his program. By the end of October, it appeared that he had succeeded in this effort. All but one of the congressional leaders immediately concerned had announced their general agreement. The Senate majority leader, John Kern of Indiana, previously equivocal on preparedness, announced he would support the administration program in all essentials. James Hay, potentially the most obstructive committee chairman, had assured Wilson, "after a careful study of the program, I can say it will receive my hearty support. I will make every effort to put it through, for I feel that it is a reasonable and conservative program." Only Claude Kitchin, the Bryanite House majority leader from rural North Carolina, hung back.[8]

In reality, despite all of the apparent support for national defense, the administration's concrete proposals for Army reform were in trouble. The keystone of the whole plan was a reserve force under total national control, which the leaders of the National Guard recognized as a threat to the integrity of their own organization. They had no intention of being displaced by a new defense force, especially after years of patient lobbying for increased federal recognition and support. William F. Sadler of New Jersey, state adjutant-general and a prominent Trenton banker, warned his friend Tumulty that "Garrison's program has made the officers and men of the Guard furious, and the President, if he endorses the program, will make more determined enemies than you know." Garrison took the Executive Committee of the National Guard

Association into conference at the end of October, but failed to relieve the fears of the Guard leaders. The secretary of war told the militia heads that the Guard might either join the new Continental force bodily or continue on as before. If the National Guard Association did not oppose the administration program, Garrison intimated, he would even support legislation that would grant Guardsmen federal pay for drill, although he could not make this part of the administration's defense program.[9]

The Guard adjutant-generals were not impressed. Peaceful coexistence with the Continental Army seemed as uninviting as absorption into it. If the Garrison plan went through, the militia would become a second-string defense organization. General Sadler wrote Wilson that what the secretary of war had proposed meant the "extinguishment" of the National Guard; he warned the Virginia-born president that the southern adjutant-generals "felt that the Continental Army in their section will be composed of negroes, the only men that can be gotten if the troops are apportioned as proposed." On November 11, the National Guard Association, meeting in San Francisco, turned down an eloquent plea by Assistant Secretary Breckinridge, and asked that the proposed reserve force consist of a federalized National Guard and that a constitutional amendment be passed which would allow the militia to be sent abroad. Meanwhile, Senator George Chamberlain, head of the Senate Military Affairs Committee, announced that he planned to introduce an amended militia pay bill. "The Continental Army," he announced, "will be an experiment, and the country can not afford to weaken the National Guard by any experiment with a new force of troops." Understandably, Wilson urged Garrison to keep a role open for the National Guard which would preserve its dignity and importance. But the gap between the secretary of war and the National Guard was never quite bridged.[10]

The formal unveiling of the defense program in early November brought out some of the disagreements that lurked beneath the surface. Both Garrison and Hay registered objections to the President's plans. After reading an advanced copy of the proposed speech, the secretary of war told Tumulty that he felt Wilson was slurring over the details of the plan and leaving it open to misconceptions. Wilson seemed to imply that the Continental Army would not be an organized force and that the National Guard could be a part of the federal reserve. Wilson coolly rejected the criticism. It was too late to change the speech, he told his private secretary, he did not feel anything he proposed to say would be misunderstood, and finally, "the plan suggested by the Secretary is susceptible, fortunately, of adaptation." The day of the speech there was an objection from the other camp. Representative Hay asked that the formal details of the plan not be officially released by the War Department. By this time it was too late to do anything, however. The President, after the release, replied conciliatorily, "I hope that now the thing is done it will turn out that a good deal of the debate can be disposed of before we actually tackle the legislation."[11]

The forum that Wilson had chosen to begin his campaign for preparedness was the fiftieth anniversary dinner of New York's prestigious Manhattan Club, which was to be held on the evening of November 4. New York was both defense-minded and a pivotal state for the 1916 presidential election; the Manhattan Club was the Democratic equivalent of the Union League, "the home of the swallow-tailed Democracy," in Henry Watterson's words, a stronghold of the very upper-class types who were the backbone of the preparedness movement. Bryan sourly labeled it "the one place in the United States where the mammon-worshipping portion of the Democratic Party meets to exchange compliments." Eight hundred well-bred partisans packed the dining room of the Biltmore Hotel to hear the President's thoughts on defense. They had to wait some time; the affair was badly managed and dragged interminably, but at last, at five minutes before midnight, the President rose to deliver his prepared address.[12]

In his Manhattan Club speech, Wilson called upon the nation to arm itself to meet any dangers "in a way that will be chiefly an illustration of the American spirit." The regular standing army would be enlarged, the President informed his audience, but only enough to cope with the peacetime demands of garrisoning America's colonial possessions and patrolling the border. The main burden of defending the nation would rest on the citizen-soldiers of the Continental Army, a challenge to America's patriotism that Wilson felt sure she would meet. The President gave a sketchy account of the proposed naval program and promised that the present "serviceable and efficient" National Guard would not be subordinated or superseded in any way. At the same time, Wilson hastened to reassure his listeners that there was really nothing specific to prepare against. "No thoughtful man feels any panic haste in this matter. The country is not threatened from any quarter.'' Perhaps significantly, the loudest applause came from this Democratic audience when he linked external defense and internal security and talked of the need for Americanism and the danger of hyphenated loyalty. Then, half of his listeners rose to their feet in a two-minute ovation, cheering and waving over their heads the small American flags with which the tables were garnished.[13]

It was a decent speech. Theodore Roosevelt rather predictably flayed the President's program as one of "adroit delay and make-believe action," but loyal Democrats were satisfied. Yet, to the skeptical but fair-minded editors of *The New Republic*, the whole speech seemed curiously lacking. Wilson had not really tried to educate the people, he had not explained how the men were to be raised or how the army was to be financed, he had not sought to relate power to policy. The President had treated the issue in a vacuum; his remarks were "resolutely confined to platitudes, to large and dull abstractions." As events were to show, some of the omissions in the speech all too accurately reflected gaps in Wilson's approach to the problem.[14]

*   *   *

In November, the country seemed committed to preparedness, but in December, when Congress met, the tide of public enthusiasm crashed against the sea-wall of congressional obduracy. Wilson had not been able to pull the Democratic party together on the issue, despite his friendly attentions to its leaders. The sticking-point for any defense program lay in the House of Representatives, traditionally economy-minded and parochial, and unmoved by the enthusiasms of the urban press. Here the Democratic majority was less than thirty, and the majority leader, Claude Kitchin, was at the head of a peace coalition, put together during the summer, which opposed any increase in defense spending. The core of the group consisted of some thirty Democratic Representatives from the rural South and West, "backwoods Congressmen," as the *New York World* described them patronizingly, "who are honest in their opinions and sincere in their almost infinite ignorance of world conditions." These men found allies in congressmen from a few Progressive and labor constituencies in the North, and enlisted the support of some midwestern Republicans from across the aisle.[15]

This group was important enough to block the functioning of the Democratic machine, and Kitchin, by virtue of his position, was able to fill the House military and naval committees with men sympathetic to his views. The House majority leader even toyed with turning the Democratic caucus around to oppose Wilson's plans, but felt he did not have the votes. In the last analysis, most House Democrats, however privately skeptical of preparedness, would fall in behind their party's President in any straight-out confrontation. On the other hand, Wilson felt it inexpedient to move against the popular and respected Kitchin, and he did not dare make the defense program a matter of party discipline through the caucus himself; this would irretrievably antagonize the Republicans on a patriotic issue, and given the mutinous state of the Democratic party, Republican votes might be needed. To complicate matters further, while the Republicans were stoutly for defense, it was only on their own terms. When Wilson invited the Republican congressional leaders, Representative James Mann of Illinois and Senator Jacob Gallinger of New Hampshire, to the White House for a conference, they declined to commit themselves to the details of the President's program. The Continental Army, Mann declared, was an ''impracticable compromise,'' and he did not intend to take orders from the President. With the Democrats divided and the Republicans partisan, the fate of the Wilson program was problematic. ''Congress,'' a National Security League official wrote, ''is a lottery.''[16]

Garrison's carefully prepared program was ground to pieces in the legislative hopper. Major General Enoch Crowder, the judge advocate general, had prepared a draft bill embodying the secretary's recommendations, and had submitted it to the military committees as a guideline. The secretary of war refrained from trying to shove a specifically War Department measure down the throat of Congress; he simply wanted the outline of his policy preserved. But, subjected to the enigmatic processes of Congress, the outline began to blur away into unrecognizability. The call for Army reform was lost in a babble of voices. Both the Senate and House Military Committees came out with tentative programs which radically differed from the War Department's and from each other.

Senator George Chamberlain, the progressive Democrat from Oregon, appealing to fears of Japanese aggression, proposed doubling the Regular Army (as the War College had originally recommended) and providing belt-and-suspenders security with both a federal volunteer force and a federalized National Guard. Representative Hay, on the other hand, recommended a smaller army increase than the one the War Department had requested. Administration supporters introduced a bill embodying Garrison's original proposal. Other congressmen had ideas of their own—it seemed to the chief of staff that every senator and representative for preparedness had a private plan. Major General Tasker Bliss, the assistant chief of staff, complained: "We are sweating blood over the rain of bills now coming to the War Department from Congress—bills on the National Defense, on reorganization of the Army, on the abolition of the Army, on unlimited fortification, on building a Chinese Wall around the United States, on creating about a million West Points, and God knows what else. It begins to look as if with all of this we would get nothing."[17]

The single most dangerous threat to the secretary of war's plan came from James Hay and the House Military Affairs Committee. In October, General Leonard Wood had predicted that Hay "will acquiesce and accede until the thing comes to Congress and then put the knife in. . . ." At the end of November, Hay broke the news to Garrison that he was not going to use the War Department's bill at all, but would hold hearings and formulate a measure in committee. The House chairman then presented the idea he had broached to Burleson the previous summer. Instead of enlarging the Army by creating more skeleton units, why not simply raise the existing regiments to war strength, as Garrison himself had recommended in 1914? This proposal, of course, would eliminate the need for new officers and new promotions in time of peace, and for reserves to fill up half-strength units in time of war. It would make the Army more ready for immediate action, but less able to expand to meet a crisis. Garrison now objected; for one thing, he pointed out, Hay's plan would create an impossible housing situation. All of the Army posts in existence had been built to accommodate peace-strength units, and regiments at full strength would actually have to be broken up between different departments, unless Congress appropriated large sums for new barracks. But Hay persisted in his approach in his tentative draft bill. Worse, although the chairman had included provisions for a Continental Army in the draft, by the second week of December he was indicating that he doubted both the support in Congress for the Continental Army and its practicability. The House Military Committee looked like a potential deathtrap for Army reform, at least along the lines desired by the War Department. As the chief of staff wrote, "nothing is going to come out of the box that Mr. Hay does not permit, and what he is going to permit, none of us know."[18]

The Continental Army was at once the heart of the Garrison proposal and its weak point. It was new and hence controversial in itself, it promised an extension of federal control into the domain of the states, it threatened the existing National Guard, and there were serious doubts as to its feasibility. It was questionable that the proposed increment of men for the first year could be obtained unless the National Guard surrendered its identity and was assimilated, something the Guard was unwilling to do. Critics pointed out that the training period was too short and the six-year enlistment commitment too long. The broad class of people from whom an army had to be raised could not take the long periods off every year for training which the plan envisaged. Summer training camps had indeed been a success, but they had attempted to enroll only a small group, they had not required a permanent engagement, and they had thrown men into the company of their own class. Major General John F. O'Ryan of the New York National Guard, shrewdly realizing that the preparedness movement rode upon an undercurrent of popular hysteria, pointed out that "a plan to be sound should not base its success on what is really temporary emotion based upon the war in Europe." Representative Mann suspected Wilson's sincerity in the matter; he told an editor that the Continental Army was being used by the administration as a litmus test of popular sentiment: if nobody volunteered, it would prove that people did not want defense anyway, and the Democrats would be off the hook. From the start, Congress manifested a massive lack of enthusiasm for the plan.[19]

Garrison was caught in a pincers attack on this issue. On one side he was pressed by those who felt that a reserve force could be created simply by federalizing the National Guard. The Guard was an already existing force of 125,000, not just a plan, and making use of it had a bird-in-hand practicality. The organization seemed reassuringly untainted by militarism. It was an old and familiar force, with deep roots in American history and a powerful political lobby. During the previous summer all but one of the state governors had declared themselves in favor of an enlarged and strengthened militia. The dominant group in the Guard was eager for federal pay and acceptance and was willing to submit to federal controls in return. To many congressmen, including James Hay, a federalized National Guard was a highly acceptable alternative to a completely new national force. To the War Department, which despaired of imposing adequate controls over a heterogeneous force of forty-eight state militias, it was not. The War Department still remembered that the militia had lost Washington, D.C. in 1814.[20]

On the other hand, the more enthusiastic and partisan supporters of preparedness continued to attack the Continental Army as an inadequate compromise, a Wilsonian subterfuge. The ultraconservative Republican Union League found itself incongruously allied in this fight with the sometime radical Progressive Theodore Roosevelt. The hard-liners and their congressional spokesmen wanted universal military training, or the big Regular Army recommended originally by the War College, or both. They denounced Garrison for discarding the recommendations of the General Staff experts and opting for a political army. Too many people wanted to go further than the secretary of war was then prepared to venture. Even the Regular Army was not united behind the War Department. Garrison was distressed to find General Wood talking up universal military training schemes as practiced in Switzerland and Australia. Such schemes might be very fine, Garrison wrote him, but it was not the War Department's plan, and "diffusion of effort almost always spells failure." But efforts continued to be diffused. Many of the soldiers and civilians who backed the Continental Army did so only because they felt it to be a halting step in the right direction, a half-way house to universal compulsory training. The problem with the War Department's plan was that, while it attracted wholehearted opposition, it received only half-hearted support. *The New Republic* wrote an appropriate epitaph for the Continental Army: "It was a pretty little child, dressed to make a good appearance in public, but it was fatally anaemic. Nobody was interested in keeping it alive."[21]

*   *   *

In December, the hopes of those interested in military preparedness had been largely shattered. Congress was in disarray, and the President, busy with remarriage, seemed to provide no leadership. In January, the Senate and House Military Committees began separate hearings on the Army bill, and it was here that Garrison's program finally withered away. Once more, the House Committee was the stumbling-block. On January 6, the secretary of war made what Scott called a "masterly" presentation to Hay's committee, but in the course of the questioning he admitted that if voluntary enlistments failed to maintain the strength of the Continental Army, conscription would be necessary. The chief of staff, in his own testimony, also raised the specter of peacetime compulsory service. The congressmen were dubious enough of the Continental Army, and the thought that its failure might inevitably pave the way for conscription caused them to shy away still more. On January 11, although the hearings still had a long way to go, Representative Hay told Wilson that the committee was irrevocably opposed to the Continental Army Plan. The committee chairman began to put forward his own plan, drawn up with the assistance of his old friend, former Adjutant General Fred Ainsworth, the *bête noir* of Army reformers.[22]

A showdown had clearly come. The following day, in a six-page letter, Garrison in turn informed the President that the defense program was at a "critical juncture." If the Hay program for reliance on a federalized militia were adopted, it would be a "betrayal of the trust of the people." The state militia was a shadow force which could never be of any use; nothing could be obtained from it but a sham army. Hay had now declared he would not support the administration's military policy. His opposition might be decisive, since Hay had great power as committee chairman, he was dealing with a subject of which the House was ignorant, and the militia scheme appealed to the personal interests of the members. The secretary of war demanded that Wilson personally intervene in the struggle and exert his leadership.[23]

The President studiously refrained from backing his secretary in any confrontation with Hay or his committee. He would suggest that the House Military Affairs Committee endorse the Continental Army, but indicated that he was willing to abide by the judgment of its members. In an interview with Garrison, the President pointed out that his only understanding with Hay was that he hoped the Committee would provide a defense plan as good as or better than Garrison's. Clearly, the President was not willing to tie his prestige to the fate of a detail like a completely national reserve force. At this development, the overwrought Garrison wrote his superior that he could only show his sincerity "by declining to admit the possibility of compromise with respect to essential, fundamental principles." Wilson coldly replied that "I do not share your opinion that the members of the House who are charged with the duty of dealing with military affairs are ignorant of them or of the military necessities of the nation."[24]

Garrison had now locked himself into an irreversible conflict not just with Hay, but with both military committees, which favored some form of federalized National Guard. When Senator Chamberlain undertook to consider a measure involving federal pay for the militia, the secretary of war wrote him: "We have come to the final parting of the ways. The passage of such a measure would fully and irretrievably commit us to a system that has utterly failed in the past, which menaces our safety now. . . . If we put the Organized Militia firmly in the saddle as is contemplated in this bill, the opportunity of adopting a sound military policy for the nation will have passed beyond recall."[25]

Secretary Garrison's zeal for defense won him credit with civilian preparedness groups and made him something of a hero to the more militant Republicans. Henry Cabot Lodge was soon to call him "a Secretary of War to whom as an American I feel under obligations." But meanwhile, the Wilson preparedness program, whose passage in some form was a political necessity, was hung up helplessly in the Democratic Congress. William Howard Taft gloated, "I think Wilson is going down hill." The politically astute Tumulty was quick to see the dangers of the situation. "Now is the time when impressions are being made," he wrote Wilson, "and the impression abroad in the country is that we are drifting." There was no enthusiasm for defense on Capitol Hill, and the nation had turned apathetic. The people needed "entertainment and guidance" on this important issue. Tumulty urged Wilson to stump the country.[26]

The President accepted his secretary's advice. He decided to recapture the initiative and rally the nation once more behind defense through a speaking trip. The campaign opened at the end of January in the Grand Ballroom of New York's Waldorf Astoria with a speech to the Railway Business Association. Wilson took pains to explain his *volte face* on the issue of preparedness since December 1914. "I would be ashamed of myself if I had not learned anything in the fourteen months." Injecting a deft note of bipartisanship the President praised the speech that Representative Mann, the minority leader, had just made in the House endorsing preparedness. He did not mention that Mann had asked for a 250,000-man Army and had claimed that England was as likely an enemy as Germany. The following day the President departed by private railway car on a ten-day tour of the Midwest, designed to meet the Bryanite opposition to preparedness on its home ground and crush it.[27]

The swing around the circle of Wilson and his small party was something of a triumph. Unlike the Manhattan Club speech, it was a deliberately nonpartisan affair. By instruction, the local Democratic committeemen stayed away, and the President was entertained not by the party faithful, but by businessmen's organizations. As the President swung across the country from Pennsylvania to the Mississippi Valley, a million people turned out to see him, often standing in the bitter cold. He talked to packed houses in cities from Pittsburgh to Kansas City, and the audiences responded as never before. Surrounded by surging crowds, cheers, and waving American flags, Wilson translated into an extemporaneous and inspirational oratory all of the vague fears and emotions that lay behind the drive for preparedness. While never mentioning a specific threat, the President eloquently expressed in his speeches the shock and alarm felt by educated Americans over a world turned upside down by war. "The world is on fire and there is tinder everywhere," he warned. "We are in the midst of a world that we did not make and we cannot alter," and again, "We are daily treading amid the most intricate dangers. . . . no man in the United States knows what a single day of a single hour may bring forth." At times the President was concrete, as when he pointed out that, because of the Mexican Border patrol, the Army was inadequately manned for the routine tasks of peace. At St. Louis, the President was carried away by the applause of the crowd and actually proposed (against administration policy) that the United States acquire a navy that would be incomparably the greatest in the world. In Milwaukee, a German-American stronghold, Wilson stressed patriotism, speaking of the lines of red in the flag as "lines of blood, nobly and unselfishly shed"; if necessary, "that flag will be colored once more, and in being colored will be glorified and purified." It was an emotionally exhilarating experi-

ence, both for the crowds and the President. Wilson was a cheerful man
when he returned to Washington.[28]

Wilson had dramatized the issue of preparedness and had scored a
personal success, but his effort had done more to capture public attention
than to put the administration's military program through Congress.
Wilson's triumph had been in the cities, and since the preparedness
movement was a distinctly urban phenomenon, he had largely been
preaching to those already converted. Newspapers and businessmen in
the West were substantially as much in favor of defense as those in the
East. The lines of division on the defense issue ran not between sections,
but between city and countryside. Hence, Wilson's campaign, though it
doubtless changed some minds and votes, was not overwhelmingly
effective against the stubbornness of a rural-oriented Congress. The
administration's real problem was not so much that Congress was unwilling to do something for defense, but that Congress was unwilling to
accept the radical departure of the Continental Army. The militia influence had too many votes. Even as Wilson toured the Midwest, the
National Guard spokesmen had had their say before the House Military
Affairs Committee and had been favorably received.[29]

On February 5, Hay broke the news to Wilson: the Continental Army
plan, he wrote once more, did not meet the approval of the Committee. It
would be possible, however, to develop and federalize the militia in such
a way "as to supply more men than the most sanguine supporters of the
Continental Army [could] hope for." Congress could specify the qualifications of the officers and the organization of the units, and it could draft
the militia bodily into federal service in time of war. Three days later,
Hay assured Wilson that he had canvassed the House and found that the
Continental Army plan would be overwhelmingly defeated. The plan had
been compromised by the testimony of War Department witnesses that
they favored compulsory training. Southerners feared it because they
believed it would be a way of enlisting large numbers of Negroes. On the
other hand, the chairman went on, the militia plan was favored by every
man on the Committee and nine-tenths of the House. Even Kitchin had
said he would not oppose a federalized National Guard. The militia plan
"will not only unite our own party. . . . but will bring the opposition to the
support of your policies;" the Continental Army would have the reverse
effect.[30]

Hay's figures were correct—a *New York Herald* poll showed that only forty-two Representatives favored Garrison's plan, half of them Republicans—and his political logic was irrefutable. Wilson bent in gracious surrender. As *The New Republic* wrote bitterly: "When the handkerchief fell, he was not proud enough to fight. He quit." The President was not particularly interested in the details of defense; rather, he favored a wholly national reserve over the militia, but not with a suicidal fondness. He did indicate to Hay that his military advisers had indicated state troops would be less efficient than national troops, but that was as far as his final stand for the program went. Wilson was quite ready to accept half a loaf. In direct conference with both the Democrats and the Republicans on the House Military Affairs Committee, the President urged the preparation of a bill, any bill, that would produce a Regular Army and reserve force that would total up to the magic number of 500,000 men demanded by the military as a precondition to land defense.[31]

*   *   *

This turn of events meant the end, of course, for Garrison, who had repeatedly and dogmatically made it clear that he felt any reserve system not under total national control would be an unacceptable sham. The secretary found another issue to speed him on his way out of the administration. Senate Democrats had just passed the Clarke Amendment on February 4, providing for American withdrawal from the Philippines within four years if the President certified that the external and internal situation so permitted. This action directly overruled the wishes of the War Department, which administered the islands, and the President once more seemed reluctant to back up his subordinates in a fight with Congress by vetoing the measure. On February 9, the secretary of war informed the President that he intended to make known in public his views that reliance on the militia for defense was impossible and that the Clarke Amendment was a betrayal of the nation's trust. "If, with respect to either matter," Garrison wrote, "we are not in agreement upon the fundamental principles, then I could not, with propriety, remain your seeming representative with respect thereto." It was an ultimatum, and Wilson gave his polite but inevitable answer the next day. The secretary of war was perfectly free to express his views by speech or letter, the President wrote back, "but I hope you will be kind enough to draw very carefully the distinction between your own individual views and the views of the Administration."[32]

Lindley Garrison submitted his resignation as secretary of war upon the receipt of Wilson's letter. The secretary stepped down partially out of disgust and partially to dramatize the issue. Like Bryan, he resigned for a principle. Henry Breckinridge, his loyal assistant secretary, also resigned, and arm in arm the two men walked down the halls of the War Department and out of the building. Garrison left Washington on the Congressional Limited without talking to reporters. The next day, appropriately, the House Military Affairs Committee terminated its long-drawn-out hearings. The new acting secretary of war was now Major General Hugh Scott. The old cavalryman gave his recent superior a sincere and touching tribute: "This is indeed a cold day for the War Department and the Army. We all feel as did my little girl Houston, who when she heard the news said 'Oh dear!' and put her head in her mother's lap."[33]

6

War in Time
of Peace

*There seems to be a preparedness germ or an epidemic
that has swept the country. Nearly everybody has it.*

—Senator George Norris

*The danger of an attack upon our country has been
made to appear very real and very imminent. It has
been painted in lurid colors—moving pictures showing
New York's splendid edifices toppling to destruction,
under the shots of enemy guns, the enemy garbed to
convey the idea that they are Germans. . . .*

—Senator Robert LaFollette

We have a new craze. It is war in time of peace.

—Chancellor James R. Day

While Congress debated defense at leisure, urban America resonated to the drums of an intense preparedness agitation. The European War had provided the army reformers and big-navy enthusiasts with the civilian base they sought. For months the war had been beating upon informed Americans through the medium of the press, and this had had its effects. As William Allen White wrote, "the thing is in every man's consciousness—not as a passing show but as a dark impending shadow of reality across their own lives." The preparedness campaign, exaggerated and silly as it sometimes was, reflected an authentic unease among educated Americans. The invasion of Belgium had shaken the faith of a generation. Now, many feared Germany, some Japan, and some professed to fear Great Britain or even vague combinations of nations. But a tremendous number of Americans were in agreement with the New York lawyer and elder statesman Joseph Choate, when he said that if the Europeans put their heads together after the war, "I don't think they could find any better game than this country, so fat and so rich and so unprepared."[1]

Preparedness was bipartisan, although Theodore Roosevelt seemed increasingly to be its standard-bearer. It was a nationwide movement, but its heartland lay in the East and its fountainhead was New York City, which was wealthy, cosmopolitan, and, in Alton Parker's words, "a little bit timid, lying out on the ocean as she does." Other reform movements in the Progressive Era had rolled in from the West; preparedness was an eastern export. (The West Coast, however, had its own long-standing reasons to be defense-conscious.) Overwhelmingly, the cause of preparedness enlisted the support of America's upper and middle classes; as Simeon Strunsky, an acute if hostile contemporary commentator observed, "the big army sentiment is strong in the clubs and weak in the cheap restaurants." William Howard Taft charged that the rage for defense was strongest in "the Clubs and smart set" of New York and Chicago, and paralleled a pro-Ally sentiment. The movement involved the middle classes in general, however, and not just the old-stock social elite. The U.S. Chamber of Commerce, other business organizations, and the bulk of the urban press threw their support to defense. Nor was the preparedness movement generally interventionist. Foreign policy was too controversial; it was simpler to campaign for increased armaments than to encourage speculation on the uses to which they might be put.[2]

This new civilian interest in defense generated, as might be expected, all sorts of fresh ideas on the subject, of varying degrees of practicality. There were many proposals for a Swiss-type citizen army, and there was some enthusiasm for an industrial army which would give vocational training to American youth. Robert R. McCormick, showing perhaps the first signs of a certain parochialism, suggested that the passes of the Rocky Mountains and the Appalachians be fortified against invasion. The noted inventor Thomas Edison wanted to set up a huge store of arms and munitions factories with a civilian reserve and then keep just a small training army in being. Somebody warned that Japanese troops might invade Chicago up the Mississippi River. In the field of naval affairs, many wanted to replace battleships with aircraft and submarines as a first line of defense; planes and subs would be cheaper and could not be used for imperialistic ventures in Latin America. Some odd ideas for saving the Republic wound up embodied in congressional legislation. Representative Kenneth McKellar of Tennessee found the moment propitious for pressing his long-standing scheme to set up forty-eight miniature West Points, with one federally funded and state-administered military and vocational school allotted to each state. California's erratic Senator John D. Works introduced a bill calling for a 200,000-man homecroft reserve to be set up on the West Coast; reservists would live on five-acre plots rented from the government, drill for one or two months every year, and work on reclamation projects the rest of the time. But all of this was just the froth on the wave. Increasingly, as the preparedness campaign wore on, there was a general consensus that expert advice must be followed. In this situation, the generals and admirals seemed the only people who knew what they were talking about. The civilians fell in line; where the military would lead, they would follow.[3]

* * *

The two agencies which did most to mobilize civilian support for defense were the press and the organized defense societies. From the summer of 1915 on, the urban newspapers were so unanimously committed to preparedness that opponents spoke darkly of "a conspiracy of class and press." There was no conspiracy, but the papers both reflected and intensified the drift of the times. The switch of the Wilson Administration on the issue had decided most of the last holdout newspapers, and by the end of the year less than a dozen papers of any size in the whole country opposed defense increases. One critic summed up the attitude of the New York press: "The *World*, the largest in circulation among morning newspapers, is moderately in favor of increased armaments, the *Sun* is emphatically in favor, the *Times* and the *Herald* are feverishly in favor, the *Tribune* is deliriously in favor." For once, the New York press was not unrepresentative; the rest of the nation's dailies mirrored the trend. The impact of this newspaper campaign was greatest on city dwellers. The passion for preparedness which so agitated the metropolitan press was absent from the hundreds of parochial county papers and triweeklies which did so much to form the opinion of rural America. Nor were the country dwellers swamped by such an avalanche of war news. Town dwellers were not completely insulated, however, for big-city newspapers did circulate throughout much of their states.[4]

While newspapers were the most important factor in making people preparedness-conscious, books also made a contribution. The European War evoked a snowstorm of paper on the nation's alleged defenselessness. The fuzzy-bearded Hudson Maxim, brother of the machine-gun maker, published *Defenseless America* in early 1915, predicting that war was inevitable and that before Americans came to their senses, "we must first put on sackcloth, ashed in the embers of our burning homes." One hundred thousand foreign troops could march across America behind a barrage of long-range artillery, like Xenophon's host, Maxim claimed. He warned that after the United States was overrun, "our wives and our daughters and our sweethearts would be commandeered to supply the women and song." (Some suggested that Mr. Maxim was trying to drum up business for the Maxim Munitions Corporation.) Richard Stockton, Jr.'s *Peace Insurance*, published at about the same time, pointed out that defense costs should be looked upon in a businesslike way as a reasonable premium on losses to be expected in any possible war. In 1915, America was paying out on defense an inadequate one-fifteenth of 1 percent of what she might lose. Stockton calculated that what the country would lose was its total wealth, about $117.9 billion, plus independence and political and religious liberty, which Stockton guessed was worth an equal cash sum. More prosaically, the Army reformer Frederick L. Huidekoper published *The Military Unpreparedness of the United*

States, which was long, relentlessly factual, copiously footnoted, and quite dull. Huidekoper attempted to demonstrate that the United States had been unprepared for armed conflict ever since the Revolutionary War. These books were among the first in a procession; some sixty titles relating to national defense were published between 1915 and America's entry into the war.[5]

The popular magazines carried their own full share of preparedness propaganda. *The Scientific American* ran an impressive series of articles called "Our Undefended Treasure Land," which was later published in pamphlet form. Admiral Bradley Fiske and General Leonard Wood repeatedly had their say in print. The young Eric Fisher Wood warned *Century* readers in "The Writing on the Wall" that a European staff officer had told him 400,000 European troops holding the line of the Hudson, Susquehannah, and Potomac could stand off the world. Magazines and newspapers carried lurid fictional serials with titles like "1917?" and "The Invasion of America." All of these efforts involved coalitions of unnamed European powers launching vast armadas of warships and troop-transports against a feeble and divided America whose defenses had been crippled by poltroons and incompetents bearing an odd resemblance to Bryanite Democrats. The partisan humor magazine *Life*, which had pilloried Josephus Daniels, published a "Get Ready" number which was more than usually explicit on just what America had to get ready for: the cover showed a map of America as New Prussia, with cities renamed Kulturplatz, Hyphenburg, and Schlauterhaus, and a Japanese settlement on the West Coast.[6]

The preparedness movement even generated transient journals of its own. The Navy League already had its own magazine, *Seven Seas*. In the fall of 1916, the new American Defense Society attempted to publish what its chairman called a "national magazine built along the lines of the organ of the German Navy League," *American Defense*. This somewhat discomfited the publisher of another new magazine in the field, who had titled his journal *National Defense*. Finally, somewhat in a class by itself, was the magazine *Electra: The National Preparedness Magazine*, devoted to defense, the electrical industry, and boosting the interests of the city of Buffalo, where it was published. The backers of *Electra* attempted to enroll readers in the "National Spiritual Reserve of the United States of America."[7]

The relatively new art of the motion picture was now available to promote the cause of defense. Commodore J. Stuart Blackton of the Vitagraph Company turned his efforts to producing a film version of Hudson Maxim's book *Defenseless America*. The result was "The Battle Cry of Peace," a picture containing, in the words of *The New York Times* reviewer, "a slender plot, a modicum of heart interest, and a great deal of flag waving." It also had a cast of thousands and rather too many shots of Hudson Maxim. In the course of the picture, America was invaded by a horde of licentious soldiery, mansions on Long Island went up in flames, Times Square, filled with swaying crowds, was bombed, and assorted atrocities were committed. The identity of the invaders, clad in specially designed uniforms and helmets, was not specified. But as the reviewer from *The Times* pointed out, "it is difficult to escape the impression that you are expected to recognize the nationality. They are certainly not Portuguese, for instance." "The Battle Cry of Peace" seems to have been very successful; by the following year the producer was planning to release a sequel, "The Battle Cry of War." There were emulators. The Patriot Film Corporation came up with a visual object lesson in preparedness urging the fortification of all frontiers, including the Canadian, with a striking motion map. The sensational novelist Thomas Dixon, whose book had provided the plot for "Birth of a Nation," collaborated with Victor Herbert on a preparedness lesson and motion picture show entitled "The Fall of a Nation."[8]

*   *   *

The real spearhead of the preparedness movement was provided by the civilian defense societies. By the summer of 1915, these included the National Security League, the Navy League, and the rather unimportant Army League. As the campaign went on, the original organizations continued to expand and new associations multiplied. With enrollments of thousands and letterheads decorated with the names of the prominent, the societies proved able to generate a good deal of attention and publicity for the defense cause. Highly visible, the societies were perhaps a little less solid than they looked. The distinguished men who obligingly lent their names as honorary officers exercised little control over policy, which was set by small groups of insiders. The defense leagues concentrated on mobilizing public opinion rather than lobbying, and they proved more noisy than adept at influencing congressional legislation. But they did provide a rallying point and a sounding-board for the middle-class defense sentiment in the country.

Detractors repeatedly accused these groups of being creatures of big business engaged in whipping up war hysteria for money. The charge was vigorously denied. In fact, the defense societies seem to have been relatively guiltless on this point. The Navy League was the oldest and most established of the societies; during the year ending March 31, 1916, it received less than $60,000, with three-fifths of the sum coming from membership dues. As the secretary's report indicated, the amount was "small for a country of a hundred million." The Army League at one point had only between $1,000 and $2,000 in its treasury. The American Defense Society, which backed Theodore Roosevelt's views, was reduced to employing a professional fund-raiser to drum up donations. The MTCA raised a little less than $82,000 in its 1916 campaign, a good part of it from Plattsburg volunteers. The National Security League did manage to take in $160,000 from all sources by the summer of 1916. But, as Stanwood Menken put it, its fund appeals were made to "identically the same groups of men who made donations to the Y.M.C.A., the Red Cross, the men who were always giving to the big movements in this country." For purposes of comparison, it should be noted that the League to Enforce Peace, oriented toward international organization rather than armaments, garnered $350,000 by 1916. This does not mean that all support for defense was altruistic. Airplane manufacturers and automobile makers like Henry Joy of Packard Motors showed a zeal for American defense which may not have been unconnected with expected profits. But the defense societies, on the whole, seem to have been above-board and were not lavishly financed.[9]

The most aggressive and influential group pressing for military reform continued to be the National Security League, which Stanwood Menken had founded in the fall of 1914. Menken had started out with some experience in organizational work and with a few good connections in New York legal circles to capitalize on. The League found itself in the right place at the right time. The respected publisher George Haven Putnam had been one of the original founding members, and the League soon enlisted John Purroy Mitchel, the reform mayor of New York,

Frederic L. Coudert, the prominent international lawyer, and ex-Secretary of War Henry L. Stimson. Presently, the League attracted the attention of the capitalist and retired general Francis Vinton Green, who provided an entrée to even more exalted circles. Green was able to introduce Menken to the elderly, wealthy, and immensely distinguished Joseph Choate, regarded by many as the first citizen of New York. With Choate's assistance, the League reached other distinguished citizens, and recruited Alton B. Parker, the Democratic presidential candidate in 1904, as an honorary vice-president. The League thus provided a prestigious and bipartisan nucleus for defense advocates to rally around.[10]

By the summer of 1915, the National Security League had hired a full-time executive secretary and was beginning to spread out across the country. Seventy branches, loosely controlled and supervised, were in existence by November, and the League was particularly strong in Chicago and St. Louis. The defense movement found a response in almost every large city. Aiming its appeal to the widest popular audience, the League carefully avoided specifying any potential enemies against whom they might have to defend themselves. As William F. Brewster, its midwestern field secretary, expressed it, America must prepare against "no one! Everyone . . . contingencies." However, when John Wanamaker, the newly elected chairman of the Philadelphia branch proposed that the United States embargo munitions exports and "buy" Belgium from Germany with the payment of a $100 million indemnity, he was speedily induced to resign. If the National Security League were not overtly pro-Ally, its eastern wing, at least, did not provide a very sympathetic climate for anything which smacked of pro-Germanism.[11]

Maintaining a nice bipartisanship, the League worked with officials at all levels of government to promote defense. New York's Democratic Mayor Mitchel took the lead, appointing Cornelius Vanderbilt to head a committee of 1,000 in New York in the fall of 1915. Some eighty mayors followed his example. The National Security League encouraged Republican Governor Charles Whitman to form a defense committee for New York State, a move which also had its imitators. (The League found mayors and governors almost solidly backing increased defense.) Finally, the National Security League decided to cooperate with the Wilson Administration on defense when the President began to develop his program in the summer of 1915. If the President's proposals were not all that could be desired, at least they could be supported as a good first step in the right direction. The League did not want to wall itself off in a policy of blind opposition; moreover, such prominent Democrats as Judge Parker might resign their posts if the League were too critical of the administration.[12]

The willingness of the National Security League to go along with the Wilson Administration angered some of the Roosevelt supporters in the organization. The League's Publicity Committee defected in the summer of 1915 and set up a new organization, the American Defense Society, with a more extreme program. The chairman of the Publicity Committee, C. S. Thompson, had been frustrated by the League's unwillingness to grapple with the administration, and perhaps also by the fact that his salary had just been cut in half. Thompson thoughtfully started the new Defense Society on Security League stationery, much to everybody's confusion, and enlisted quite a number of people under misapprehension. Relations with the National Security League were understandably chilly.[13]

The American Defense Society proudly carried Theodore Roosevelt's name at the top of its letterhead, called for a big army and a huge navy, and fished for members with the help of the remaining machinery of the Progressive party. However, members were slow to come in, the prestigious advisory board was never asked for any advice, and the Society never realized any financial benefits from its support of Roosevelt's cause. A private detective agency was soon to observe that "there is an underlying current about Thompson and the affairs of this Society which does not spell confidence." Caught up in a struggle to publish a monthly magazine, with its proposed military exhibit an empty store, the Society turned to a professional fund-raiser named George Baxter to raise money on a commission basis. It soon developed that Baxter, a genuinely talented solicitor who had brought in $60,000, had been one of the most notorious members of the "We Boys" ring, a group of confidence men which pushed fraudulent philanthropies. Baxter was fired in a messy squabble and the Defense Society's management suffered an abrupt change. By this time, in 1916, the Defense Society's once extreme program was being taken over by other preparedness groups.[14]

At about the same time that the American Defense Society struck out on its own in the summer of 1915, the Aero Club moved into the forefront of the defense movement. The New York-based club was a collection of what one Congressman called "high minded, enthusiastic, patriotic faddists." Its members may have been less than experts—Philip Roosevelt, for example, who was active in the defense movement and should have known, told his cousin Theodore that "none of them in fact can fly, or know why a machine does fly." Nevertheless, they were ardent supporters both of military aeronautics and defense in general. The Aero Club fathered the American Society of Aeronautical Engineers, in order to get representation on the Navy's new Board óf Inventions. The Aero Club offices provided the site for the founding of the Conference Committee on Preparedness, which united, or rather claimed to unite, the National Security League, the Navy League, the Automobile Club, the Aero Club, the Red Cross, the American Legion, the American Institute of Engineers, and the Institute of Radio Engineers, all under one umbrella. The Conference Committee does not seem to have done too much in the way of uniting preparedness activities; the existing organizations retained their identities and a certain distrust of one another. But it did raise into prominence the Committee's chairman, Henry Wise Wood, the son of New York's disreputable Civil War mayor. A bellicose and pushy Quaker inventor and businessman, Wood was reactionary in social views, turgid in prose, and aggressive in personality. Philip Roosevelt was later to comment that Wood was "a man whom I have seen a good deal of in the past year and I do not trust him for a minute." Wood became one of the most vocal and extreme civilian agitators for defense, and his views soon carried him into a break with the Wilson Administration. On December 22, 1915, he resigned his position as delegate of the aeronautical engineers on the Naval Consulting Board, protesting the insufficiency of Secretary Josephus Daniels' program.[15]

This action was symbolic of the growing gap between the organized defense societies and the Wilson Administration. As Wilson seemingly wavered on defense, the societies took a harder and more independent line. The National Security League scheduled its first general congress in Washington in January 1916 as a device to put pressure on Congress. Acting against the advice of George Haven Putnam, one of the founders of the League, Menken and Henry Wise Wood secured as their chief speaker the colorful and controversial Theodore Roosevelt, Woodrow Wilson's archenemy. The whole League congress was structured around

Roosevelt's speech—the former President's availability was the ultimate factor even in determining the city where the convention would be held. At the end of its sessions, the League voted to endorse Roosevelt's demands for universal military training. Garrison's departure from the Wilson Cabinet in February eliminated the last major administration figure acceptable to the civilian defense movement. The societies now put their trust in Roosevelt, rejected compromise, and demanded a total and ideal preparedness. By March, Thomas Robins, the vice-chairman of the Naval Consulting Board, was attacking the National Security League as a partisan organization, hostile to the administration. "Everybody knows that the National Security League has overdone its work."[16]

As the defense movement accelerated its demands, there was also a renewed effort to coordinate its component organizations. The movement was still fragmented and chaotic. General Leonard Wood confessed, "we are a little swamped with the multiplicity of societies." Former President William Howard Taft defined the problem in personal terms: "There are so many Associations that it is very difficult to know what to join. I am a member of the American Legion, but not of the National Protective Society. I believe I am a member of the National Security League." This was obviously an undesirable situation, and the National Security League congress saw an attempt made to unify the preparedness drive, a task made easier by the recent change in the management of the maverick American Defense Society. George Hewitt Myers, secretary of the Army League, suggested that a new coordinating committee be formed. General Wood was in favor of this suggestion and put forward the name of Robert Bacon, Roosevelt's former secretary of state and a perennial Plattsburger, to head it. Bacon was practically a living embodiment of the whole preparedness movement. Not only was he a connecting link between the Plattsburg group and the civilian defense societies, but he was also on the Executive Committee of the Navy League, the Army Committee of the National Security League, and was Theodore Roosevelt's choice to straighten out the tangled affairs of the American Defense Society. As a coordinator, Bacon never fully succeeded, but at the National Security League convention in May, when Menken declined his unanimous reelection, it was Robert Bacon who became president of the League.[17]

The choice of Bacon, a man completely identified with the cause of universal military training, emphasized how far the defense movement had come since the fall of 1914. The National Security League had started out with demands for a simple inquiry into the nation's defenses. It now had committed itself to following the desires of the Army General Staff. Universal military training had become the key demand of the whole defense movement. The Plattsburgers supported it, and a new and single purpose pressure group, the Association for National Service, had been set up to campaign for it by a newspaper referendum drive. Universal training had been massively endorsed by the U.S. Chamber of Commerce and by a conference of city heads which Mayor Mitchel had gotten up in St. Louis in March. The defense movement no longer would be content with asking for a bigger army and navy; its advocates now wanted the moral exhilaration of a whole nation under arms.[18]

*   *   *

While the defense societies mobilized public opinion, some people, caught up in the fever of preparedness, took both practical and impractical steps to get ready. The eccentric Philadelphia philanthropist, A. J. Drexel Biddle, organized a military corps of 8,000 men, and other Philadelphia businessmen raised and equipped units of up to regimental strength from the ranks of their employees. New York life insurance clerks were put to drilling during the noon hour on the roof of their office building. The benefits of military drill were extended to newsboys and the convicts of the Maryland State Penitentiary. Yachtsmen organized a Volunteer Patrol Squadron of motor launches. By 1916, a number of *ad hoc* militia units were in existence, outfits unrecognized by their state's National Guard and which trained without pay.[19]

There was also a move to bolster the nation's defenses by private funds, to let private initiative take over where the government failed. Wealthy magnates, including Elbert Gary and Henry Clay Frick of the steel industry, presented a squadron of armored cars to the New York National Guard. The Arctic explorer, Admiral Robert Peary, suggested the establishment of an aerial coastal patrol in 1915, an idea which was taken up by John Hays Hammond, Jr., and the ever-active Aero Club. Money to set up patrol stations manned by naval militia was raised by private subscription. The Aero Club also sponsored a drive to buy planes for the National Guard and to give flight training to militiamen and civilians. Beginning in 1915, the National Aero Fund raised $171,000 in cash by the end of the following year, along with a doubtless optimistically overestimated $200,000 worth of planes and flying lessons. One philanthropist, the New York Banker Emerson McMillen, gave nearly $34,000 in matching grants, and the Glenn L. Martin and Curtiss aircraft companies each donated a plane. Curtiss also provided flying lessons for one National Guardsman per state. On a less serious level, a thirteen-year-old Brooklyn schoolgirl attempted to start a fund to purchase a battleship with a donation of ten cents in stamps to the *New York Tribune*. (The $20,000 ultimately raised went for a naval marksmanship prize.)[20]

The preparedness movement was not confined to men, but swept up women and even children in organized activity. Women's clubs scrambled to get aboard the preparedness bandwagon, and new groups sprang up. The National Woman's Special Aid Society embraced the cause of defense with a vengeance, compiling lists of sewing clubs and nurses, making specimen kits of items that would be useful to the individual soldier, and even preparing summer cottages for use as military hospitals. Ladies of the Civic Federation fought with the American Red Cross for control over the distaff side of preparedness. The Women's Section of the Belgian Relief Commission metamorphosed, with some fitness, into the Women's Section of the Movement for National Preparedness. The newly founded Women's Section of the Navy League was an instant success. The Socialist magazine *The Masses* carried an irreverent account that "an alarmed patriotism has appealed to the ladies of the Boston Auxiliary of the National Security League to 'register their automobiles for the purpose of carrying the virgins inland in case of invasion.' "[21]

There was even a female equivalent for the Plattsburg Movement. A Woman's Preparedness Camp was held at Chevy Chase, Maryland, near Washington, in the spring of 1916, and some 250 uniformed ladies threw themselves vigorously into the task of military training. (The marine cooks in charge of the mess declared that the women students ate twice as much as the marines.) Mrs. E. Vandercook-Browne founded the American Women's League for Self-Defense in New York. Its members drilled in uniform weekly at the Ninth Regiment Armory. The question of proper uniforms for women occasioned some controversy. The League's commandant, Mrs. General J. Hungerford Milbank, felt it would be best to wear skirts out of deference to husbands and sweethearts, but this argument was quashed when Miss Anne Higgins, a breeches advocate, cried out, "Think no longer of husbands and sweethearts. Think about dirt and barbed wire fences. . . . This is the age of the new woman." Mrs. Milbank then founded a new organization, the International Order of Military Women, and announced plans for a coeducational army camp. "It is very lonely for the young men to go into camp by themselves," she stated.[22]

There were also movements to give military training to teenagers, both for its own sake and as a school for patriotism. Arthur S. Hoffman, the editor of *Adventure Magazine* and co-founder of the American Legion, came up with a plan for a National School Camp Association, which would give military and industrial training to boys about twelve years of age, thus organizing and disciplining the majority of children who had been forced to leave school. Lest the camps smack of charity or threaten the boys' sturdy independence, one of the Association's backers announced, "the cost of the movement will be borne almost entirely by the boys themselves." Hoffman and his friends were not alone in their ideas as to the benefits of military training for the young. Weightier voices would soon call for a training program on an official level. By the end of the summer of 1916, there would be 1,200 secondary school boys drilling under Army auspices at the junior Plattsburg Camp at Fort Terry, New York.[23]

*   *   *

The agitation for preparedness went on at a high pitch through the early months of 1916, as Congress debated military legislation. In the spring of the year, it found some new methods of expression. An aviator named De Lloyd Thompson staged a one-man mock attack on Washington with fireworks bombs in April to show the capital's vulnerability. (Repeating the demonstration above the Woolworth Building in New York City, the intrepid flyer narrowly escaped blowing a wing off his Day biplane when a bomb exploded prematurely.) And the nation was swept by a cycle of great civilian preparedness parades.[24]

The preparedness parade was an appropriate, highly visible, and quite easy method of dramatizing the defense issue. Parades succeeded in mobilizing the enthusiasm of the middle classes for defense, and took advantage of the availability of large numbers of captive white collar workers who could be marched by defense-minded employers. The first parade took place in New York City in May. Its organizer and grand marshal was Colonel Charles Hitchcock Sherrill, a former Republican ambassador to Argentina, who had served as marshal for the great Sound Money Parade of 1896. After six weeks of preparation (and some attempts to quash the idea by a cautious Wilson Administration), 135,000 marchers streamed down Fifth Avenue twenty abreast for nearly twelve hours. Josephus Daniels called it "the greatest petition of the ages"; a preacher solemnly noted that "the day was less a holiday and more a consecration than any pageant the city has witnessed in our time." Although the Wilson Administration had worried about German-American reaction to the march because of the contemporaneous *Sussex* crisis, the German language press had in fact endorsed the parade.[25]

More was to come. The New York parade inspired imitation all over the country. Walking for defense had a certain irresistible charm, and was certainly more appealing than enlisting. On June 3, 350,000 Americans were out marching for their country in ten cities across the nation. The paraders in Chicago that day were 130,000 strong, and included several hundred telephone operators garbed so as to form an immense moving American flag, and a contingent of uniformed goose-stepping playground directors. America had become preparedness-conscious.[26]

The defense movement was now a part of American popular culture. Preparedness filled the newspapers and flooded into the streets. The advertisements for innocuous products featured pictures of soldiers or battleships, and men's clothing stores put out uniform displays for prospective Plattsburgers. Daisy Air Rifles came out with a new military model, with sling, adjustable sights, and a "detachable rubber-tipped bayonet." That summer, the popular colors in fashion would be red, white, and blue.[27]

7

The Large
Regiment

*The political issue of 1916 is the issue of a thoroughly
disciplined Americanism.*

—Frederick M. Davenport

*The soldier is no longer a tradesman in war, but is part
of that large regiment which includes his entire country.*

—Newton D. Baker

Preparedness was a symptom as well as a movement; it was the
expression of a deep unrest beneath the surface of American life. In
Europe, the warring nations had set up a new standard of efficiency,
cohesion, and purpose amid the storm of battle, while America sat
ignobly on the sidelines, a mere sponge for wealth. In comparison to the
disciplined combatants, the United States, in Walter Lippmann's words,
now seemed a "straggling democracy," recklessly individualistic, point-
lessly violent, and filled with unassimilated national groups. "Through-

out the uneasiness of America," Lippmann wrote in 1916, "there runs the sense of our own relative incompetence." Consciously or unconsciously, men turned to preparedness as a moral equivalent for war. Preparedness, in its wider sense, was at once a tool to integrate America and a way to express national vigor and purpose.[1]

The uneasiness in the country was real and palpable. In the backwash of the European War, Americans wallowed in self-deprecation. "Above the stomach, this nation scarcely exists as a nation," mourned Henry Osborne Taylor in *The Atlantic Monthly*. A correspondent complained to General Hugh Scott that the United States was not a country, "just a huge jelly fish of a settlement." Roy Howard, the president of United Press, told Amos Pinchot that the preparedness movement would all be worthwhile "if it only served for a time to lift this nation out of the sordid pot-bellied, fat joweled state into which it is getting as a result of its orgy of money-making." Even labor leader Samuel Gompers declared that "many indications mark a decline of national virility." It was small wonder that the thoughtful Progressive, Herbert Croly, felt what the nation needed was "the tonic of a serious moral adventure." For some, the discipline of military preparedness seemed the needed medicine. Their light at the end of the tunnel was a gleam of steel.[2]

In particular, Americans seemed drawn to matching their country against the arch-villain of the European drama. As one businessman wrote, "Eighteen months ago some of the lessons of the war had begun to emerge in tangible shape. Above them all loomed the lightning-bolt example of German efficiency." It was the challenge of Germany which haunted men's thoughts. Former Secretary of War Henry L. Stimson felt that America had to prove "that a democracy like ourselves can, under the proper methods and with the proper spirit, product efficient results comparable to those which have been produced by the autocratic methods of Germany." Theodore Roosevelt warned his patriotic listeners in Detroit in the spring of 1916 that "in many ways Germany furnishes us an example we may do well to heed." Germany was preeminently armed, an obvious success, and a standing reproach to America as a society. Preparedness could make America over into the image of her rival. As William Lyon Phelps of Yale dryly noted, "I feel that those persons who most loudly curse Germany are most anxious that we should follow her lead."[3]

Increasingly, Americans saw preparedness as a way to transform America and reshape her whole society, to homogenize a drifting mass of immigrants, rationalize her industries, and ennoble her spirit. "The political issue of 1916 is the issue of a thoroughly disciplined Americanism," wrote one professor and journalist. Croly noted that "Americans who are advocating 'preparedness' are basing their approval largely upon the better order, which it is expected to impose upon our time honored internal chaos." Stimson was in striking agreement. If the preparedness drive produced only additions to the naval and military establishments, he wrote, "the nation will have lost a great opportunity. The real need of the country is a change of ideals in all respects." Preparedness united old-fashioned patriots with reformers. The integrating impulse behind the defense movement had an immediate attraction for some Progressives. *The New Republic* was not alone when it felt that preparedness could be a Trojan Horse which would bring overdue social reforms to America.[4]

This quest for a greater national unity was a generalized reform sentiment which found echoes in all parties. While the Wilson Administration hung back from some of the wider implications of preparedness, it did worry about consolidating the country. As the tensions of the European War stirred up German-American protest at home, and fires broke out in munitions plants, an increased demand for loyalty and uniformity swept the country. The Wilson Administration called for the psychological mobilization of "Americanism." As early as October 1915, Colonel House was contemplating making "Americanism" the main issue of the 1916 campaign. Significantly, Wilson stressed the importance of national unity in his Manhattan Club speech devoted to defense. Americanism too was part of preparedness. In fact, as Theodore Roosevelt put it, "Preparedness and undivided Americanism are one."[5]

If Wilson endorsed some aspects of this deeper preparedness, its undoubted leader remained Colonel Roosevelt, that American Bismarck who united martial vigor with social reform. By 1916, Roosevelt seemed more relevant than ever. The proposals which had frightened businessmen at Ossawatomie now could be put forward as simple necessities for the home front. As an admirer wrote, "Wall Street, that hated Roosevelt in 1912, accepts him with his whole social program today because it vaguely senses the need for solidifying the nation." Rejected at the door, progressivism seemed to be coming in through the ammunition hatch. For a moment in 1916, Roosevelt seemed to embody urban America's craving for authority, discipline, and order. A Newer Nationalism was in the wind. To refashion America on proper lines, preparedness advocates turned to programs of universal military training and industrial mobilization.[6]

*   *   *

Universal military training had obvious appeals to the Army as a far surer method of raising the necessary manpower than the volunteer system. The Army reformers of 1912 had taken the small professional volunteer army of Great Britain for their model. But now Britain seemed to be floundering under the shock of war, groping toward conscription herself. By 1916, American soldiers and civilians alike were inclined to dismiss the British tradition of volunteer enlistments as, in the words of *Everybody's Magazine*, "the ghost of that dead system" which had taught Englishmen "to slack at home and to let hired Tommies and eccentric volunteers do their fighting for them. . . ." The harsher model of the Continental military machines now seemed appropriate and compelling. Even when the Army was pledged to support Garrison's Continental force, the possibilities of better things danced before the generals' eyes. Leonard Wood had been an early and public advocate of universal military training. But even Army Chief of Staff Hugh Scott, a man of a markedly different intellectual stripe, edged up to the subject. In January 1916, he told a congressional committee that universal training would be necessary if the Continental Army failed.[7]

"I looked for the sky to fall in on me for talking about universal service here," Scott wrote a friend after his testimony, "but it does not seem to fall for some reason, and I have been amazed at the spread of such doctrine." The fact was that the idea of universal military training had found a broad civilian constituency by 1916. It had become the latest reform of the Progressive Era, backed by newspapers, businessmen's associations, and defense leagues, as well as soldiers. To the military, universal training was merely a code word for conscription, "a happier phrase," as a War Department memorandum put it, than "compulsory military service." But many civilians endorsed the idea as a way of disciplining and strengthening American youth and ordering American society, not as a conveyor belt to bring grist to the military mill. Although military training would be compulsory, the real fighting in the event of war, they fancied, would still be done by volunteers. Universal military training was offered to the public as a school for citizenship. Ellery Sedgwick, the editor of *The Atlantic Monthly*, had shrewdly forecast the approach shortly after the outbreak of war in Europe. "If militarism is unpopular in this country, education is the national religion." *The New Republic* agreed: "If the American democracy has always revolted at the idea of compulsory military training, it has explicitly accepted the idea of compulsory education." Despite all of the talk about preparedness, the thought of actual battle seemed far away from many defense advocates.[8]

Universal military training now seemed a panacea for America's social and economic ills, making the nation fit for competition in peace as well as war. Theodore Roosevelt, its most notable advocate, declared that the measure "would not be of prime military consequence, but of prime consequence to us socially and industrially." The Progressive economist, Richard T. Ely, enthused that "the moral effect of taking boys off street corners and out of saloons and drilling them is excellent, and the economic effects are likewise beneficial." Will Culbertson of the Federal Trade Commission felt military training would generate "a profounder sense of responsibility and a deeper appreciation of the meaning of discipline." Business circles were particularly interested in this reform. Sedgwick claimed that most of the men in charge of America's organized industries believed German industrial efficiency was the result of compulsory military training. The popular writer Frederick Palmer predicted that the adoption of universal training would make America 20 percent more productive in twenty years. The U.S. Chamber of Commerce felt it would "take up this slack of idleness in the industrial field and substitute a period of helpful discipline for a period of demoralizing freedom from restraint." In short, as Julius Rosenwald of Sears, Roebuck put it, universal military training would be "far more important as preparedness for peace than preparedness for war."[9]

The drive for universal training enlisted both the dreams and the fears of the Progressive movement. It held out the promise of democracy. The sons of the rich and the sons of the poor would be gathered under the same tent for a common patriotic effort. "Universal military training is the

most democratic thing in history," one of Roosevelt's correspondents
wrote. Universal military training would stifle any danger of militarism.
"A Democracy must avoid a military caste," Ralph Barton Perry told his
readers, "which it can best do by making the people its own army."
Senator William Borah, a western progressive Republican who showed
some skepticism about preparedness in general, declared that universal
service would be good because "a democracy should not only be self-
governing, but self-protecting." Conscription had been transformed into
a high duty of democratic citizenship, and opponents of preparedness
moaned with some justification over "the rape of our best phrases."[10]

Universal military training promised social efficiency. It would
homogenize an America that seemed dangerously divided in a military
pressure cooker. The country, Leonard Wood warned, was showing
"lines of cleavage and rupture whenever the pressure is put on, as you see
all about you today." The Army was the social institution which could
break down class lines and assimilate and nationalize the immigrant.
Frederick Palmer urged citizens to "go over to the East Side of New York
and watch the crowds. Go into an American town and see the loafers
hanging around the street corners" and then visualize the benefits of
military training. In Henry S. Breckinridge's words, universal training
was "the only way to yank the hyphen out of America." It was not just
the immigrants who would benefit. The Cowles newspapers warned that
"the prisons, the reformatories, the ever-enlarging army of deserted
wives, the ever-increasing grist of the divorce mills—all speak of an
excess of so-called 'personal liberty' and lack of wholesome discipline
over the country's youth." In short, universal military training offered
middle-class America social control as well as democracy, a chance to
discipline minds as well as bodies. Ralph Barton Perry bluntly wrote
about the place of the pacifist in this system: "If his conscience is
offended, so much the worse for his conscience. What he needs is a new
conscience." The *Chicago Tribune* editorialized: "The fact that universal service would bring a degree of mental conscription with it is precisely
the reason that it is desirable in this country."[11]

Finally, universal military training seemed to offer an emotional
catharsis in a time of stress, a chance to sacrifice, at least vicariously.
Perry, the Plattsburg philosopher, eloquently expressed some of the
motives behind the growing agitation when he wrote: "There is a spread-

ing belief that if we are to take part in the making of history, we must acquire the strength to do it. Military training, or some other exercise to make oneself fit for national service, is a natural outgrowth of the desire to *act* in this great crisis when every good thing is in jeopardy." The Philadelphia lawyer George Wharton Pepper declared, "What we Americans need . . . those of us who are well to do—is to take a course in real hardship." Middle-class Americans yearned for a taste of the Spartan mode; while some went to Plattsburg, others were interested only in military training for other people. Well-fed and prosperous men over fifty at dinner parties were particularly enthusiastic, the head of the New York National Guard noted skeptically. But the impulse was there, and it tugged at the heart as well as the head. In the spring of 1916, Theodore Roosevelt stumped the country; he drew the wildest applause when he mentioned universal military training. When he spoke at the Detroit Opera House in May, *The New York Times* reported, "The crowd was on its feet cheering, and when quiet was restored, a woman on the balcony . . . called in a clear, ringing voice: 'I've got two sons to go.' "[12]

This demand for universal military training spilled into the halls of Congress. The maverick Democratic Senator George Chamberlain, head of the Senate Military Affairs Committee, took the lead by introducing a training bill at the beginning of 1916. Chamberlain's proposal was clearly modeled along the lines of the Swiss military system, which had received much popular attention. Under the terms of the bill, all American males would receive military training from age twelve to twenty-three, beginning with a Citizens Cadet Corps and ending in a Citizens Army. The actual provisions of the legislation made the program sound less formidable: the Citizens Army would drill for only 120 hours a year, and the Citizens Cadet Corps could be trained through the Boy Scouts. The Citizens Army would be subject to civilian courts rather than to military discipline.[13]

The Chamberlain bill was more an attempt to generate discussion of the issue than anything else. Chamberlain's own committee at this time was considering the administration's proposal for a Continental Army, into which the senator's scheme scarcely fitted. As the senator admitted privately, "I fear for its fate." Moreover, professional military men shot the proposed legislation full of holes. The plan would not fit anybody to fight. By spring, however, with sentiment growing for the idea, Chamberlain thought that the prospects for at least getting a report on universal military training legislation from his Senate committee had brightened. And he had obtained professional military assistance to draft a revised bill. Inevitably, any plan of universal military training would be shaped by the General Staff, not by civilians.[14]

Meanwhile, there were efforts at the state level to give military training to the young. Governor David Walsh of Massachusetts advocated compulsory military education for all boys over fourteen, with one week of camp a year. Massachusetts and New Jersey both created commissions to study military training in the public schools in 1916. New York State, always a stronghold of preparedness sentiment, acted more dramatically, passing a complete program of legislation. At the end of the legislative session, the state hastily adopted the Welsh and Slater bills. (Unkind critics suggested the legislature was largely drunk at the time.) The Slater Act set up a three-man State Military Training Commission headed by Major General John O'Ryan of the New York National Guard, provided for three hours of military training a week for boys sixteen to nineteen, and created juvenile camps on the Plattsburg model. The Welsh Act ordered a program of physical education for boys and girls between eight and sixteen, to be supervised by the Military Training Commission. The New York commissioner of education, a statutory member of the Military Training Commission, was passionately opposed to the Slater law he was supposed to administer. Since the appropriations for the Plattsburg-type camps amounted to only thirty cents a student, *Everybody's Magazine* concluded, "the believers in military training were too long on sentiment and too short on practical sense. They may possibly have been also short on sincerity." The *Independent* accurately summarized the New York legislation as "a characteristically American piece of hocus pocus." But it indicated the forces that had started to work in America.[15]

The drive for universal military training did not affect all Americans equally. The Wilson Administration, with its generally liberal orientation, remained cool to the idea, although individuals like Secretary of the Interior Franklin K. Lane approved. Congress was indifferent, an attitude that almost surely reflected the feeling of the mass of American voters. Still, there were signs that the agitation was having some effect in changing the political climate. In May, Wilson's new secretary of war, Newton D. Baker, rather ambiguously endorsed "universal training through voluntary service.'' (But this may simply have been a rhetorical substitute for the ''citizenry trained and accustomed to arms'' which Wilson himself had loftily advocated back in 1914.) On the other flank, the cautious and conservative William Howard Taft had initially held back too. In January 1916, he had written a close friend: ''Roosevelt is rushing into conscription. Of all things, conscription would be the most unpopular thing in the entire country that could be devised. Either I am crazy or somebody else is crazy, and as yet nobody has proposed a committee of lunacy for me.'' By June, however, the ex-President was telling graduating students that compulsory military service would be good for the country whether it gave preparedness or not, although he still feared that its adoption might trigger a backlash against defense by workers and farmers. Universal military training as a reform had clearly captured the imagination of the urban middle class, and the traditionalists were on the defensive.[16]

A few advanced thinkers questioned the basic assumptions of the universal training advocates. It was Herbert Croly, one of the most far-seeing of the Progressives, who pointed out that the United States was not, after all, a larger Switzerland, but a major power, whose defense problems might require something other than a home guard. An army, Croly warned enthusiasts, was not ''a vehicle of civic grace,'' nor was it a democracy. Rather, it was ''a delicate and dangerous instrument which may be called upon to perform the terrible work of killing and submitting to being killed.'' This was a point, in all the zeal for new-modeling America, that many were inclined to overlook.[17]

*   *   *

Another widespread demand at this time was for some form of industrial mobilization. Here Germany provided a model of organized, disciplined efficiency. The demand came from both military and civilian sources. Leonard Wood pointed out that ''the Army and Navy are only the cutting edge of the blade;'' that nation would survive which could ''most skillfully combine the implements of industry with the implements of war.'' But industrial mobilization seemed to offer other benefits, which caught the imagination of civilian Progressives as diverse as George Perkins and Newton D. Baker. Perkins asked Theodore

Roosevelt to emphasize industrial preparedness as much as military preparedness in his speeches. He told his chief that it was as important to organize for readiness ''against the industrial wars we are sure to have than for the war at arms that we may possibly have.'' Baker was just as enthusiastic. He proposed an industrial and even a spiritual mobilization which would be ''as valuable and as vital in times of peace as in times of conflict.'' The secretary of war went on to tell his readers: ''We have the impulse and the opportunity to give our daily life a national purpose. Every occupation in America now takes on a patriotic aspect.''[18]

On this front the Wilson Administration proved unexpectedly responsive, and the vague yearnings for a Newer Nationalism were translated into concrete actions. The first steps were taken by the Navy. In July 1915, responding to pressures from within and without the armed services, Navy Secretary Josephus Daniels set up a Naval Consulting Board of engineers and inventors under the chairmanship of Thomas A. Edison. Originally, Daniels had informed the press that he intended to work with ''a board of only a few men, probably just four or five, but men whose names are known everywhere, the very leaders in their professions.'' By the time the final list had been prepared, however, there were twenty-three men on the Naval Consulting Board, representing eleven scientific and engineering organizations. Incredibly, Daniels' critics in the defense movement scoffed at the Board because it was composed of civilians. ''Naval people see little hope for practical benefits,'' Admiral Bradley Fiske observed gloomily. The armed services were still parochial in 1915; it was one of the accomplishments of the preparedness movement that it helped break down the distinctiveness between the military and the greater society. *The New Republic* was more perceptive: it praised the move as ''the first intelligent attempt to utilize the inventive genius of the country for essentially national rather than commercial ends.''[19]

There had been some thought that the Naval Consulting Board, with the famous Edison at its head, would be simply a committee on inventions, a sort of collective Tom Swift. But the Consulting Board soon transcended this role, its interests spreading far beyond the Navy. Newton D. Baker would later recount the process: ''As fast as they learned to spell one word, Europe propounded another, and so the board was driven from the simple and elementary task of merely suggesting ingenious and newly invented devices to the Navy, and began to realize . . . that the

whole industrial and commercial forces of the nation had to be organized.'' The Board first met in October 1915. By November it had
spawned a Committee on Production, Organization, Manufacture, and
Standardization, headed by Howard Coffin of the Hudson Motor Car
Company, a man who had done much to standardize the automobile
industry as president of the Society of Automotive Engineers. Renamed
the Committee on Industrial Preparedness, this group would come to
dwarf its parent in importance.[20]

Demands for some form of industrial mobilization were already in the
air. Businessmen, generally sensitive to preparedness, had come to
realize that the nation was not organized for war. Allied war orders had
brought the scope of the problem home. As the president of the Cleveland
Chamber of Commerce stated, ''the thing that has stirred up the business
men, particularly of the Middle West—and I suppose in the East . . . has
been the experience that we have had, the manufacturers particularly,
with this question of producing materials.'' In the summer of 1915,
Martin Gillis, president of the Wisconsin-based Mitchell Wagon Company, had circulated a plan among government officials for the procure-
ment of military supplies in time of war. Gillis proposed that the President create a General Honor Board of American businessmen from
representative industries, which would survey the productive capacity of
the country, standardize equipment, and prepare the necessary dies and
samples. In the event of war, military contracts would be let out to private
industry at cost plus 6 percent, thus eliminating the problem of excess
profits. Gillis's plan got wide circulation, was approved by the Army
War College Division, and was endorsed by the Chicago *Tribune*. Although never formally adopted, it foreshadowed much that was to come
after. It was roughly along these lines that the Committee on Industrial
Preparedness began to work.[21]

In December, the Committee resolved to call upon the presidents of the
nation's five great engineering societies to survey the country's industrial
capacity for war. As manager for the campaign, the Committee acquired
Walter S. Gifford, the chief statistician for the American Telephone and
Telegraph Corporation, and it set up its offices in New York City. In
January, Woodrow Wilson wrote on behalf of the Committee to the heads
of the engineering societies, and the campaign was on. Each society
nominated a representative for every state to help in the survey; this

network of 240 or 250 men carried the brunt of the work. By the middle of the summer, the Committee had acquired thousands of files and the nation had accumulated an unprecedented knowledge of its industrial base. All of this work was done by voluntary contributions of time, labor, and money. The Naval Consulting Board had no legal status and no funds. The expenses of the Committee's central office were borne personally by Coffin; the state committees financed themselves or extracted money from sympathetic business corporations. The Associated Advertising Clubs ran free advertisements boosting the survey; the U.S. Chamber of Commerce did its part to help by framing resolutions exactly in accordance with the Committee's proposed program in a referendum to its voting members.[22]

Business and the government—or, rather, the government's unofficial proxy—were working hand in hand on this survey, a triumph of patriotism united with enlightened self-interest. The Chamber of Commerce fell in with the Committee's plans so readily because the Committee's recommendations seemed to embody everything the Chamber of Commerce desired. Under the plans evolved by the Committee, industrial preparedness would mean not only nationalization and standardization, but educational orders in peacetime and the assurance that war orders would be equitably distributed all over the country in time of emergency. The charms of the cost-plus contract or government leasing on relatively generous terms would make cooperation with the military machine profitable as well as patriotic. Howard Coffin explained the mutual benefits of these schemes: "We are giving to the Government a thousand strings to its bow where it now has a few . . . we are laying once for all the bugaboo of the munitions lobby at Washington."[23]

Working independently, a different group of men attacked another aspect of the mobilization problem. Encouraged by Leonard Wood, Dr. Hollis Godfrey, the head of the Drexel Institute, and Dr. Henry Crampton of the American Museum of Natural History were engaged in a study of the nation's biological and material resources. As in the case of the industrial survey, the work had never been done before, and was outside the scope of the Army General Staff's concerns. Godfrey and Crampton were supported by private funds, which Wood helped to secure. Their investigation involved taking each product necessary for national defense and scheduling its integral parts. The scientists found out its ingredients, where the ingredients could be procured, and how they could be put together. All of this information was assembled on great illustrative charts. A third research group was to enter the field in the summer of 1916, when the National Academy of Science organized a National Research Council, at the President's request, to study further the problems of industrial and scientific mobilization.[24]

By the spring of 1916, pressures were building up for a more formal government involvement in this process of industrial mobilization. Initiatives came from a number of directions. In the summer of 1915, the prominent Democratic financier Bernard Baruch had proposed to General Wood and to Wilson that he organize a committee of great businessmen to aid the government in purchasing supplies and transportation in any emergency. At the end of April 1916, Baruch broached his proposal for a businessman's commission to Colonel House, stating that he believed the U.S. government could acquire an organization "that could vie with, if not surpass, the much vaunted German efficiency." House had already been thinking along these lines himself, even to the point of attempting to secure the names of potential commission members. By May, Baruch had been put in touch with the secretary of war.[25]

Meanwhile, early in April, Baker had independently proposed a mobilization plan to Wilson. He urged that the work of the Coffin Board be pursued on a continuing basis. It should be "brought to some national agency which could coordinate it, prevent duplication, and provide for its continuation." Baker suggested the creation of a "council of national strength," consisting of Cabinet members and captains of industry, which would control a staff for industrial mobilization. Echoing the concerns of the Council for Industrial Preparedness, the secretary proposed that plants be given educational orders in time of peace and that they be leased by the government in time of war. To ensure a stable labor supply, workers at the defense plants would be drafted into the service in an emergency. Government arsenals could be used as experiment stations, and would train a cadre of men to reinforce the workers at nationalized defense plants when war came. The whole scheme, Baker felt, would provide for crisis and have the effect of enlisting "the sympathetic and voluntary cooperation of the industrial interests of the country in defense." Baker had discussed the matter with Josephus Daniels and had even drawn up a tentative bill.[26]

The industrial mobilization plan actually adopted by the government, however, seems to have evolved from proposals which Drs. Godfrey and Crampton had presented first to Lindley Garrison and then to House. Their ideas were shaped into a piece of draft legislation by that shrewd Republican lawyer, Elihu Root, while further detail work on the subject was done by Dr. Crampton and his staff. Unlike Baker's original proposal, this plan envisaged a coordinating council for economic mobilization made up only of selected Cabinet members. Businessmen and others would advise this council, but would not have direct executive control. It was this plan that the secretary of war came to support, and the bill was brought to the attention of Representative Rollin B. Sanford of New York and Senator John W. Weeks of Massachusetts. By late May it was a part of the Army bill. The nation's industry would be another military resource. Preparedness had been extended back into the whole economy and the whole society.[27]

Other elements in America besides industry were being mobilized, not the least important of which was the medical profession. An Army Medical Reserve Corps had been in existence since 1908, but until the European War, it had consisted only of some 1,400 patriotic doctors with neither military training nor organization. As the preparedness movement caught hold, the American Red Cross began to organize base hospitals for emergency duty on a military basis, using Medical Reserve Corps personnel. This was done under the supervision of Colonel Jefferson R. Kean, the new Red Cross director of military relief. Additional Medical Reserve Corps personnel were enlisted from lists provided by the cooperating American College of Surgeons. In the spring of 1916, a Committee of American Physicians for Medical Preparedness emerged. The tangible results of all this activity were thirteen base hospitals ready for emergency service by midsummer 1916. A similar zeal for service was shown by the engineering societies, which, in addition to carrying the brunt of the industrial survey, had been demanding the organization of an army engineer reserve force since 1915.[28]

America was consciously pulling together and organizing for preparedness, as the government linked up its activities with the energies of great private associations. Almost unconsciously, America was being effectively mobilized by the European War itself. The war provided more than an incentive for America to become unified, disciplined, and efficient. It also provided an insatiable demand for armaments which was steadily restructuring the American manufacturing plant to military needs. As the New York *World* pointed out, the United States had "reached a state of preparedness of which too little account is usually taken." What the administration had neglected to provide in the way of arms, Britain and France had encouraged in the way of munitions plants. Theodore Roosevelt observed, "Whatever the motive of the munitions makers may be, they have rendered, and are now rendering, some real, and in addition, a very great potential service to the United States." By 1915, the Army was accepting the resignations of officers in the elite Ordnance Corps so that they might accept employment in private munitions plants. The War Department now felt its experts could do more for national defense as civilians than as soldiers.[29]

*   *   *

By the summer of 1916, industrial mobilization was starting to become a reality, and universal military training remained an enticing fancy. The country was clearly traveling down the road to a Newer Nationalism, searching for some way in which, as Newton Baker phrased it, the preparedness agitation could be "captured and capitalized into a policy tendency to strengthen and consolidate our national life." To survive in war or peace, America would have to become a species of democratic anti-Germany, organized, efficient, disciplined, and armed. William McAdoo's new twenty-five cent pieces suggested something of the spirit. On the face was the goddess of liberty, with an uncovered shield as well as an olive branch; on the reverse, "symbolical of unity," as the Treasury secretary put it, a fasces.[30]

8

Pacifists and Jeffersonians

The true traitor, the real traitor today, is the American who clamors for a larger Army and Navy and who would make us faithless to our belief in Jesus and to our belief in everything Godlike in man.

—Oswald Garrison Villard

No, the metropolitan press is not the voice of the nation; you can no more measure the sentiment of the peace-loving masses by the froth of the jingo press than you can measure the ocean's depths by the foam upon its waves.

—William Jennings Bryan

When our country really needs soldiers to defend her, millions of patriots will rush to arms and rally to the flag.

—Representative Percy E. Quin

121

Not all Americans joined the ranks of the preparedness movement. Even after the summer of 1915, some men, walking a lonelier road, continued to maintain an active opposition. These men were radicals and conservatives, pacifists and Jeffersonian democrats, from country and from town. Though outnumbered in the press and derided by opinion-makers, they voiced the deep feelings of millions of common Americans. While the cause of preparedness gradually advanced, it was not without a brisk fight against a vigorous rear-guard opposition.

There were many reasons why Americans could fight increased military and naval preparedness. The impact of the European War had changed many assumptions, but some still clung to the old belief that armaments led to war. Republican Senator T. Coleman DuPont of Delaware deplored the public clamor for a military policy "that will drain the public treasury and educate the public mind for an enemy to conquer." The highly conservative *Commercial and Financial Chronicle* stated flatly that "by the law of the case an armament party is a war party." Liberals, too, warned that America could be dragged into war by the weight of her massed armaments. America had no need to tumble down that blood-stained path. By arming, we should only intimidate our friends and provoke other nations. Preparedness, claimed Oswald Garrison Villard, the patrician editor of the intransigently reformist *Nation*, would only "complete the vicious military circle of the world," and thus "deprive the world of the one great beacon-light of a nation unarmed and unafraid."[1]

Preparedness would also burden the taxpayers of the nation. House Majority Leader Claude Kitchin calculated that if the admirals and generals got what they wanted, the nation would be paying out 70 percent of its revenues for defense and war pensions in four years. Young Clyde Tavenner, another House Democrat, warned that "the cost of living has been increasing just about in proportion to the increase of the cost of the Army and Navy." All this money drained from the pockets of the citizenry might be squandered, the Illinois congressman warned. The Army and the Navy had already spent enormous sums on defense, and yet the country was still unprotected. Before the outbreak of the European War, Britain had spent $135 million a year to get 255,000 regular and 450,000 territorial troops; the United States had managed to pay out $104 million for an army of only 85,000 men. Preparedness advocates, Representative Warren Worth Bailey charged, "want more money spent under precisely the same methods that have prevailed during the last 15 years, with results which they themselves admit to be in the last degree unsatisfactory." Democrats like Bailey had special reason to be concerned with defense costs: not only were higher taxes unpopular with the voters, but the need for more governmental revenues might force the Democrats to open the issue of tariff readjustment and thus play into the hands of the protectionist opposition party.[2]

Preparedness would take from the poor and give to the rich. This was a progressive era, ringing with battles against the trusts, and yet the preparedness movement seemed to emanate from what *The Nation* described as "the very classes that have heretofore battened on special privilege." The millionaire Progressive Amos Pinchot warned that the preparedness crowd was mostly composed of "the big employers and monopolists." Congressmen charged on the floor of the House that the Morgan interests had bought up all the newspapers of the country to spread preparedness propaganda. The Midwest, as a knowledgeable priest reported to one of Roosevelt's friends, "begrudges—Oh how it begrudges . . . the Steel Trust, the munitions makers and the Dupont family every cent they are making out of the war and that they are likely to make out of American preparedness." The common suspicion that the preparedness movement was tinged with greed and pelf was a useful weapon for critics.[3]

Most significantly, the antipreparedness men were able to argue that the defense programs which had been proposed were ill-conceived. The Wyoming Republican Walter Mondell pointed out to the House of Representatives that "if we stand in the danger that the alarmists claim we do, the great and ambitious military programs running into the distant future are pathetically and ridiculously inadequate to meet the situation. . . . A continental army five years from now will never save us." Villard reminded his readers that preparedness would not be accomplished merely by passing congressional legislation; it took years to build armies and navies. *The Saturday Evening Post* agreed that the immediate impact of any defense program would be slight. "The taxes . . . will be real. The soldiers and armaments will be mostly paper." And, in fact, the opponents of preparedness claimed, there was no real military threat from abroad anyway. By the end of the war, the nations of Europe would be too broken down to make any such effort. At the very worst, the *Commercial and Financial Chronicle* pointed out, "we should have on our side the vast factor of time." An invasion would be destructive, but so would a volcanic eruption on Staten Island; and one was as likely as the other.[4]

*   *   *

The mass base of this opposition to preparedness came largely from four overlapping groups: farmers, organized labor, German-Americans, and Socialists. Of these, the farm bloc was the largest and most important. Isolated from the press and the main currents of public opinion, the farmer was not caught up in the sweeping changes of sentiment which gripped the city. He remained suspicious of great corporations and militarism, concerned about taxes, and sturdily indifferent to the hue and cry over defense. As the master of the Ohio Grange succinctly put it: "Those in the cities who have followed the disastrous conflict across the water have more nearly lost their bearings than the man and woman who are on the farm."[5]

Everywhere the country districts proved overwhelmingly unresponsive to the preparedness drive. Farm organizations repeatedly condemned the hysteria for armaments, and farm journals largely went on record against preparedness or remained noncommittal. A Kansas editor reported letters against preparedness "now form a large part of his office furniture"; his readers, he guessed, were ten to one against the issue. Reporters noted that Senator Robert LaFollette got more and more support for his stand against major defense increases the further he moved into rural Wisconsin. A Michigan political expert observed: "The Michigan farmers . . . may be said to look askance at the prospect of unusual expenses for military preparation. In this they seem to be agreed with the farmers of the middle west generally." The South was in the same condition; a journalist graphically described the plight of a southern member of the House Military Affairs Committee: ". . . on his desk is a pile of letters from the folks back home that causes a clammy sweat to moisten his brow as he reads them. They are mostly in cheap envelopes, with no printed returns. A good many of them are superscribed in pencil. . . . They express the fixed opinion of hard-headed, even if wrong-headed people." In the far Northwest, the country districts around Spokane were polled as three to two against increased defense appropriations.[6]

Organized labor, with a long-standing distrust of the military as a tool of established interests to suppress the workingman, seemed equally sullen. The president of the American Federation of Labor, the conservative and conciliatory Samuel Gompers, did support defense. At the end of 1915, he told the National Civic Federation, "I want to say for the American workingman that we have no intention of working for disarmament." Instead, Gompers announced, "the American workingman looks cheerfully upon war for his country as one of his burdens." This sanguine approach was not so evident at the lower levels of the labor movement. John P. White, president of the United Mine Workers, said a little later at the United Mine Worker's biennial convention that laboring men were "unalterably opposed" to preparedness, which "means war"; William Green, the union's secretary-treasurer, was enthusiastically applauded on the same occasion when he announced labor's opposition to the defense agitation. By the summer of 1916, the secretary of the National Civic Federation gave a gloomy appraisal of Gompers' position: "He is having all he can do to keep his leading people in line for preparedness of any kind . . . he certainly has no small task. The labor leaders in nearly all the large cities have been completely captivated by the Pacifist crowd, some for sentimental reasons and some from sympathy with Germany in the present war." A straw vote in Cleveland in 1916 showed the dimensions of labor's disaffection from the preparedness movement: union members voted to condemn militarism by 4,432 to 565. At the end of that year the American Federation of Labor Convention went on record as being opposed to militarism, despite Gompers' protests.[7]

As might have been expected, German-Americans evinced a certain dubiousness about the defense agitation. Although military preparations were supposed to be directed equally against all foreign countries, their possible application against the Fatherland was all too evident, as was the pro-Allied bias of many of the most vocal advocates of preparedness. German-Americans were not united on the issue; observers in German-American communities gave conflicting reports about the sentiment for defense among the inhabitants. Even when opposed, German-Americans were not necessarily motivated by ethnic considerations. Many, after all, were conservative Republican farmers and others were Socialists. Moreover, the conference of German-language newspaper publishers which met in Chicago in May of 1916 did endorse preparedness. The fact was, however, that many Americans questioned the real attitude of German-Americans toward defense. It is also true that important German-American oriented newspapers like the *Milwaukee Free Press* showed a remarkable ingenuity in finding reasons why preparedness was a bad thing. Theodore Roosevelt summed up a common feeling when he wrote: "There is one very sinister thing that I don't like at all among the German-Americans here. The Illinois Staats-Zeitung, for instance, has carried on an active campaign against preparedness. Many of the professional German-American leaders have done the same thing." Even pacifists suspected the motives of the German-backed antimilitarist organization, the Friends of Peace.[8]

Finally, the small American Socialist party largely placed itself in opposition to preparedness, though not with complete unanimity and not without floundering among possible ideological positions. There were a number of plausible attitudes which American Socialists could adopt. As realists and patriots, Socialists could favor an inevitable preparedness, especially since their own doctrine proved that capitalism meant war. As Marxist determinists, Socialists could accept militarism as a final stage in the downfall of capitalism, which by disciplining the working class would actually help to bring about the Socialist order. Or, as radical internationalists, Socialists could oppose military preparedness on high principle and denounce armies as a threat to labor. In practice, Socialists generally opted for the last choice, though not without some division and confusion.[9]

Eugene Debs, the charismatic leader of the party and its 1912 presidential candidate, took a strong antimilitary line. Preparedness, he declared, would "transform the American nation into the most powerful and odious military despotism in the world." Debs seemed to speak for the bulk of his party; in a 1915 referendum, Socialists voted 11,041 to 782 for a constitutional provision which would expel from the party any elected official who voted for military and naval appropriations. As the Socialist *New York Call* declared, "the overwhelming majority of our rank and file are decidedly opposed to the preparedness policy."[10]

Some prominent Socialists, however, endorsed preparedness. At the 1915 convention of the Intercollegiate Socialist Society, Charles Edward Russell, a leading candidate for the party's presidential nomination in 1916, declared, "I believe that America ought to be able to defend itself as the last bulwark of democracy." Russell predicted that America would be forced to go to war against Germany, and he struck out at pacifist assumptions with the apparatus of socialism. "When Dr. David Starr Jordan talks about armament bribery as the cause of the war and peace advocates prattle of peace, I'd like to ask them about this unconsumed surplus." Another distinguished Socialist spokesman, W. J. Ghent, questioned the referendum vote against military appropriations. The issue, he felt, was unrelated to socialism, it set a precedent for ideological screening, and the size of the majority was suspiciously large. Ninety-three percent of voting Socialists had declared themselves opposed to preparedness, when only 72 percent of party members had been willing to condemn sabotage in a previous referendum. Some of the voters, Ghent warned, "unquestionably were German-American Socialists who ardently believe in preparedness in Germany but bitterly oppose it in the United States."[11]

Russell's stand on preparedness may have cost him the nomination. The Socialist party rather clearly defined its position in 1916 by nominating the journalist and pamphleteer Allan Benson, who was especially outspoken in his opposition to preparedness. Still, the issue would not go away. Benson had obtained his support from the radical agrarian Socialists of the plains; conservative urban Socialists, even those who were by no means as pro-Ally as Russell, were uneasy at the intellectual and political problems presented by preparedness. Socialist doctrine held that the capitalist international order was an armed jungle of competition. While debating Congressman Gardner on defense, the New York Socialist leader Morris Hillquit had been forced to admit that if one accepted the danger of war, "we must accept the conclusion that the country is woefully unprepared." Unarmed pacifism was therefore a position of questionable intellectual respectability, and not without other drawbacks. As Upton Sinclair pointed out, the pacifist program was "Tolstoyan rather than Marxian; incidentally, it is to put ourselves out of public life for a decade, possibly for a generation." The head of the Milwaukee branch of the party, Victor Berger, while ambivalent on the issue himself, sneered at the referendum vote against preparedness as the act of "civilians who imagine they can stop a military engine with hot air and paper wads." The whole question, a Socialist columnist had stated gloomily, "threatens to prostrate us as it did the European Socialists. It is a Sphinx riddle in the sense that we will die if we cannot answer it." In the end, the riddle was not satisfactorily solved, but the bulk of Socialist opinion, after some tossing about, lined up against preparedness anyway.[12]

*   *   *

The opposition to preparedness found expression in Congress in a relatively small but vociferous antipreparedness wing, whose most prominent leader was Claude Kitchin. Most active in the House, this antimilitarist bloc consisted of some midwestern Republicans, a number of western and midwestern Democrats, and a small group of Democrats from the South. Most of these men were disciples of Jefferson and William Jennings Bryan, rural congressmen suspicious of taxes and standing armies; the rest were a varied assortment of reformers and labor spokesmen. The list included Frank Buchanan of Illinois, under indictment for assisting German efforts to hamper munitions shipments to the Allies; the child-labor reformer Fred Keating of Colorado; the single-taxer Warren Worth Bailey of Pennsylvania; and the lone Socialist, Meyer London of New York. In the Senate, extreme opposition to militarism seemed less pronounced, but men like John D. Works of California, Robert LaFollette of Wisconsin, Albert Cummins of Iowa, and James K. Vardaman of Mississippi clearly rejected the appeals of the enthusiasts for armament. The small group of active antimilitarists in Congress formed only a part of the picture. The unpopularity of preparedness as an issue with rural America was generally reflected in Congress as a whole. It explains the slowness with which Congress grappled with the defense problem, despite the feverish urgings of the metropolitan press.[13]

The congressional opponents of preparedness were antimilitarists; that erratic peace man, Senator Works, doubtless summarized a good deal of popular opinion when he described the Army as "essentially a large body of idlers under the influence and control of military despotism." But they were not pacifists. Works himself backed a plan for an army made up of western homesteaders. William Jennings Bryan, the patron saint of congressional opposition to defense, had proposed in 1915 that defense money be channeled into building twelve great coast-to-coast highways: these would be beneficial in time of peace and would allow civilian volunteers in motor cars to rush to meet any invasion. Representative Percy Quin of Mississippi, a vigorous opponent of the General Staff's schemes, promised, "when our country really needs soldiers to defend her, millions of patriots will rush to arms and rally to the flag." The colorful Oscar Callaway of Texas flatly declared at an antimilitarism rally, "I ain't any pacifist."[14]

All this meant that congressional opposition to preparedness was not irreconcilable. Opponents shared many characteristics with those congressmen who were lukewarmly willing to follow Wilson in support of preparedness. Both groups feared a big army and conscription, but proposals for strengthening the National Guard and the coast defenses were not without a potentially broad appeal. If the rural bloc which most congressmen represented opposed dreadnaughts, militarism, and taxes, it generally favored building up the militia and constructing submarines—anything that had an aura of home defense about it and would be cheap. Thus, in the end, the Jeffersonian-oriented opposition to defense would join with the Jeffersonian majority in support of a compromise bill.[15]

*   *   *

Outside of Congress, there was also a vigorous opposition to the preparedness movement from pacifist groups which operated in a somewhat different tradition. As a contemporary commentator explained it: "In Bryan there is religion, idealism, provincialism and a red blooded American eagerness to come forth and start to slay the enemies of the United States just exactly as soon as it is too late. In most of the Eastern Pacifist leaders there is no blood at all." For the preparedness agitation called into being a countervailing force in the form of organized antimilitary activity which, despite recurrent setbacks, managed to gather together under one umbrella social-welfare Progressives, radicals, and religious pacifists.[16]

The shock of the European War had done much to break up the old-line peace movement, which had flourished amid Carnegie grants in prewar years. Nor was the peace movement really antipreparedness. The Quaker lawyer, L. Hollingsworth Wood, complained: "A good many of us who have been members of peace societies ever since we can remember, have been disgusted with their unwillingness to take a determined stand at the present time." But as soon as the first voices endorsing military preparation were raised in Congress in the fall of 1914, an active opposition pulled itself together, led by a small group of social workers, including Paul Kellogg, the editor of *Survey*, the famous Jane Addams of Hull House, and Lillian D. Wald of the Henry Street Settlement. The so-called "Henry Street Group" found a wide spectrum of allies. In December 1914, a committee of notables which included Miss Wald, Oswald Garrison Villard, Hamilton Holt of the *Independent*, David Greer, the Episcopal bishop of New York, and Nicholas Murray Butler, the autocratic president of Columbia University, issued a call to business and professional men to meet at the Railroad Club for the purpose of organizing a national anti-armament association. The result was the American League for the Limitation of Armaments. The League had urged America to give the world moral leadership by setting an example of military restraint, and it had vigorously supported President Wilson's refusal to be "stampeded by the hysterical craze for additional armaments."[17]

The *Lusitania* incident and its aftermath undercut the League's influence. The President's moral authority was now on the other side of the question, and conservative support for the American League for the Limitation of Armaments tended to fall away as the country became more defense-conscious. The League to Enforce Peace, founded in the summer of 1915, served to deflect the energies of many former peace men to the cause of force used for righteousness; efficient preparedness was not only consistent with the League to Enforce Peace's platform, but even essential. Political considerations also played a role in changing some attitudes. Nicholas Murray Butler had been permanent chairman of the American League for the Limitation of Armaments, but he was also a leader of the New York Republican party. By 1916 Stimson was writing with some satisfaction: "I was rather surprised at the extent to which [Butler] had subordinated his pacifist proclivities in the treatment of the preparedness question." Conservative opposition to preparedness was reduced to a matter of a few idiosyncratic individuals and publications.[18]

What remained in the way of organized resistance, as the American League for the Limitation of Armaments faded wanly from the scene, was the left wing of the peace movement. As a popular magazine writer huffed: "The new lot of peace organizations are offshoots of socialistic or anarchistic groups who use the peace propaganda to circulate the radical ideas of life." The first of these groups in the field was the Women's Peace party, founded in January 1915 by Jane Addams and the suffragette Carrie Chapman Catt. The party fought against preparedness and aggressive American foreign policies under the slogan "War against War," but its effectiveness was naturally limited by the fact that membership was restricted to women. Shortly thereafter, the radical Unitarian preacher John Haynes Holmes founded an Anti-Enlistment League. The most significant of the new organizations, however, was the antimilitarist committee which began to form at the end of 1915 on the nucleus of the Henry Street Group. This committee would soon become the American Union Against Militarism, the most formidable and intelligent of the antipreparedness lobbies.[19]

The committee was put together just as the preparedness agitation reached its crest and when the arrival of the eccentric millionaire automobile manufacturer, Henry Ford, on the peace scene seemed to hold out the promise of ample financial backing for any organization that would resist the currents of militarism. The first organizing meeting took place at the office of Villard's newspaper, the *New York Evening Post*. Paul Kellogg, the editor of the social-work magazine *Survey*, explained to the group that the plan was to form "a junta, made up of active people, acting as individuals rather than as representatives of organizations." Kellogg had talked to Ford's representative Louis Lochner, and Lochner had indicated that there might be a chance of getting Ford money; the automobile manufacturer had subsidized the Women's Peace party, and he might be more willing to back an organization with men in it. As finally organized, the Anti-Militarism Committee which emerged from the *Evening Post*'s offices was headed by Lillian Wald. Other officers were Mrs. Florence Kelley of the National Consumers League and the Quaker L. Hollingsworth Wood.[20]

By the beginning of 1916, the Committee had changed its name to the Anti-Preparedness Committee, added members like John Haynes

Holmes, the Socialist Allan Benson, the famous reform rabbi Stephen Wise, and the radical writer Max Eastman, and established offices in Washington. The Committee itself remained a New York group; a mixed collection of women, social-uplift Progressives, radical clergymen, and Socialists, with much overlapping among all these categories. The proper *New York Times* sniffed "something like one-half of them are known as Socialists." The Committee was not a broad cross-section of America, nor did it have very much money. The initial operating funds had been put up by two of the founding committee members themselves, Lillian Wald and Alice Lewisohn, and while Ford cooperated with the Committee, he did not finance it. As Crystal Eastman Benedict, the group's new treasurer, dryly observed in May, "To date the assets . . . including the promised check for $500,000 from Mr. Ford amount to $1,226.32. . . ." The philanthropist Samuel Untermeyer had been counted on for a donation of $5,000, but opted to support the Wilson defense program instead, a "terrible blow" for Mrs. Benedict. The bulk of contributions to the antipreparedness forces came in small amounts, much of it from Quakers. But if the Committee remained small and poor, it did have a headquarters strategically located in Washington. It found an uncommonly gifted executive director in Charles T. Hallinan, a Chicago publicity man who had formerly worked with the National American Woman's Suffrage Association.[21]

The Anti-Preparedness Committee conducted a vigorous lobby against increased defense. With its own headquarters and a permanent office force, it was able to serve as a mouthpiece for groups like granges and labor unions which otherwise would never have been heard. In Hallinan's words, the Committee united "the pacifist, and his profane Jeffersonian ally, the antimilitarist." The Committee worked with sympathetic congressmen, circularized 1,601 newspapers, and managed to distribute 600,000 pieces of propaganda by the summer of 1916. In the spring, in conjunction with a nationwide speaking campaign, the Committee changed its name yet once more to the American Union Against Militarism, broadened its base, and turned into a mass organization, with 6,000 members and associates, and with local committees in twenty-two states.[22]

Wilson had challenged his opponents to hire large halls and air their differences; it was this challenge that the union took up in April 1916. At first, the Union held mass meetings in Carnegie Hall, addressed by a varied assortment of speakers, from urban radicals to Oscar Callaway, about as profane a Jeffersonian as the halls of Congress could produce. Then a flying squadron of Union speakers toured ten cities of the Midwest, preceded by an advance man, a giant paper-maché armored and brainless dinosaur named "Jingo," and a trained parrot called "General Wood" which incessantly shrieked "Preparedness." The tour was a deliberate attempt to counter Wilson's own swing around the circle for preparedness. The antipreparedness speakers drew thousands of people, but only in a few cities did a noticeable percentage of the audience come from the middle class; significantly, this happened in Cincinnati and St. Louis, both cities with large German-American populations. In most cities, as the sympathetic magazine *Survey* noted, "the audience was a group of protestants drawn from the wage-earning population." As usual, the eastern press gave the meetings limited coverage; antipreparedness agitation was being stifled under a blanket of silence. But the speakers were encouraged by the response of the crowds. Villard wrote that he and his colleagues had been "perfectly amazed" to find in the West a skepticism about Roosevelt and a "deep-seated feeling against militarism and the preparedness movement, as another form of special privilege."[23]

With the success of the western trip, some antipreparedness leaders thought of organizing politically. "They realize that this is the fight of a generation and they are going in for it from that point of view," Villard reported. Rabbi Wise declared a third party would be in the field if the Democratic and Republican conventions endorsed military armament. Suddenly, Henry Ford seemed a rallying point. The automobile maker had entered, and unexpectedly won, the Republican presidential primaries of Nebraska and then Michigan, showing the vulnerability of preparedness. Hallinan, the Union's imaginative executive secretary, wanted to distribute anonymously, "Henry Ford for President" stickers in Pennsylvania. Ford was much in the public eye that spring; a Union member had induced him to sponsor enormous full-page newspaper advertisements decrying preparedness, using material taken from the ringing speeches of Representative Clyde Tavenner. But the Ford boom died down. When looked at closely, the millionaire pacifist did not after all have the makings of a suitable national leader; in fact, the radical John

Reed noted, he seemed "a very ignorant man." All the Ford advertisements did was precipitate a $100,000 libel suit against him by the Navy League for printing an injudicious speech by Congressman Tavenner before it had appeared in the *Congressional Record*.[24]

Instead, the antipreparedness forces made a direct appeal to Wilson. The President had once been the hero of the peace forces, and pacifists had always secretly doubted the depth of Wilson's commitment to armaments. One of Amos Pinchot's liberal newspaper friends had written him encouragingly, "The administration hasn't got any preparedness program. . . . The administration cannot be judged by its words on this any more than anything else. Its heart is for peace at any price, but the political exigencies are making this slogan embarrassing." Oswald Garrison Villard confidently announced to an executive meeting of the Anti-Preparedness Committee that Colonel House had told him the Wilson defense program was "put up to be knocked down." Surely the liberal President had only succumbed to political pressures, and an interview pointing out the amount of antimilitary sentiment in the country could set him right. At any rate, the American Union Against Militarism, enthused by the results of their recent tour, decided to try. Lillian Wald asked for and received an appointment with the President for an American Union Against Militarism delegation.[25]

The six-member delegation selected by the Union included Miss Wald, Rabbi Wise, and Amos Pinchot. Their interview with the President was designed to be simple and political in character, and restricted solely to the issue of defense, lest the delegation be bathed, as Hallinan put it, "in the typical Wilsonian speech, all generalities and righteousness." The American Union Against Militarism petition asked assurances from the President that he would not break with American traditions, and requested Wilson to point out to the American people the sinister and even sordid motives behind preparedness, come out against compulsory service, and make clear he had no intention of building the greatest navy in the world. The writer Max Eastman, a last-minute addition to the delegation, would later describe the ensuing scene with the President: "We sat in a circle around his desk——several distinguished citizens. . . . Each made a little lecture, to which Wilson replied with that facile gift of abstract diction which floated him so securely above the flux of fact."[26]

The President, it developed, was polite but disconcertingly unsympathetic. The American Union Against Militarism was thrown back on all fronts. In well-turned phrases, Wilson pointed out, reasonably, that bodies of opinion were hard to assess—while the Union claimed the nation's heartland was opposed to defense, the mayor of New York had just toured the same area, and had come back declaring the country was unanimous for preparedness. Militarism was not a practical problem for the United States; the only question which had to be considered was the right size for the Army. "Unless you regard it as a prophecy," Wilson warned, "there is nothing extravagant in an army of 250,000 men." Nor was the growth planned for the Navy abnormal. American forces would be needed to defend the whole Western Hemisphere or to join with other nations in keeping peace throughout the world. The President gave the delegates the same vague but ominous warnings he had imparted to his audiences in the Midwest. "This is a year of madness. . . . It is a year of excitement, more profound than the world has ever known before. All the world is seeing red. No standard we have ever had obtains any longer." As for universal service, the exchanges brought out, while Wilson opposed anything that would "lock people into a military organization and make it subject to autocratic use," he did not feel it was against American tradition for the people to know how to defend themselves. In fact, Wilson told the delegates, "my mind is to let on the subject."[27]

Disconsolately, the committee departed. The President, it appeared, was sincere in his desire for preparedness after all. Rabbi Wise solemnly informed his wife: "The President has undergone a grave moral deterioration."[28]

*   *   *

The hard fact was that, despite their vast potential constituency, opponents of preparedness were on the defensive. Wilson's switch had been decisive in changing the climate of opinion. The major remaining leaders of the peace forces, men like Bryan and Ford, could be dismissed as parochial cranks; others were scored off as Socialists, impractical idealists, or worse. It was overwhelmingly clear that the other side had the opinion leaders, the newspapers, and the bulk of the financial resources. "The forces we are fighting have unlimited funds," an American Union Against Militarism appeal cried plaintively, if inaccurately. The pressure for preparedness was massive and inexorable, and it began to show an ugly edge.[29]

By 1916, public antagonism toward opponents of defense was rising. "The war has broken all the restraints of civilization," a Cleveland lawyer warned Ohio's antimilitarist Congressman William Gordon, "and Europe in its entirety has gone right straight back to primitive man and savagery. . . . Everybody is on a feather edge. . . . our own people are becoming in their turn free from the restraints that have hitherto held them, and are becoming intensely intolerant of opposition to what they believe ought to be done here at home." Representative Warren Worth Bailey mourned that "in all the correspondence I have had during recent months there has not been a single champion of the militarist program who has not almost deliberately indicted me as an enemy of my country, as a friend of the kaiser or as anything except a good citizen with proper impulses." A popular magazine writer warned ominously, "when war breaks over us, Uncle Sam and his millions of little nephew Sammies will go crazy. Some of these pacifists will be lynched."[30]

The pressures for increased defense were so great that many antimilitarists realized that they could not be denied, but only deflected into more acceptable forms. As Representative Fred Keating had written earlier to his friend Bailey, "I believe we can accomplish more by attempting to turn the enemy's flank than by insisting upon a frontal attack." Some Progressives proposed to transform the military into a constructive force. In the influential social-work magazine *Survey*, Charles Johnson Post advocated that the Army be made into a social service organization, with West Point becoming a great federal university. After an initial period of military training, soldiers would spend the remainder of their enlistment learning useful civilian trades. The popular columnist, Herbert Quick, similarly proposed an "Army-which-would-give-the-Boys-a-Chance," where thousands of school dropouts could be educated and trained "in great school barracks, in which the article manufactured will be American citizenship, with an army on the side." The Society for Constructive Defense, a body including such active pacifists as L. Hollingsworth Wood and Stanford University President David Starr Jordan, proposed a large army of road-builders working under the Corps of Engineers. Plans for various types of industrial or working armies were introduced in Congress by a number of western senators, but these schemes, by their nature, tended to fall through. Representative Hay strongly questioned the willingness of the average soldier to enlist to dig ditches. The Army, while mildly interested in vocational training, was much more interested in producing soldiers.[31]

Instead of trying to remodel the armed forces along peaceful lines, many antimilitarists, especially in Congress, devoted their main efforts to urging the government manufacture of munitions and making sure the burden of new defense taxes fell on the rich. Since to many Populists and Progressives the whole preparedness program sprang full-blown from the collective mind of the munitions trust, these tactics had a certain logic to them. When the malefactors of great wealth found they would have to pay for additional armaments and would not be able to derive any profits from them, surely the clamor for preparedness would die down. In practice, this approach was less than completely successful. The rich could be soaked, as the Revenue Act of 1916 would demonstrate in the summer of that year, and appropriations for government munitions plants would be foisted upon the defense bills. But these actions did not seem to stop preparedness, though it doubtless provided symbolic satisfactions. Moreover, there were necessary limits to what could be done. That angry young congressman, Clyde Tavenner, might cry out, "what I am advocating is that the Government take private profit out of war and preparation for war," but this proposal was in practice impossible. The government already operated arsenals, but the Ordnance Bureau had calculated that a work force of 750,000 men would be necessary to turn out military materials in time of war. Like it or not, the country's defense needs had become too great to be met by the public sector of the economy alone. Moreover, as Socialists pointed out, while government manufacture of all arms might satisfy "such a bourgeouis anti-militarist as Congressman Tavenner," it could actually strengthen the nation's capacity for armament and aggression. Such flank attacks on preparedness never succeeded in coming to grips with the main issue.[32]

Despite everything, the Jeffersonians and pacifists of the anti-preparedness coalition continued to fight their lonely rear-guard action. The battle was not without its successes; the Continental Army plan had gone down to defeat, and Congressman Bailey wrote, "there is some satisfaction in believing that the efforts in which I have joined have not

been entirely in vain." The final House bill was a compromise so
innocuous that all the antimilitarists except Socialist Meyer London were
able to agree to it. Yet the military legislation which Congress finally
passed in 1916 owed more to the influence of the National Guard lobby
than it did to the efforts of the antipreparedness forces; it was a triumph of
congressional inertia and rural apathy rather than of positive resistance.
By the time the fight was over, in fact, some thoughtful pacifists were
unsure whether, after all, they had gained a glorious victory or had
witnessed the hatching of a Frankenstein's monster.[33]

9

Congress Disposes. . . .

If there is the danger which the President would have us think exists, that plan of defense which he suggests is absolutely ridiculous, and if there is no danger it is wholly unnecessary.

—Senator Wesley Jones

This is a peace bill, as we understand, from the report of the committee. All will agree, however, that the bill would not have been reported, and if reported would have no chance of being enacted, if it were not for the war in Europe and the Mexican situation.

—Representative Joseph Cannon

A bill that would suit nobody was the only one with a chance to be enacted into law.

—The Springfield Republican

The resignation of Lindley Garrison in February 1915 did not seriously change the balance of forces working toward preparedness. By the beginning of March the knowledgeable Colonel House was writing: "Garrison is already forgotten. His resignation made a splash and after a few ripples, all was calm again." General Hugh Scott stepped in as acting secretary of war, the first military man to hold the job since General Sherman. Wilson soon found a permanent replacement for Garrison in Newton D. Baker, the reform mayor of Cleveland. The boyish-looking Ohio Progressive with his Gatling gun speech was an admirable choice. The new secretary of war possessed a disarming reputation as a moderate uncrazed by militarism and even showed a flair for high-minded Wilsonian rhetoric (he described himself as a pacifist, "so much so that I would fight for peace"). At the same time, Baker was an able and forceful administrator and had a charm which won over his military subordinates. General Scott thought him "delightful," and felt "the whole service will be fond of him as soon as they get to know him." More flexible than his predecessor, Baker proved ideally fitted to preside over the enactment of Wilson's moderate defense policies. Meanwhile, as the War Department rather helplessly looked on, a preparedness program slowly ground its way through the mills of Congress, its course shaped more by recurrent crises and the habits of the Democratic party than by the observations of the General Staff or the agitation in the press.[1]

Garrison had hoped that his resignation would alert the country to defense; in fact, it did have its positive aspects. The abdication of the martial-minded and outspoken secretary of war cleared the air and put new pressure on congressmen to reach an agreement on defense. The dangers that the Republican party might have a winning issue were all too clear. Some forty Democratic representatives sent word to the White House that they would support the President. Although Speaker Champ Clark still dismissed as "arrant nonsense" any talk of demoting Claude Kitchin from his post as House majority leader, there were obvious strong influences on dissidents to meet the President half-way and pull the party together. By February 18, Kitchin had apparently become resigned to the prospects of some kind of increased preparedness, for he told the House Democratic caucus that defense expenditures would probably be high. The Democratic leadership in Congress did not embrace defense, but positive opposition in the House seemed to ebb.[2]

Garrison's Continental Army plan, as a popular magazine had said, "was not the backbone of preparedness; it was only one of the floating ribs." With Garrison out of the way, the Wilson Administration followed the lead of House Military Affairs Committee Chairman James Hay and embraced the idea of federalizing the militia. This decision was made at the highest levels, and at first, without consulting the War Department. The President took his advice on the matter from Postmaster General Albert S. Burleson, Treasury Secretary William G. McAdoo, and Attorney General Thomas W. Gregory. Wilson personally studied the draft that Hay had prepared to make sure that the government would have sufficient control over the National Guard in time of peace. Opposition within the War Department to this course continued unabated, on legal as well as practical grounds. Enoch Crowder, the judge advocate general, questioned the constitutionality of the plan, as did Garrison and former Secretary of War Henry L. Stimson. A hundred years before, the Supreme Court in *Houston* v. *Moore* had issued an aside to the effect that the national government was necessarily dependent on the states for officering and training the militia. The nation's whole defense structure might hang on a disputed point of law. But Secretary of War Baker, when he entered the scene, disagreed with Crowder's judgment and lined up with Wilson and Hay.[3]

On March 6, the House Military Affairs Committee at last reported out its bill with what would turn out to be a rather spurious show of unanimity. The bill embodied many of the original provisions of the War Department bill, including the modest and gradual increase in Regular Army strength to 140,000 that Garrison had requested. A greatly expanded and federalized National Guard would provide the nation's second line of defense. Hay did not bother to seek the approval of the War College Division for this piece of legislation. Shaped with the help of General Ainsworth, Wood's old enemy, the Hay Bill was a minimum response to a new national mood. In 1912, it would have been welcomed. By 1916, however, events seemed already conspiring to overtake and render inadequate any preparedness legislation whatsoever. Military readiness was fast becoming more than a theoretical proposition.[4]

Three days after the committee reported its bill, the forces of Pancho Villa raided Columbus, New Mexico. The fiery lava of the Mexican Revolution had at last splashed across the border, with lethal results. The cavalry unit on guard had been taken by surprise, the standard Army machine gun, it developed, was loaded only with great difficulty after dark, and it took days to organize a pursuit column under Brigadier General John J. Pershing. War with Mexico was a real possibility, and the country was clearly unprepared. With its mobile forces strung out along an 1,800-mile border or committed to the chase in Mexico, and with no reserves behind them, the Army was seriously overextended. General Tasker Bliss warned the chief of staff that it could not "reasonably guarantee American territory from hostile invasion and American citizens and property from injury." The border was in an uproar; the governor of Arizona demanded 3,000 Krag rifles and ammunition for his citizens. As a result of this crisis, Scott asked that the Regular Army be raised to maximum strength immediately and that the militia be sent to the border. Four hundred thousand troops would be needed in case of war, the Army calculated. But there was no war, the militia stayed home, and Pershing's brigade column continued unmolested ever deeper into Mexico, its tiny air force breaking down under the stress of operation. Long after the initial panic had passed, the continued presence of this expeditionary force in Mexico would continue to strain the resources of the military establishment and threaten peace. "Every source of information leads us to believe that the Mexican generals are certain of our entire lack of preparedness," Baker was warned by Scott and General Frederick Funston in May.[5]

The military and political pressures generated by the Mexican situation cleared the way for speedy consideration of defense legislation. It was obvious that something would have to be done at once to strengthen the Army, and so the day following the Columbus raid, Hay introduced a resolution authorizing the President to recruit the regular forces to their maximum enlisted strength of 120,000. This measure quickly passed both houses. At the same time, an alerted House leadership agreed to sidetrack the immigration bill that was pending and consider the proposed defense bill. Hay's 91-page draft went before the House on the next day.[6]

In the confused and ill-attended debates which followed, three things became clear. First, the facade of unanimity with which the committee had reported out the bill was only paper-thin. Not all of the representatives who had signed the report even agreed on the constitutionality of militia federalization, and it was thoroughly understood that any committee member who felt the Army should be larger was at liberty to try to amend it. Thus, committee members turned around and attacked their own child. Second, it was evident that preparedness advocates were dissatisfied with the provisions of the proposed bill. Representative Augustus Gardner sneered that "this bill makes a noise like preparedness, but it is not a noisy noise," and pointed out that in 20,000 words the bill provided for just two regular soldiers per word. The National Security League published full-page advertisements asking Congress to defeat the bill, and the *Chicago Tribune* raged "we do not want ignorant inaction to be replaced by ignorant action." Third, the House was in real confusion as to whether the Army bill was supposed to be a long-term measure or a response to present and possible emergencies. This dispute largely pitted Democrats against Republicans, and would continue to haunt the struggle for preparedness.[7]

All of these facts were pointed up when Julius Kahn, the minority leader of the House Military Affairs Committee, introduced an amendment to allow the strength of the regular forces to be increased immediately to 220,000 men. The German-born California congressman acted at the prompting of Army staff officers like Lieutenant Colonel William Johnston and Major Douglas MacArthur; for if the War Department remained quiescent in the fight, individual officers emphatically did not. Members of the War College Division now pressed for the big regular force they had originally wanted. In supporting the Kahn proposal for a big army, House Minority Leader James Mann linked Army legislation with the problem of Mexico and the storm in Europe. It was America's duty "to prepare now an army which will add to the weight of the reasons and the suggestions which we may make." The President of the United States had gone to the country and alerted the public to preparedness, Mann went on, "not as a matter of a permanent policy of a country in time of peace, but as an emergency matter in the face of possible international complications." And what had been the response of Congress? A proposal to increase the Regular Army by 10,000 men in the following fifteen months.[8]

Chairman Hay remained unmoved. The War Department bill had been framed as long-term legislation, and the President and Commander-in-Chief had indicated no dissatisfaction with Hay's approach. Scornfully, Hay pointed out: "Gentlemen talk about emergency. Emergency? Why my friends, does anyone presume that if an emergency arose 220,000 men would meet it? If we had an emergency, it would take a million men, not 220,000.'' If passed, the Kahn Amendment would prove the impossibility of raising such a force. The Military Affairs Committee chairman scoffed at the danger of war and deprecated the opinions of the experts. Other small-army representatives made the point that the Kahn Amendment would be almost useless in time of war and would saddle the country with an expense of seventy or eighty million dollars a year in time of peace. On the first vote, the Amendment went down to defeat 183 to 103. The action of the House backed up Hay's stand that ''we are speaking now of a peace proposition and not a war proposition.''[9]

On the other hand, the preparedness forces won minor victories. The original War Department bill had proposed that reserve officers be procured by setting up cadet companies in which candidates would serve as enlisted men for a year. Upon second thought, no one found this solution, which had been carried into the Hay Bill, very attractive. Ever since 1913, land grant and military colleges had been pressing the government to set up a reserve officer training program in their schools. This plan, which would give the Army access to a big and desirable manpower pool of college-educated men, had won the approval of the War College Division and ultimately that of Secretary Garrison. Ohio Democrat Warren Gard introduced an amendment providing for a Reserve Officers Training Corps, and this passed with the approval of Representative Hay. Similarly, Kahn and Gardner successfully introduced a provision which stipulated that an enlisted man could be released to the reserves after a year's training with the consent of his commanding officer. This provision embodied an old hope of military reformers like Wood and Stimson that a short enlistment period would attract a higher class of enlisted man into the regulars for training. The most significant addition to the bill, however, was inserted, almost unnoted, by Congressman Hay. It provided for war-time conscription—a step which even preparedness enthusiasts like Representative Gardner professed to shun.[10]

On March 17, the day debate opened, Hay had proposed that ''the President be given power in time of war to draft every man between the age of 18 and 45 in this country.'' Years later, Hay was to claim that he had made this proposal at the instigation of Wilson, but the President's correspondence never reflected this claim. At any rate, the proposal did not go through, but a committee amendment prepared by Carl Hayden of Arizona did. The amendment, modeled on existing Arizona legislation, provided for National Guard reserve battalions; in time of war, if there were not enough enlistments, the President would be authorized to draft into these units the "unorganized militia." This meant, quite simply, every man between eighteen and forty-five. This approach was an indirect one, but the thin edge of compulsion had at last been introduced into the federal system. The draft was passed amidst such popular inattention that even the pacifists would not grasp what had happened until the late summer; Wilson himself seems not to have known what was going on. [11]

Moreover, popular sentiment and the Mexican imbroglio seemed to be having their effect. While the Kahn Amendment had been overwhelmingly defeated in the committee of the whole, it lost by only twenty-two votes on a roll call on March 23. Eastern Republicans and Democrats had been for it, whereas western and southern Democrats, aided by a few Republicans from the Midwest, had formed a solid bloc against. A switch of twelve votes, preparedness supporters noted, might have changed the result. The final bill was passed by a vote of 403 to 2, with only the Socialist Meyer London and a lone preparedness advocate from Illinois balking. The bill was now in the court of the Senate, which had proved to be more defense-minded. The Senate, Army backers hoped, would write a bill sufficiently strong to force a tradeoff; at least the House might let a larger regular force through in order to get the pork-barrel it wanted for the militia lobby. The Hay Bill was not an end but a beginning, merely a device to rope off the arena for the fight. As a congressman had pointed out earlier, "We are not going to make the bill here. We are simply going to pass it. In another place they are going to take the 'innards' out of the bill and put in an entirely different set of works, and then we will appoint a conference committee. . . . We are simply the mechanics that are starting the operation." The process had at last begun. [12]

*   *   *

In the other house of Congress, enthusiasm for preparedness was more ardent. The Senate was less parochial than the House and more susceptible to business influence. George Chamberlain, the energetic chairman of the Senate Military Affairs Committee, was a hard-liner on defense, unsympathetic to Wilson's moderate position. The Oregon Democrat was a firm advocate of universal military training and of a Council of National Defense to coordinate national security policy. Far from scoffing at the threat of war, Chamberlain felt that the Monroe Doctrine would be endangered at the end of the European conflict. He even wanted to bring Great Britain to account for her interference with American commerce while the war was going on. Impatient with America's apathy to the defense issue, the senator at times seemed to welcome a military catastrophe; he once wrote that only an invasion by a "first-class military power" could snap the country out of its torpor. Understandably then, the bill which Chamberlain's committee produced was much stronger than the House bill. It provided for a Regular Army of sixty-five infantry regiments, twenty-five cavalry regiments, and twenty-one artillery regiments, backed up by engineers and supporting troops—the same unit strength recommended by the War College Division in its *Statement of a Proper Military Policy*. The force would be built up in increments over a five-year period. The peace strength of this army would be 178,000 men, but the expansive principle was maintained, and the force would be raised to 250,000 in time of war. The bill provided for short enlistments, a reserve officer training corps, and federal aid and supervision for the militia. Most interestingly, it brought the defunct Continental Army back to life under a different name. [13]

This proposition seems to have been the private idea of the judge advocate general, Enoch Crowder, rather than of the War Department. Crowder had told a number of Republican House leaders in late February that he could draw up a six-line compromise bill for a federal volunteer force which would avoid any of the rigidities of the Continental Army plan. Since a volunteer law providing for federal organization of troops in time of war had been on the books since 1914, the President should be authorized to organize, maintain, and train such a force in time of peace. Regrettably, "the War Department was headless," Crowder felt, and could not push the plan. This did not prevent the judge advocate general from using his own political connections. The provision crept into the Senate bill. Under this plan, 261,000 federal volunteers would be organized and would be given thirty days' training a year. This force would supplement the federalized militia. [14]

The volunteer army proposal captured the imagination of preparedness advocates. While the Continental Army had aroused little enthusiasm, the federal volunteer force now became a prime legislative goal for the defense lobby and big-army Republicans. The plan was more flexible than the Continental Army, and it did not bear the stamp of the administration. Moreover, it seemed the only thing that might prevent the complete triumph of the militia. The Military Training Camp Association had already achieved its goal of federal support for the summer training camps in both House and Senate bills; now it turned its energies into the support of what it saw as yet a wider extension of the Plattsburg Idea. The federal volunteer force, once created, might lead by easy steps to universal military training. Secretary of War Baker warned Grenville Clark that he "deprecated our training camp organization getting into the fight about it and said we could do better work in the long run by sticking to our own line." Undismayed, the Military Training Camp Association battled on for Section 56, the volunteer provision.[15]

But the volunteer army plan did not please the militia, and when Senator Chamberlain at last introduced his Army Reorganization Bill to the Senate on March 29, a covey of militia generals was sitting attentively in the Senate gallery. Their leader was Adjutant General J.F.C. Foster of Florida, one of the eighteen National Guard generals from that state. The National Guard executive council over which Foster presided was a rather unmartial body of politically appointed state adjutant generals, some of whom weighed in at three hundred pounds apiece. But this group was influential. The militia which its members spoke for was the country's traditional home guard, and it also represented a goodly bloc of voters. Furthermore, a number of congressmen were sympathetic National Guard officers, including no less than four members of the House Military Affairs Committee. The Guard was able to produce on demand a barrage of telegrams from home states; whatever its liabilities as a military force, it was adept at political infighting. "There is no doubt about it that the average Congressman is afraid of them. . . ," the chief of staff admitted. With its vital interests at stake, the National Guard lobby had presided over the military bill since February like a hovering angel. In getting rid of the Continental Army, the House had given the National Guard all it wanted. The Senate draft, although Chamberlain himself had been a Guard officer, was less appealing. The Senate had allotted no federal pay for senior Guard officers. And the volunteer force which the

Senate bill proposed was as unappealing to the militia as the Continental Army itself.[16]

This sentiment, to be sure, was not universal. Henry Cabot Lodge, a stout supporter of federal volunteers, declared "the tone of the National Guard of New England has been extremely good." The adjutant general of Massachusetts declared, "Every man that I know in the Militia wants to be a United States soldier and not a state soldier." In April the Massachusetts legislature passed a bill authorizing the state's Guard to come into the federal service under the volunteer provisions of the Chamberlain Bill. But this was a minority view. For the most part, the National Guard and the supporters of the proposed volunteer force regarded one another with the natural and implacable hostility of two scorpions in a bottle. The National Guard wanted federal support and control, not annihilation, and feared any competitive reserve force. General John F. O'Ryan, head of the efficient and progressive New York National Guard, declared that if Chamberlain's plan were adopted, "in the very nature of things there would begin a war between the Federal Volunteers and the Federal National Guard—a war for public esteem, for appropriations, and for everything else that concerns the two forces." Leonard Wood agreed. "There can be no doubt that these rival organizations will be operating against each other." The federal volunteer force held other hazards for the Guard. Henry L. Stimson wrote that with such a force in hand, "if we get a good Republican administration in the War Department, we can make the National Guard walk Spanish!" So the militia lobby remained adamantly opposed, and it was a group with more grass-roots support than the high-minded Plattsburgers.[17]

The ensuing debate on the bill in the Senate once more showed Republicans and Democrats at cross-purposes over whether this was to be a war or a peace measure, and once more was overshadowed by international crisis. On March 24, the steamer *Sussex* had been torpedoed in the English Channel, in an apparent violation of Germany's solemn pledge to refrain from sinking passenger vessels without warning. The forces of the hurricane continued to press in on an unarmed United States even as the talking went on. As the month of April proceeded without a resolution to the crisis, German-American relations were slowly strained to the breaking point. The administration fretted over the disposition of the Army; nightmare pictures of internal subversion flickered through the heads of responsible officials. Baker and Secretary of State Robert Lansing at one point wanted to withdraw troops from Mexico to guard American cities. There were only 3,000 soldiers available to protect New York City from fifth-columnists without leaving Boston unprotected. The police commissioner of New York asked for 5,000 Springfield rifles for his men. "There are more German reservists here than I thought," House worried. All of this came only indirectly to the Senate, if at all. But the general crisis atmosphere would have a cumulative impact.[18]

Even before the *Sussex* affair, some Senate voices had proposed that what the country needed now was an army in being, not a master plan for the future. In particular, Hoke Smith of Georgia had asked that the Regular Army be doubled immediately, with a force enlisted for two years. On April 1, with the submarine controversy beginning to heat up, Republican Senator Frank Brandegee of Connecticet proposed an amendment to the committee bill providing for an immediate increase in the regulars to 250,000 men, the size recommended by Theodore Roosevelt all along. Brandegee also endorsed the volunteer army provisions, but objected to the thirty-day time limit on training. What was needed was a large force in being. "I am rather inclined to think that might have some effect in making some diplomacies more successful than the mere conducting of literary correspondence on the subject."[19]

Brandegee's proposal did not win immediate approval. The War Department itself had proposed increasing the Army over a five-year period rather than all at once. Also, the amendment involved thrusting an unasked-for and Republican-made sword into Wilson's hands at a delicate moment. Besides, not all senators wanted an army to enforce American rights here and now; as Senator Porter J. McCumber of North Dakota put it, this meant "offensive, not defensive preparedness." It was easier to get consensus on a peacetime Army bill, although comments on the irrationality of this procedure were not lacking. Washington's republican Senator Wesley Jones declared that the proposed legislation demonstrated the President's "wonderful facility in riding two horses going in opposite directions. He leads the shouting host of preparedness and at the same time he stands upon a program of peace." If the country were in danger, "that plan of defense which he suggests is absolutely ridiculous and if there is no danger it is absolutely unnecessary." With some accuracy, the Washington Republican declared that the President "is simply taking advantage of the excitement to secure what the military authorities have not been able to secure in the past."[20]

Even the volunteer army plan had a hard time. National Guard pressure was strong, and the volunteer force stayed alive on April 6 by only a two-vote margin. The chief of staff wrote gloomily, "We greatly fear the turning over of the Army to politics completely." At any rate, the Army bill had been turned over to politicians, and the Senate, ignoring the pending crisis, proceeded to amuse itself by decking out the original bill with an amazing variety of amendments. As Senator John Sharp Williams observed, "everybody seems to be using this bill as a vehicle whereby to transport into the public attention some favorite idea of his own." James Reed proposed setting up military high schools; Hoke Smith demanded vocational training in the Army; others proposed industrial armies. Thomas Hardwick of Georgia advanced an ingenious scheme to create a schoolboy army trained by soldiers detached to every high school with fifty willing boys. The Senate ventured even further afield when Oscar Underwood of Alabama demanded that any defense bill contain provisions that would secure a suitable supply of nitric acid for the government. A government nitrate plant, conveniently enough, could also be used to manufacture cheap fertilizer for farmers. With great enthusiasm, the Senate spent a week debating the merits of Muscle Shoals. In despair, Senator Lawrence Sherman of Illinois declared: "The Senate has embarked on a course where we will have embraced everything. I think amendments have been offered now for everything except a rural-credit bill, possibly a parcel-post bill and a hard roads system, and I look for them to come on apace in due time. If we are going to provide for the manufacture of nitrates to fertilize the soil, it is certainly consistent that we should give them some soil to fertilize."[21]

On April 18, the U.S. Senate and external reality at last intersected. President Wilson announced he would address a joint session of Congress on the German crisis the following afternoon. The news came just as the Army bill moved toward a final vote. With a complete break in diplomatic relations with Germany apparently imminent, Senator Brandegee reintroduced his amendment for a 250,000-man army within the hour. This time, the impact of crisis carried the day. The Brandegee Amendment passed by a vote of forty-three to thirty-seven, with southern

Democrats and midwesterners from both parties providing the bulk of the opposition. The crisis also may have saved the volunteer army provision, which squeaked through on a vote of thirty-six to thirty-four with much the same alignment of forces. The hard-line Army men seemed to have carried the day. But the Senate bill, loaded down to the water's edge with amendments, was a weaker bill than it seemed, a combination of military grab-bag and spasm response to emergency. It was not certain that the large Regular Army it provided for as a permanent military policy could ever be recruited. With the Senate so divided and the House so opposed, it was doubtful that the volunteer army provision, as Hoke Smith pointed out, could survive conference committee. The bill imposed vocational training requirements on the Army which ignored military needs. Senator Hardwick's schoolboy army, which would have denuded the Regular Army of officers, had been incorporated into the final bill. The sheer size of the projected force, however, did hearten preparedness advocates.[22]

*　　*　　*

On April 19, President Wilson, addressing a joint session of Congress, solemnly warned Germany that her international conduct was unacceptable and that the submarine campaign would have to stop. Although the United States refrained from breaking diplomatic relations, the two nations were obviously on a collision course. At this juncture, the President at last displayed some more interest in the passage of preparedness legislation. Writing Hay the day of his speech, he requested the House to reconsider the numerical strength of the Army. Wilson told Hay that while "the *peace* strength provided for in the Senate Bill seems to me much too large," he felt that the total number of units created by the Senate was just about right. Wilson especially wanted specialized components, such as artillery and engineer troops. What the President had in mind was "an ample skeleton and unmistakeable authority to fill it out." Fourteen months after *Lusitania*, the President still thought of preparedness largely in the future tense. Despite the threatening international situation, the President asked from Congress only a blueprint, not a gleam of steel. The United States would not arm now, but would only move to keep its options open for a later mobilization. Predictably, Theodore Roosevelt denounced all this as a "crime against the nation."

Men might talk of standing behind the President, but as for Roosevelt, ''I wish to speak for the men who in the event of war will stand in front of the President.''[23]

With the international crisis still at fever pitch, there was a clamor for the House to pass the Senate Army bill at once. The New York *World*, a firm administration supporter, declared that ''the passage of the bill within forty-eight hours would emphasize every word of the American note now under consideration in Berlin.'' Instead, the issue became tangled in a parliamentary maze. James Mann, the Republican minority leader, attempted to force the Senate version through by refusing unanimous consent to send the House bill to the conference committee; Mann wanted the bill recommitted and the House conferees instructed to accept the Senate amendments on the size of the Army, the volunteer army provisions, and the nitrate plant. This approach led to much wrangling, but it did not produce the desired congressional display of strength and unity. Ironically, Mann, who had recently accused the President of trying to force war with Germany, was now accused of disloyally using obstructionist tactics by *The New York Times*. The issue was finally resolved when the Republicans were outflanked; Meyer London, the lone Socialist member of the House, was recognized on a move to recommit the bill without instructions, and when this was predictably defeated by a vote of 248 to 1, the bill went to conference. The episode proved as much as anything the truth of Champ Clark's complacent dictum that ''no man can bull a proposition through the House by main strength.'' At least no Republican could.[24]

Conference produced only deadlock. On May 5, the day after Germany bowed to American demands on the submarine question, Representatives Hay, Kahn, and S. Hubert Dent, the House managers, reported that after ''full and free conference,'' they were unable to agree with their opposite numbers, Senators Chamberlain, Warren, and J.C.W. Beckham. The House agreed to one last debate on the three critical propositions of the Senate bill. Eighty minutes would be allotted to discussing the provisions for an enlarged Regular Army and volunteer force, and eighty more for discussing the nitrate plant; this division of labor seemed to show where the real interests of the members lay. Once more the legislative wheel had turned to the House, once more Republicans cried for a force in being to meet the emergency, and once more the Democrats made clear that they were voting for a peace bill. As Hay had told the opposition earlier, "if you believe that by voting for these 250,000 men you are going to prepare for an emergency, you believe what is not true and what you know is not true. You are voting for it in response to a fear of your constituents, and not because you believe you are going to get the men under it." Hay again emphasized the fact that the bill would have no connection with what would have to be done if war should break out in the next few months.[25]

As usual, the President remained above the battle, except to send down word that he wished the House would accept the nitrate plant. Wilson had already privately indicated to Hay his desire for a compromise plan rather than a big army. Republicans like Mann might cry out "the emergency is now," but the President declined to toot the trumpet or beat the drum on their behalf. The evident peace sentiment in the country had had its impact: "It would be hard to exaggerate the effect on the House of the Ford victories in Michigan and Nebraska," wrote the American Union Against Militarism's director. Preparedness forces were weaker there in May than they had been in March. The volunteer army and the 250,000-man regular force died on the floor of the House, buried under an overwhelming vote. The nitrate plant, that bow to progressivism and boon to farmers, stayed in.[26]

Many newspapers were enraged. The slow lurching of Congress toward defense in a time of crisis had already produced a drumfire of criticism against allegedly piffling and pork-barrel-minded politicians, and now a preparedness-minded press was in a frenzy. The New York *World* cried out, "It is intolerable that a Congress should be so blind and so stupid, so sordidly indifferent to its grave responsibilities and duties." *The New York Times* declared that "Representatives of an enemy's nation could hardly do worse for us." Tumulty apprehensively reported the storm of criticism to the President: "I spoke to you a few days ago about the apparent dissatisfaction of the country with regard to the attitude of Congress on preparedness. You seemed to feel it was not nation-wide. I send you herewith an editorial from the *Milwaukee Journal* . . . which has supported you on everything. It denounces the action of the House as 'criminal folly'. . . ."[27]

But Wilson remained calm. At no time had he attempted to drive Congress forward under the spur of crisis; instead, he had politely suggested and guided. James Hay declared that the President "was never impatient and never dictatorial." Wilson's motives for this course are obscure, but he was in fact without military enthusiasms and was apparently satisfied to obtain a minimal preparedness for future shocks without splitting his party or the country. Perhaps too he feared that an immediate call to arms would irretrievably commit the nation to bellicose policies in Europe and Mexico. At any rate, he soothingly wrote a critic that "the truth must be admitted that not all of the country feels alike upon the questions of detail involved, and the matter is being handled by men who have had the greatest familiarity with the elements involved for a great many years." The President added that "no doubt we are all going to be more or less disappointed"; it seems clear from his handling of the issue, however, that he was less disappointed than many.[28]

The Army bill that was finally hammered out in conference was a compromise along the lines which Wilson had suggested to Hay. While the House chairman continued to believe preparedness was a humbug, he proved willing to go along with the tactful demands of his party leader. The bill provided for an eventual Regular Army of sixty-five regiments of infantry, twenty-five regiments of cavalry, and twenty-one regiments of field artillery, the same force which the original Senate bill had provided for. These units would be maintained at a peace strength of 165,000 men, but could be filled out to 216,000 men in an emergency. In addition, provisions were made for 31,600 supporting troops. Although the President was given power to raise the whole force in a crisis, this program was essentially long range. Short of national emergency, it would take five years for the force to reach full strength. As the General Staff had originally recommended, the Army would be built up by annual increments, a provision which was pleasing to Representative Hay. The Virginia congressman told the House that when the war in Europe was over and the hysteria abated, "then Congress can cut off these increments and make the standing army of the United States any number it pleases."[29]

In addition to this buildup of the regular forces, the bill served as a vehicle to satisfy the dearest wishes of many preparedness lobbies. While

Senator Hardwick's brainchild of a schoolboy army was dropped from the measure, the National Defense Act of 1916 did provide for a federally regulated and financed National Guard of 457,000 officers and men as a second-line defense force. It introduced ROTC and an enlisted reserve of technical specialists who could be called up in time of war. Provisions were made for industrial mobilization. For the first time, the Plattsburg camps received official recognition and money. Sixteen hundred new officers were authorized, to be recruited by examination from the civilian population. The umbrella of the federal government had at last been thrown over the civilian auxiliaries that men like Leonard Wood had labored to encourage. The day of the amateur was passing.[30]

There were also hidden drawbacks. The bouquet which Mr. Hay had thrust upon the Army was not without thorns. A concealed provision struck at the authority of the General Staff; another, while increasing the number of General Staff officers, ordered half of them out of Washington. A carefully drafted section created a position for one of Representative Hay's personal friends, and there was even an attempt to deprive General Wood of his Congressional Medal of Honor.[31]

* * *

The National Defense Act of 1916, in the words of one distinguished historian, was the "resentful response of rural and progressive isolationists to tremendous political and social pressures." As much as anything, it was a decision that the United States would *not* arm immediately to meet the menaces of a world at war. With a target-date set five years ahead, the bill was a peacetime measure produced by wartime demands. But if it was remarkably unrelated to the foreign policies of the country, this fact owed something to the lofty unmilitarism of the President and the whole approach of the expert General Staff. Although it had been framed by politicians, the act was far more intelligible when looked upon as an implementation of the Army's peacetime demands than as a response to world war. The bill did give the Army the total force it had originally thought necessary to deal with a threat to the continental United States, and it provided for a larger Regular Army than Garrison's War Department had dared to ask for. While the General Staff was by no means enthusiastic or even united over the merits of the legislation, the official General Staff memorandum described the act as the "first comprehensive legislation for national defense," and the "best military legislation that the country has ever had."[32]

The bill was politically acceptable, though, to be sure, not everybody was satisfied. "Congress has done almost its worse," *The New York Times* cried; the Army bill was an "unspeakable apology" which the President could never sign. Representative Gardner, the original tubthumper for defense, described the legislation as a "fake preparedness bill that every pacifist in the House can support." But in fact, the administration's tactics had succeeded in massing a broad and bipartisan congressional coalition behind its compromise program. One of the virtues of the bill was that almost everybody could at least live with it. The National Defense Act passed the House on May 21 by a lopsided margin. Only an oddly assorted group of twenty-five extremists held out, ultrapacifists for once joining hard-core preparedness men like James Mann to vote against the measure. The Senate had already agreed to the bill without a fight. Although preparedness forces called for a veto, Wilson signed the National Defense Act into law on June 3, 1916.[33]

The nation now had a land defense policy, although the funds still had to be found. The military, diplomatic, and political imperatives of the times seemed to have been met. An additional supplement was on its way. With administration prompting, Hay introduced a bill providing for a Council of Executive Information, which would consist of a Cabinet committee and a civilian advisory council to consider problems of war mobilization. The Wilson Administration was moving to capture the rising demands for organizing the civilian economy for defense, and it was acting before election-time.

This legislative action was as ashes to the disappointed preparedness forces. In the feverish atmosphere of the spring of 1916, they had dreamed of great citizen armies planned by military experts. They had obtained a peacetime Army bill framed by southern Democrats, the most salient feature of which seemed to be a huge windfall for the militia lobby. Even before the National Defense Act became law, Senator Chamberlain had announced he would wheel out his old hobbyhorse of a universal military training bill. The preparedness hosts, unsated, were still in the field, and international events still beat upon the United States with jarring force. As the ever vigilant American Union Against Militarism warned its members, "there is a certain tide to be reckoned with." Congress had passed a piece of legislation, but it had not disposed of the preparedness movement.[34]

10

Summer Maneuvers

The Republican party made no real fight on the vital issues. Among the leaders there were just about three men, in addition to myself, who stood straight.

—Theodore Roosevelt

Preparedness is not an issue in the platforms of the two great parties.

—Senator Warren Harding

The trainloads of men in uniform carrying arms they know nothing about and going to be introduced to animals they have never seen, all in the presence of a possible enemy, gives one a very vivid idea of the public's conception of preparedness.

—Major General Leonard Wood

In the summer of 1916, the military preparedness movement rather noticeably died down. Congress had temporarily settled the whole matter

158

with the National Defense Act of 1916, and a weary country settled back to the joys of conventional politicking and a presidential election campaign which did not revolve around the issue. Meanwhile, the National Guard, newly federalized by Congress, was undergoing an immediate test on the Mexican border. By the end of 1916, with Wilson back in the White House, Congress in session, and the National Guard coming back home, the stage was set for a fresh effort. The preparedness movement rose up again with a new and urgent demand for universal military training—a demand which would only be stifled, ironically enough, by the onset of World War I.

*   *   *

To many it had seemed that the elections of 1916 would inevitably revolve around the twin and overlapping issues of preparedness and Americanism. As former Secretary of War Stimson expressed it, "the great dominant issue of this campaign seems to be that of American nationalism, including within it as the pillars of its central structure the questions of preparedness for both peace and war. . . ." Both parties had attempted to clamber onto this bandwagon with Theodore Roosevelt providing the rhetoric and the incumbent administration some tangible legislation. But preparedness as an issue suddenly seemed to go limp.[1]

The process began at the Republican Convention in Chicago that June. The logical standard-bearer in a campaign of all-out preparedness and straight Americanism was obviously Theodore Roosevelt. While this possibility aroused patriotic ardor in the hearts of the Union League, it promised to go over less well in the farm belt, and Roosevelt still had a gaggle of enemies left over from 1912 among the professional politicians. Some friends of General Wood saw presidential gleamings about their man, but a professional soldier would be even less acceptable to the rank and file than a Roosevelt. The nomination therefore went to Charles Evans Hughes, a bearded and moderate Progressive who had just stepped down from the bench of the United States Supreme Court and who had no identification with sensitive subjects. The Republican platform was also toned down to straddle the preparedness issue, which now appeared divisive. The original document, drawn up by a nine-man subcommittee headed by Lodge and including the inevitable Robert Bacon, had called for a 250,000-man army, universal military training, a navy second to none, and straight Americanism. Such zeal was quenched by the full resolutions committee. Universal military training was struck from the platform by a vote of twenty-three to nineteen, and the other hard issues were deftly blurred. The Republicans had produced, as a friend of Roosevelt told him, "about the same sort of platform as Harding's keynote speech." A Republican leader frankly explained that "if we go anywhere near the other extreme on this matter of preparedness, the voters will think we are for war, and they will beat us. No sir, we will soft-pedal this preparedness stuff long before election day." Only the Progressives, with their commitment to Roosevelt and a disciplined national order, came out for full preparedness. The Progressives were jettisoned by Roosevelt himself in the interests of Republican unity.[2]

The same trend away from the martial impulse was evident later at the Democratic Convention, where the delegates frantically applauded the keynote speaker when he told of all the times the United States had refused to go to war. "Whenever he got back to Americanism, on which all the great applause of the convention was supposed to hang," *The New York Times* reported in surprise, "the convention lost all its ardor. . . . The plans of the Democratic leaders went all agley today." Even after the conventions, both House and Tumulty felt that national defense would still be a main campaign issue, but this failed to materialize. It was generally realized that the Republican party had backed away from preparedness; Theodore Roosevelt's continuing efforts on behalf of the issue served only to make a generally lackluster Republican campaign schizophrenic. Both parties had adopted similarly innocuous and meaningless platforms. As Senator Warren Harding, the veteran Republican wheelhorse, confessed in September, "Preparedness is not an issue in the platforms of the two great parties." As for patriotism, the fight was only between "Americanism versus Americanism," one paper observed.[3]

Part of the Republican failure to make political capital out of preparedness stemmed from the internal need of the party to conciliate the large numbers of rural and German-American voters upon which it depended. But part of it was due to the fact that the Wilson Administration had preempted the issue. During the summer the administration moved to strengthen the Democratic position. Congress had already passed the National Defense Act, and the President had personally signified his commitment to defense, after the fashion of the day, by marching in the Washington preparedness parade wearing ice-cream-colored pants and carrying an American flag. The Army Appropriation bill passed in August, actually funding the proposed programs, totaled some $267.5 million, a 250-percent increase over normal expenditures. In addition, Congress voted to strengthen the ever-popular coast defenses. When the legislative branch created the Council for National Defense to coordinate the armed forces and the civilian economy, the Wilson Administration selected as head of the Defense Advisory Council Walter S. Gifford, the leading advocate of industrial mobilization and a former Roosevelt supporter. The administration embraced the enlarged and now officially recognized Plattsburg Movement. Addressing a training brigade in camp, Secretary of War Baker implicitly accepted General Wood's views when he told the volunteers, "It is your duty to mold public opinion on army legislation." Assistant Secretary of the Navy Franklin Roosevelt announced a series of naval cruises for civilians with the words, "the navy has taken a leaf from the notebook of our friends in the army . . . we are trying to create a Plattsburg of the sea."[4]

By smoothly co-opting the movement for military preparedness, the Democrats undercut the Republicans, and one of the Republicans undercut was General Wood. If the administration endorsed the Plattsburg camps, it did not support their godfather, who continued his own campaign for defense. After the abortive presidential boomlet in his favor, Wood was now a marked man, irrevocably tainted with politics. The maverick general had overstepped too many boundary lines in fighting for his beliefs. A newspaper correspondent now warned him that the administration refrained from relieving him of his command and placing him on standing orders only for fear it might become a campaign issue. As one officer wrote the chief of staff, "General Wood is in the historic *cul de sac* of distrust into which so many administrations have forced the senior general of the Army." Ironically, as the defense movement succeeded, the personal fortunes of its most zealous uniformed backer declined.[5]

The Wilson Administration's most important defense step of the summer came in the field of naval armaments, when the President personally intervened to help push through Congress an immense, accelerated naval-building program. As the first line of defense, the Navy was traditionally popular with the public. It failed to conjure up the age-old fears that a standing army did. While Americans were divided on military preparedness, the New York *World* reported, "there is hardly any division of opinion in respect to the sea side." This hopeful statement was more than a little exaggerated. Some Progressives had a great abhorrence of a large navy, which they saw as both a vehicle for imperialist aggression and a bonus for the steel trust. Combining with big-navy Republicans, a small knot of rural Progressives in the House Naval Committee had been able to hold up Josephus Daniels' projected five-year naval program. The Republicans wanted a big crash program, the Democrats as little as possible. In the ensuing deadlock, the matter did not come to Congress for debate until the Army bill had been passed; as Idaho Senator William E. Borah had pointed out, Congress had been compelled to shape the last line of defense without knowing what the strength of the first would be.[6]

Here fate intervened. The Democratic House caucus decided in late May to pass the Navy bill before the Democratic Convention (which it assumed had been packed with preparedness supporters) assembled. With a piece of legislation thus enacted, the Convention would be confronted by a *fait accompli*, which it could not repudiate without rejecting its own party in Congress. On June 2, the House passed a compromise committee bill calling for the construction of five battle cruisers—heavily armed scouting vessels presumably less obnoxious to antimilitarists than battleships. Just after the vote, news of the Battle of Jutland reached the United States. In the first large-scale fleet action of World War I, the British and German fleets had battled inconclusively. But in the course of the fighting, three of the thinly armored British battle cruisers had been sunk, while the modern battleships on both sides remained relatively unscathed. Obviously, the House of Representatives had decided to put America's naval eggs in one rather fragile basket. The small-navy program of the Democrats was sunk along with part of the British fleet.[7]

After the conventions, the Wilson Administration moved decisively to retrieve the situation. The Senate voted by a big margin for a speeded-up version of the Daniels program which would involve constructing ten battleships and six battle cruisers in only three years. Wilson placed the prestige of his office behind this program. If the administration had been relatively passive in the fight for Army legislation, it showed a real zeal on behalf of the Navy. Colonel House had pointed out to the President the uses of a strong fleet in promoting international peace and defense. "We have the money and if we have the will," he wrote, "the world will realize that we are to be reckoned with. Its effect will be far reaching and it will give us the influence desired in the settlement of European affairs, make easier your South American policy, and eliminate the Japanese question." It would also be awkward, House mused privately, if trouble should come after the war and the administration find itself still unprepared, after all of the warnings. On July 27, the President invited the House members of the conference committee to the White House and pleaded with them to accept the Senate bill *in toto*. Lemuel Padgett, the Tennessee Democrat who chaired the House Naval Committee, resisted for a while. But when Wilson told him the Senate bill was imperative, Padgett surrendered. The committee chairman personally moved that the House adopt the Senate version in mid-August.[8]

The huge cost of the proposed Navy appalled many representatives; others protested the abrupt Democratic *volte face*. But with party discipline at a premium under the shadow of the approaching election, the administration steamroller crunched triumphantly on. Opposition to a big Navy was probably never as strong as opposition to a big army. Anyway, the House yielded to the tremendous pressures. "A good many of these men are talking one way in the cloakroom and voting the opposite way on the floor," an American Union Against Militarism observer wrote in discouragement. "The forces on the other side are too great," Warren Worth Bailey lamented. Sweetened by the Hensley Resolution, which provided that the whole program could be stopped after the European War in the interests of international disarmament, the Navy bill passed the House by a vote of 238 to 51, with many abstaining. Congress then moved to satisfy disgruntled Progressives by raising the income tax. If the rich had foisted a big navy on the people, they would have to pay for it.[9]

By the end of the summer it was clear that the Wilson Administration, with the new military and naval programs, had knocked the preparedness weapon from the hands of its opponents. Even Josephus Daniels, who had been a *bête noir* to preparedness advocates, had now been transformed into a navy statesman. Republicans had nothing to offer. "Wilson has captured your preparedness issue bodily,'' a Louisville lawyer told Theodore Roosevelt. Another correspondent of Roosevelt's succinctly commented, ''when the Democrats appropriated $630,000,000 for armaments, they broke the backbone of the Republican campaign.'' There were signs that the public was becoming a little tired of the whole thing; the sales of defense literature fell off, and 40 percent of the applicants for the expanded Plattsburg camps failed to show up. Ben Lindsay, the famous Colorado juvenile court judge, counseled the former President that ''You will find it is practically impossible to get up much enthusiasm here on the preparedness or Mexico issues.'' While Roosevelt still kept the field valiantly, he fought almost alone. Preparedness was shoved to the periphery of the political campaign. Henry Wise Wood, the aggressive head of the Conference Committee on Preparedness, complained that he was not even allowed to campaign for Charles Evans Hughes, the Republican presidential candidate. ''The Defense Movement has been deliberately sacrificed to what was thought to be the anti-preparedness sentiment of the pro-German element,'' the manufacturer sulked.[10]

With both parties trying to stand on the same ground, Wilson's narrow victory in November proved nothing one way or the other about popular sentiment toward preparedness. Some felt that the hawkish reputation of the Republican party had helped to injure Hughes in the West. On the other hand, the Navy League was able to rejoice in the defeat of some of the defense movement's active opponents. Oscar Callaway and ''Cyclone'' Davis had been defeated in the Democratic primaries, and Warren Worth Bailey, Frank Buchanan, and Clyde Tavenner had all failed to be reelected. But Buchanan had been linked with disloyal elements, while both Bailey and Tavenner were Democrats elected from heavily Republican areas because of the breakaway of Progressive voters. With the return of eastern Progressives to the Republican fold, these men were politically doomed anyway. However, a cluster of Ohio antipreparedness men stayed on. Robert Bacon had failed in his preparedness-oriented campaign for the Republican senatorial nomination in New York. Claude Kitchin had demolished his primary opponent. Despite all of the accusations against him in the metropolitan press, James Hay had been renominated to his seat without opposition, from where, however, he was elevated to the Court of Claims in July by the Wilson Administration. (Whether this appointment was a reward for faithful service or a device to remove him from the House Military Affairs Committee is not really certain.) Overall the election results hardly proved that the American people were obsessed with the preparedness movement.[11]

* * *

Although defense had been largely sidelined as a political issue, America's military readiness was being put to an actual test, which in the end would revive the whole debate. General Pershing's expeditionary force was still deep in Mexico. Its presence served only to exacerbate international relations, and the threat of raids against border towns remained. On May 10, President Wilson had called up the National Guards of Texas, Arizona, and New Mexico, a force of some 4,500 men. The militias of these southwestern states were not at peak efficiency. The New Mexico National Guard was forced to make an unofficial appeal to the American Legion for help in securing its quota of enlistments. The Texas National Guard had been plagued by embezzlements, 1,000 men on its muster rolls did not exist, and at least one of its companies had been formed as a front for a bottle club to avoid local prohibition laws. One hundred and sixteen Texas Guardsmen initially refused to take their oath of service. This situation, coming just as the Hay Bill was on its way to passage, had spurred Senator Chamberlain to announce the introduction of universal service legislation. More was to follow.[12]

In June, the Mexican situation deteriorated further. With Pershing confronted by what amounted to a Mexican ultimatum, Wilson felt compelled to mobilize. The Army had already demanded a force of 150,000 additional men to guard the Mexican border in case of any serious trouble. Under the law, there was only one place to which the President could turn. So, just sixteen days after the Hay Bill had been signed into law, President Wilson called up the National Guard of the United States. Three days later, a bloody brush between American cavalrymen and Mexican forces at Carrizal threatened full-scale war.[13]

Thus, the National Guard, just federalized on paper, was put to an immediate and unfair test. Until the passage of the Hay Bill, the Guard had practically been a collection of forty-eight miniature state armies.

The efficiency of these almost completely state-controlled forces was highly variable. New York State had outfitted a complete and well-regarded infantry division. Other states had been content with a few ill-equipped skeleton units officered by political appointees. In some states, the quaint custom persisted by which junior officers were elected by their men. One National Guard cavalry troop was described by its inspecting officer as not so much a military unit as "an agglomeration of men, three of whom wear shoulder straps, some of whom wear chevrons, and some are privates. In that the command was without horses, its efficiency in connection with mounted work was not able to be observed." South Carolina had no National Guard at all; Governor Cole Blease had mustered out the entire state militia in 1915 in a fit of pique at the War Department. In no case had the Guard units been given more than one week of field training a year. It was upon this motley assemblage that the federal call fell. Many of the Guardsmen had not yet taken their oath as federal volunteers under the Hay Act. This did not matter, for the President had not drafted the National Guard into federal service, but merely called it out to perform its constitutional functions as state militia. The federal broom impartially swept everybody up. The Guard did have one thing to offer: at least it was there to be called upon. As a Guard officer and magazine writer had previously observed, "A national guard in the armory is worth two volunteer armies in the bush."[14]

The call was met at first with enthusiasm, for it was a patriotic age. The troops marched down to their railroad stations to the accompaniment of bands, flags, and cheering crowds. Ninety-one members of the Yale graduating class, members of the college artillery unit, turned up in khaki at Commencement. The Fighting 69th paraded down Fifth Avenue in New York City with the band playing "The Girl I Left Behind Me," senior officers on horseback, and the Union League standing bareheaded at attention on the sidewalk. At the state mobilization camps the situation became less amusing. Many camp sites proved to be ill-chosen. It became clear that numbers of troops were reporting without weapons and equipment, and some even without uniforms. It took an agonizingly long time to pull the assembled Guardsmen into military units fit for service.[15]

One of the problems was manpower. Of the 95,000 enlisted men on the rolls of the National Guard units who were called up, half never made their way to the border. Although all but a few states had theoretically adopted Army standards of physical fitness for their militia, federal authorities rejected over 18 percent of all Guardsmen who reported, on medical grounds. In one National Guard company, 77 percent of the troops flunked the federal physical. Thousands of militiamen failed to answer the call. The equivalent of an entire infantry division vanished from the rolls in various ways which the War Department could not explain. Despite a rush of civilian volunteers in the first flush of enthusiasm, Guard units in most states were severely understrength. In Kentucky, reformatory inmates were paroled into the Guard to fill up the ranks.[16]

The mobilization clearly spotlighted the deficiencies of the National Guard. It also showed up deep flaws in the approach of the War Department to defense. Like the Regular Army, the National Guard had been organized on the expansible principle. The sixty-five-man peace strength companies were ordered recruited to full war strength for mobilization. Inevitably, this meant that Guard units would be packed with raw recruits, or understrength, and often they were both. Moreover, the Army Quartermaster Corps failed to give the assembled National Guard adequate logistic support. All of the necessary equipment for a militia mobilization had been stockpiled in a single depot in Philadelphia. Naturally, when the crisis came, there was incredible confusion and delay. Much of the equipment itself was wholly unsuitable. In the middle of mobilization, the Army was forced to rush out onto the open market and buy essential supplies. "The Quartermaster Department crumpled up like an eggshell," Wood wrote.[17]

Because of the crisis, the War Department decided not to wait until the entire National Guard had been assembled and trained in rear base areas. Instead, individual units would be flung into the breach as soon as they were ready. (Some never got to the border at all.) Even this process took time. "The Militia are fearfully slow," Scott fretted. The first regiments began to entrain from their state mobilization camps at the beginning of July amid scenes of some confusion. It took hours and days for inexperienced units to load up their trains, which then lumbered off for the front at a government-dictated thirty miles an hour. Since not enough Pullman cars were available, most of the troops spent days sprawled awkwardly over the seats of day-coaches. The sides of the troop trains were chalked with unit names and destinations, as well as decorations and slogans; the

National Guard was ''going forward as silently and surely as Barnum and Bailey,'' a reporter noted. To the confusion of the War Department, several regiments were reported to have run out of rations, although they were supposed to have ten days' supplies for a four-day trip. ''How they could use up ten days rations . . . unless they threw it away, I do not know,'' the chief of staff wrote. These problems were lavishly publicized by an uncensored press. ''The train-loads of men in uniform carrying arms they know nothing about and going to be introduced to animals they have never seen, all in the immediate presence of a possible enemy, gives one a very vivid idea of the public's conception of preparedness,'' General Wood wrote. But the beginnings of an army did begin to take shape on the border as pink-cheeked northern boys, sweltering in wool uniforms, moved into tent cities on the dusty plains.[18]

The military situation now aroused a storm of protest. Appalled by the hasty dispatch of the National Guard, former Secretary of War Stimson accused the administration in print of ''rushing untrained levies . . . to the border.'' But on this point Secretary Baker stood firm. The militia was the nation's only reserve force in being. It could be trained at the border as well as anywhere else; in fact, a workout under combat conditions supervised by professional soldiers would be the best thing for it. Moreover, the mere presence of troops on the border would exert a calming influence. Military necessity dictated taking some risks. The chief of staff took an even harder line. The danger to women and children on the border was so great that ''inaction could not be justified so long as we had a rifle and a cartridge.'' The National Guard might not be able to hit anything, he wrote grimly to another friend, but ''they could act as a scare crow.''[19]

In General Wood's words, the National Guard mobilization had been a ''rather heavy spring to arms.'' By the end of the summer, a force of 128,000 men had been assembled on the border. While half of these men already had sketchy militia training, 60,000 were brand-new recruits who arrived without any previous military experience. Only 37 percent of the troops had been members of the units to which they were assigned on the date of the callup. Just 21 percent had qualified as first-class shots. Even so, most units were far below their designated wartime strength. China could scarcely have done worse, Stimson mourned. Paradoxically, although the United States now had more men under arms than ever before, the country seemed more unprepared than ever. Fortunately, this half-baked force was not committed to the furnace of war. Even as the National Guard assembled, diplomacy cooled down the Mexican situation. The Guard's mission became one of training and passive border defense.[20]

The dull routines of garrison duty began to take their toll of morale. The Guardsmen had marched out with flags flying to throw back the Mexicans; all they encountered were the monotonies of peacetime soldiering. The drawbacks of being first-line reserves now became more apparent. As a Guard officer wrote dramatically about his colleagues, "they were sent down into a wilderness too wild for maneuvers, they were kept in dismal boredom while their jobs were lost, their opportunities missed, their rivals established." Some of the Guard units dispatched to the border were "crack city regiments," like New York's Squadron A, the Seventh New York Infantry, and the First Illinois Field Artillery. These were outfits of considerable social tone, their ranks filled with prominent businessmen. The members of these elite units suddenly developed a keen distress at the prospects of spending an indefinite period executing squad rights in the Southwest. Their sentiments were shared by others. It is hard to know how widespread the disaffection was, for troops always gripe. Once on the border, the militia was well-supplied and in fine health, and General Tasker Bliss, a not unperceptive observer, found the men in "excellent spirit." There was an undertone of grumbling, however, which was magnified by sensation-conscious newspapers and by enemies of the administration and of the National Guard. An exasperated secretary of war told one complaining congressman in General Scott's hearing that "he had gotten everything the militia needed now but nursing bottles, and he would have to get them before long."[21]

Nevertheless, the National Guard had reasons for·discontent. The unpleasant fact was that the militia was now stuck with a dirty job which no one wanted to share. Despite all of the preparedness parades, enlistments for both the regular forces and the National Guard lagged. "The spirit was rife to let somebody else do it," the chief of staff commented with unwonted cynicism. When there seemed some prospect for action, civilians had flocked to the colors, but between July and October, only 15,000 new men were recruited for the National Guard. (In defense, Guard advocates pointed out that the War Department had ordered Guard recruiting parties to go to the border with their units, thus seriously hampering the obtaining of replacements.) The Military Training Camp Association did propose to help organize a "Plattsburg" volunteer force for use in any real crisis, but this was merely a stalking horse, a device, as General Wood admitted, "to indicate to the country they were ready to go and answer the hidden innuendo that they were not willing after all to serve their country." It was accepted that Plattsburgers would participate only as officers in a general emergency. Meanwhile, National Guard recruiting parties were not allowed to enter the camp. While the preparedness movement had produced a fervent desire to sacrifice for the nation in the abstract, it did not generate men to police the Mexican border.[22]

National Guardsmen with dependents found themselves in awkward straits indeed. Many state governors had tried to release such men in advance of mobilization, only to be told it was illegal. In June the House of Representatives passed a bill authorizing a monthly support payment of fifty dollars for Guardsmen with wives and families, but the measure fell into limbo on the floor of the Senate. Senator Chamberlain scorned such financial support on the grounds that it would introduce invidious distinctions between the National Guard and the Regular Army (which received no family allowances). It would simply be "a charity offered to a soldier to perform his duty that he owes to his country." Besides, the senator taunted, "the National Guardsmen themselves asked for the legislation that requires their being drafted into service." The War Department thus was reduced to ordering department commanders to discharge enlisted men with dependent families; Baker had a lively idea of what "the spectacle of a great number of wives and children made objects of community charity" would do to the popularity of the National Guard. As Blair Lee, the Guard's most articulate Senate supporter, pointed out, this too would be demoralizing, for it would tend to strip the militia of all of its experienced men. In late July, the Senate at last agreed to support dependents.[23]

Another factor gave Guardsmen some unease: the suspicion that the border mobilization had been politically motivated, designed either to force training on the National Guard or possibly even to discredit it. Circumstances lent plausibility to this belief. In the springtime, a number of voices had urged just such a practice mobilization. When the commander of the New York National Guard division, Major General John F. O'Ryan, told the troops in July that they would be staying on the border until 1917, *The New York Times* knowingly reported that "the reason for the long stay is to make the guardsmen into first line soldiers [as] . . . the first effective move toward real preparedness." In the fall, the Republican governor of New York threw fuel on the flames by reviving these charges. These suspicions were unfounded. Of course, the Guard mobilization was a golden opportunity to whip the reserve force into shape. As a staff officer wrote Wood cheerfully, "this war problem is a fine one for us all, and for the first time, short of war, we have been given full power and punch." But the training was an accidental byproduct of the mobilization, not its intent. Because of the danger from Mexico, the War Department wanted a covering force of 150,000 men on the border to screen the frontier towns. Because of the small size of the Regular Army, the National Guard got the job. Police action, however, seemed harder for Americans to accept than war.[24]

*   *   *

The National Guard performed its useful and necessary function in the summer and fall of 1916. Despite all of its deficiencies, it had been ready as a force in being and had met the unglamorous military requirements of the nation. There were ominous indications that the whole experience had been a little too much for it. The Guard felt that it had borne the whole burden of the nation's defense, and had borne it alone. As the regiments began to trickle back from the Mexican border in late 1916, after the situation had grown less tense, the National Guard showed signs it might be coming apart. In a three-month period ending October 25, nearly five hundred National Guard officers had resigned. The *Seventh Regiment Gazette* of the New York Guard reported stridently that "almost without exception every man in the Guard to-day, when his period of enlistment is up, is through for all time." Of the Guardsmen contacted by the New York Mayor's Committee on National Defense, 84 percent stated flatly that they would not reenlist. The situation was aggravated by the fact that many militiamen at the border had not yet taken the six-year federal reenlistment oath prescribed by the Hay Act, and numbers refused to take it after they got home. In three Illinois regiments, *The Nation* reported, less than 20 percent of the returning Guardsmen would take the oath. A Plattsburger wrote General Wood that when one returned militiaman was asked what the effect of the mobilization would be on the National Guard, he replied, ''There isn't going to be any National Guard.'' Another cycle of the preparedness movement was about to begin.[25]

11

A Certain
Tide To Be
Reckoned With

A combination of Great Britain and Japan could put us out of business just as rapidly as they could march through the country.

—Colonel Edward House

We must get our men so that they are machines, and this can be done only by means of a process of training. . . . The recruits have got to put their heads into the military noose.

—Major General John F. O'Ryan

The spirit was rife to let somebody else do it.

—Major General Hugh Scott

The core of the National Defense Act of 1916 was the provision federalizing the National Guard to provide for the necessary military reserve force. By the fall of 1916, much of the public had been persuaded that this federalization had proven a disaster. Secretary of War Baker did not share in this belief. But the chief of staff assumed that the point had been amply made on the border that the Hay Act was unworkable. *The New York Times* editorialized that thirteen years of the Dick Act had not made the state troops fit for exacting military duty, and there was no reason to believe the Hay Act would do any better. *The New Republic* announced that the Mexican border experience had demonstrated the failure of the recent legislation with "satisfactory finality." The National Guard mobilization, claimed the *American Review of Reviews*, "was worse than a failure; it was a black tragedy."[1]

Much of the criticism was not only harsh but hasty. The National Guard obviously had had no time to profit from the benefits of federalization before it was mobilized. The militia, as the only force in being, could have and would have been sent to the border without the Hay Act; indeed, it was never drafted formally into federal service. Nonetheless, all of the forces which had been opposed to militia federalization in the first place fell on the National Guard with a vengeance. This time they had allies within the Guard itself. The Guardsmen were unhappy at having been forced to carry the weight of the nation's defense alone. A poll of 612 National Guard officers and first sergeants taken by General J. Franklin Bell revealed that five hundred now favored universal military training. The attitudes of the returning Guardsmen told their own story. The spirit indeed was rife to let somebody else do it. The discontent found a ready and sympathetic response. Charles Evans Hughes, the Republican presidential candidate, had piously announced in August that "we are too great a country to require of our citizens who are engaged in peaceful vocations the sort of military service to which they are now called." The New York Mayor's Committee on National Defense noted that business circles now wanted "a system to which business could fairly adjust itself," rather than having Guardsmen called up from offices and factories. As General Wood stated, there was a growing demand for "a force which can be turned out without asking great sacrifices of certain classes to the advantage of others."[2]

This ideal force was more easily described than found. One solution might have been a substantial increase in the Regular Army. Higher pay would surely have brought in more men. As it was, with private's pay at fifteen dollars a month, the Army had not yet been able even to recruit to the strength of 120,000 authorized after Villa's raid. This avenue of approach the Army was unwilling to try. It would increase costs too much, and the General Staff had its own plans for any cash which could be pried from Congress. Instead, the defense movement turned to plans for universal military service. This solution was popular but not entirely rational. As General O'Ryan pointed out, the hard fact was that many of the National Guardsmen who clamored to come home from the border in the absence of excitement were young men in precisely the group that would be doing the same thing under a system of compulsory service. Inevitably, in any limited war situation, a part of the nation would have to carry an unfair burden. Moreover, the mobilization of any reserve force would surely involve taking its officers and senior NCOs from their established jobs in civilian life. Enthusiasts ignored all of these drawbacks. The defense movement was in the mood for a panacea, and it seemed a happy solution to take the burden of defense from the Guard and dump it on the shoulders of the young and voteless still outside the economic system. With Wilson elected, Congress back in short session, and the militia coming back from the border at the rate of 6,000 a week, a new agitation for universal military training began.[3]

The drive was reinforced by a dramatic reversal on the part of the General Staff. The force levels set up by the National Defense Act of 1916 had essentially been based on calculations made by the War College Division in 1911. In October, the chief of staff, General Scott, asked for a reappraisal of America's military needs in the light of changed conditions; in December, this project was put on a crash basis. The Army was finally taking World War I into consideration. In response to Scott's request, the War College Division produced a report which concluded, with a certain narrowness of vision, that "the changes that affect the present study are really limited to two countries, namely Great Britain and Japan." The huge forced growth of British and Canadian forces meant that America's military problem was no longer merely that of preventing a hostile landing on the coast. "Our northern neighbor has become a military power," the report warned. The United States had to be ready to repel an Anglo-Japanese attack from Canada. To do this, the country needed 1,500,000 men under arms at the outbreak of war and another 1,500,000 ready in three months. The military requirements of the United States had just been multiplied sixfold.[4]

Scott brought this new development to the public eye in his testimony before the Senate Military Affairs Committee in December 1916. Broaching the newly discovered need for three million soldiers, the veteran old cavalryman told the senators, "At present we are practically defenseless before the veteran armies of our northern neighbors and could quite easily be crushed by the existing coalition of these island empires." Such a huge force, of course, could only be raised by universal training. Not only was the volunteer system, in Scott's words, "undemocratic, unreliable, inefficient and extravagant," but it couldn't produce three million men.[5]

Scott's testimony was not uncritically accepted. The possibilities the chief of staff suggested, while no doubt breathtaking, also seemed a little far-fetched. The New York *World* pointed out, quite properly, that "the moment the General Staff conjures up military combinations against the United States and provides aganst them, there are no conceivable limits to the defense requirements." Going further, *The New Republic* accused the chief of staff of "abominable levity," and felt it would be best if he were prevented in the future from disclosing "the mischievous folly of his political opinions." This was a little unfair; Scott and the General Staff had operated on the basis of calculating foreign capabilities, not intentions. The chief of staff personally seems to have felt a postwar alliance between Germany and Japan would be the most likely threat to the United States. Even more important was the fact that the speculations of the General Staff paralleled the real, if secret, fears of high American policymakers.[6]

By the end of 1916, America's relatively good wartime relationship with Great Britain seemed to be coming unraveled. The United States was increasingly annoyed at British intrusions on American neutral rights, while the President's dream of arranging peace in Europe threatened to conflict with Allied plans for victory. In the disoriented world of 1916, these developments cast monstrous shadows. Colonel House seriously discussed the possibility of an Anglo-Japanese attack with the President. It would be possible, he told Wilson, for the British to destroy our fleet and seize part of the United States with the help of

Japanese troops. The President, with good reason, expressed his doubts at the likelihood of the prospect. If we actually were invaded by enemy troops, he supposed that they would have to stop somewhere. On being informed of Wilson's reply, Frank Polk, the counsellor of the Department of State, remarked that they might well be stopped around the Gulf of Mexico. "We are on the verge of war," House wrote in his diary, "and not a move is being taken in the direction of immediate preparation." These fears may have shaped the report of the General Staff, or at least accounted for the fact that the analysis was given crash priority over all other subjects in early December.[7]

*   *   *

The National Guard mobilization and the new demands of the General Staff brought the clamor for universal military training to its highest pitch. With a big navy now assured, universal military training became the central demand of a suddenly revived defense movement. By the end of 1916, the groups which had earlier supported preparedness in general had rallied around to the cause. The Chamber of Commerce and the defense societies had already endorsed universal training in the spring. The 1916 Plattsburg camps had turned out over 16,000 gratuates, "all for universal service and . . . of forceful influence," as Scott reported. Now leaders of the medical profession and students at Ivy League schools went on record in its support. In the summer, the National Educational Association, formerly opposed, had heard out General Leonard Wood, and then assented to the proposition that the state had a right to put military training in the school. At the first meeting of the Wilson Administration's newly created Defense Advisory Council, six of its seven distinguished members favored universal military training; only Samuel Gompers of the AFL held out against it. Encouraged by the usual General Staff lobbying ("I am working very hard with my newspaper men. . . ," Major Douglas MacArthur reported), the metropolitan press increasingly supported universal military training. The War Department compiled a file of fifteen hundred newspaper clippings from coast to coast, and found 90 percent in favor of the proposition. The newspapers themselves began to take straw polls on the subject and reported encouraging results: from 80 to 99 percent of their respondents favored universal military training. It seemed to some defense leaders that the time for the culmination of the preparedness movement had now arrived. In a year, the Mexican border mobilization would be forgotten and the war in Europe might be over. This was the time to strike.[8]

The organized defense societies cast themselves heart and soul into the struggle; the fight for universal military training was now their *raison d'être*, and there was even a little intramural scuffling over the custody of the issue. The Plattsburgers, of course, had always worked for this goal, although the Military Training Camp Association did not endorse it formally until November. Now the National Security League embraced the cause, staging a big Congress of Constructive Patriotism in Washington and launching an extensive leaflet campaign. This activity somewhat annoyed General S.B.M. Young and his Association for National Service. The Association had been the first civilian lobby formed to support the idea, and Young resented the way the Security League had elbowed in and "cribbed some of our best literature." Finally, there was a new and well-financed organization in the field, with its own concrete plan and with good connections in both the political and military spheres. This was the Universal Military Training League, which seems to have been organized around the Union League Clubs of Chicago and New York in the summer of 1916.[9]

The Universal Military Training League had the advantages of talent and money. As executive director, the League was able to obtain the services of the veteran lobbyist, Howard H. Gross, a man one of Roosevelt's correspondents described admiringly as a "real live wire." A portly, folksy, and unhurried resident of Chicago, Gross was a skilled professional with a couple of very solid accomplishments to his credit. He had helped to pass the Smith-Lever Act through Congress and had headed up the Tariff Commission League in its successful campaign. Now Gross was ready to run a well-heeled fight for the next Progressive cause. The resources at his disposal were substantial. The plan of the League was to secure founders who would subscribe $2,500 apiece and underwrite a sum of $2,500 more. This plan seems to have succeeded. At the outset, the UMTL netted the support of Robert Bacon, John T. Pratt, Charles G. Curtis, George H. Perkins, and the great white whale of finance, J. P. Morgan himself. By September, $65,000 had been subscribed, and $100,000 more apparently was raised in Chicago at a single dinner in October. The campaign would start off with an ample war chest.[10]

While the Association for National Service had propounded only an abstract idea, the Universal Military Training League from the beginning had searched for a feasible and definite plan on which to center its efforts. The scheme the League quickly hit upon was the product of an able young staff officer, Captain (later Major) George Van Horn Moseley. The Moseley plan called for six months' service, all in one dose, for all able-bodied eighteen-year-old boys. After their initial period of training, the youths would go into the reserves and would be liable for military service in case of war for a ten-year period. The plan was in line with the thinking of military Progressives like General Wood, which held that troops could be trained in six months of concentrated work. The short training period also made the plan pleasing to civilians. As the father of two boys, Moseley explained to Senator Chamberlain, he had no wish to see the United States burdened by a long-service conscript army like the nations of Continental Europe. Extreme militarization was unnecessary; the United States Navy would always provide the margin needed for further preparations. "In these times of hysteria," the captain urged, "let us catch the pendulum as it swings from a condition of unpreparedness and stop it at a position of reasonable preparedness."[11]

This moderate plan for universal service was accepted both by the League and by Senator Chamberlain, and was endorsed, after a little hesitation, by the leaders of the National Security League and the Association for National Service. The whole civilian defense movement seemed to swing into line behind the plan. Senator Chamberlain readily agreed to strike out everything after the enacting clause on his own universal training bill and substitute the Moseley proposal. The drive for universal military training was becoming more serious as well as more coordinated. Chamberlain's original bill, drawn up without professional assistance, had been in the nature of a patriotic gesture. The senator had proposed setting up only a watered-down version of the Swiss military system, a play army under civilian discipline with an absolute minimum of training. The new Chamberlain Bill was a serious attempt to create a usable military reserve force. The bill was now the centerpiece of the whole preparedness movement. Chamberlain's draft, embodying a slightly modified version of the Moseley plan in which the training age was raised a year, was reported out favorably from the Senate Military Affairs Committee in February 1917.[12]

The Chamberlain Bill did not, however, satisfy the Army. The military was rabidly in favor of universal training. Scott had conducted a one-man guerrilla campaign against Baker on the subject all winter, ambushing him with favorable newspaper editorials daily. But the Army had no intention of letting the defense pendulum stop at the center. Most officers demanded a longer training period than Moseley's proposal envisaged. The militarily conservative chief of staff had written to a friend that "the Germans and the French are not able to make a soldier in under two years, and I do not know how we can do any better." This was not exactly true; the Germans and the French had imposed long-term service on their conscripts to keep a force in being, not to train the men. But the comment reflected a general military sentiment. With universal military training at last a real possibility, the Army wanted to submit its own plan and control its own destiny. On December 12, 1916, after he had received the new estimate of military requirements, General Scott ordered the War College Division to come up with a blueprint. Disdaining political considerations, the military would demand that only its own needs be considered in the framing of defense legislation.[13]

Generating a universal service plan proved to be an agonizingly difficult task for the War College Division. The National Defense Act of 1916 had cut the effective strength of the General Staff by half. The remnants, overworked and perhaps defectively organized, sputtered for two months toward a satisfactory solution as the short session of Congress hastened toward adjournment. Scott fretted, "it is possible we may lose out because we have not a plan ready just at this psychological moment." Even working Sundays, the War College Division Committee assigned to the job was not able to produce a first draft until the end of January. When the plan finally emerged, it was an uncompromising one. The Army, the committee report declared, would have to "ignore the individual whenever his interests conflict with those of the Republic." Each year 500,000 men would be given eleven months' training in sixteen localized training divisions. Recruits would be paid a highly nominal five dollars a month. No educational or occupational deferments from training would be granted.[14]

Unfortunately, this scheme presented certain problems. Under the

General Staff plan, it would still take eleven years to create the force of three million men that the Army had claimed to be necessary. The plan stated that no reservists could be trained until the training personnel were obtained, but the 300,000 man Regular Army required for this purpose was supposed to be recruited from already trained reservists. As General Joseph Kuhn, the commander of the War College Division, admitted, "its cost is prohibitive, and it is a practical certainty that it will not be adopted by Congress." General Bliss urged that the Army develop a spectrum of alternative plans, instead of placing all its eggs in one basket. "If we submit our best plan, with no alternative proposition, we will get nothing." General Scott stubbornly clung to the War College Division's proposals, however; perhaps it was now too late to do anything else. In February, they were submitted to Baker as the Army's plan for universal military training. [15]

*   *   *

The tide for universal military training was at the flood by the beginning of 1917. But it was still contained by massive dikes. The Army and its civilian allies had not been able to agree on a common plan. Universal training, like preparedness in general, made its strongest appeal to business circles and the urban upper-middle class, and these were not the whole nation. Many Americans remained unconvinced. The prospects for universal military training in Congress were not good. The House of Representatives was still controlled by rural southern Democrats, and while the Army had five loyal supporters on the crucial House Military Affairs Committee, a majority of committee members remained opposed to any grandiose military schemes. As one of them wrote William Jennings Bryan, "I do not think the 'militarists' will find it so easy to frighten this Congress into additional expenditures for the Army and Navy as they did the last one." The defense-minded Otto Kahn felt it would be a good idea to give the militia system a further trial. Despite Scott's belief that the time was ripe, Senator Chamberlain admitted that no legislation on the subject was possible during the lame-duck session of Congress. George Van Horn Moseley, for one, showed that he did not believe the campaign for ultimate preparedness would be a short one; serving on the border as a colonel with the Pennsylvania National Guard, he offered to resign his commission eventually and work permanently for the Universal Military Training League. Finally, neither the secretary of war nor the President was yet reconciled to the idea.[16]

While the chief of staff had been allowed to express his enthusiasm for universal military training in the 1916 *War Department Annual Reports*, the secretary of war had been careful to disassociate himself from it. In his own report, Baker had asked only for a stronger corps of engineers and a system of preparatory schools for West Point. It would be politically premature, the Cleveland Progressive felt, to condemn the federalized National Guard as a failure until all the facts were in. Despite the metropolitan papers' clamor for universal military training, Baker told the President, "the general public have not really taken up the situation for consideration." The best policy would be one of watchful waiting. "When the next session of Congress convenes we can go very much more sure footedly into the question of what a wise military policy requires," Baker concluded at the end of January.[17]

This line of thinking suited the President well. Wilson was maneuvering for a peace without victory in Europe, not for a military system at home. In fact, the President had just tongue-lashed a delegation from the Maryland League of National Defense which had presented a memorial attacking the National Guard and claiming that the United States was "in actual present danger of being involved in a European war." With indignation in his voice, the President said he deplored snap judgments and he defended the militia system. Nothing but a standing army could prevent men from being taken away from their jobs. "These things are of the utmost intricacy and difficulty, and are not to be settled *ex cathedra*," the President had warned. The moment for universal military training, it seemed, was not yet.[18]

The moment would never quite arrive. Even as the campaign for universal training peaked, the idea was becoming obsolete. Universal military training had been the dream of peacetime theorists, but it was too inefficient and expensive to meet the needs of actual warfare in an industrialized age. As *The Scientific American* had written, the lesson of the European War was "that certain men are too valuable to be placed on the battlefield," Bliss, with one of the best minds in the Army, had already hit upon this point. If the country were contemplating the possibility of an emergency in three years, he told the chief of staff on the last day of January, there would be large numbers of men in each of the contingents subject to call under any system of universal training and service that would have to be immediately returned to their normal work. On the other hand, "If there be a possible emergency confronting us in the not distant future, we should not waste time, energy or money in the training of people who are not to be immediately called into active service in the field." The secretary of war had similar thoughts. He felt that the available military resources of the nation must be so constituted that they would not disorganize the industrial life of the country or the operations of its government when they were called into service. Perhaps the long-range answer to America's peacetime military problem would not after all be universal military training, the secretary mused, but some form of "selective compulsion."[19]

As it happened, the 1916-1917 campaign for universal military service was cut short by immediate events. By the time the Chamberlain and General Staff proposals had reached their final stages, the nation was no longer in urgent need of a long-range peacetime military policy. For on February 1, 1917, the Imperial German Government declared unrestricted submarine warfare against its enemies, in defiance of American neutral rights. The face of the final enemy had appeared from the shadowy and indistinct menaces conjured up by the preparedness movement. At last, the emergency was now.

12

A Pause Between
Two Breaths

From a military point of view, America is as nothing.

—Imperial German Naval Minister
Eduard von Capelle

"Cold and windy day," General Wood wrote in his diary on February 3, 1917. "Relations broken off with Germany. General satisfaction. . . ." The Wilson Administration had accepted the German challenge. Now the United States had begun to edge down the road to a war for which it was still unprepared. Wood had observed the day before, "Country unready, completely so." This opinion was shared by other circles. Germany had decided to launch her submarine campaign in the belief that America would be powerless to strike back. As Admiral Eduard von Capelle, the German naval minister, summed things up on the last day of January, "from a military point of view, America is as nothing." Germany was gambling that Great Britain could be beaten from underneath the seas long before America's weight, even if it developed any, could be added to the balance.[1]

A curious interlude followed the break of diplomatic relations with Germany. As Newton D. Baker put it, "We are all between two breaths here. We have taken one breath and are wondering whether we will have to draw the other one." Americans rallied behind the President; William Howard Taft hailed "an exhibition of patriotism that we have not seen since the days of the civil war." But the fury was not on us yet. American merchant shipping stayed close by its ports for weeks, and there were no immediate submarine incidents. In this twilight situation, the Wilson Administration made imperceptible gestures at preparation, agonizedly conscious that a false step might tip the scales in favor of war. Meanwhile, with the country half-way over the precipice, the preparedness debate went on in a near vacuum; incredibly, congressmen still talked in terms of peacetime armies.[2]

The theory of the National Defense Act of 1916, Baker had written the President in December, was that "it was not safe for a country to wait until it was in a great emergency to make its preparations." Unfortunately, that was just what had happened. The National Defense Act was only a piece of paper, a long-range authorization which had not yet been fleshed out; it had not been designed in any case to meet the requirements of a European intervention. Now the country had to arm in the presence of the enemy. The Wilson Administration proved noticeably cautious in its initial approach, partially out of a desire to avoid provocation, partially, perhaps, from an underlying skepticism about the need for a military solution. As late as February 15, Wilson told his Cabinet members at dinner that he was not in favor of any great preparedness. The War and Navy Department staffs did go into a frenzy of activity, and Wilson visited Baker and Daniels in early February to discuss and review preparations. But the secretary of war told Wood that the President deemed it imperative that no troops be moved around "in a manner which will excite apprehension or suggest anticipated trouble"; Wilson was especially concerned that "no basis shall be given for opinion abroad that we are mobilizing." The final demobilization of the National Guard was announced in February, although department commanders were under secret instructions not to muster out any more militiamen. Secretary of War Baker even dissuaded the President from calling an immediate meeting of the Council of National Defense, since "this might lead to the suggestion of immediate and active preparations on the part of the country."[3]

Not only was there hesitancy in beginning preparations, but there was also considerable confusion over what preparations to make. The preparedness movement had fixed men's minds in certain grooves which were hard to escape. Blotting out the international situation, some assumed that America's natural military response in any crisis would be to go on an armadillo-like defensive. When the Defense Advisory Council met, the War College Division indicated that it might be necessary to consider evacuating the North Atlantic ports and fortifying the line of the Appalachians. Rear Admiral Bradley A. Fiske, the little fighting-cock who had led the naval wing of the preparedness movement, warned members of the Lotus Club that "In case an attacking force is sent against us, we shall have only three weeks to get ready to fight." Work crews began construction on gun emplacements at Rockaway Beach off New York City. Not everyone was oblivious to the presence of the Allies between the United States and Germany, but it was by no means certain just how the United States would take part across the oceans in a European War. The military expert of *The New York Times*, for example, predicted that America's contribution to the war would be in terms of naval, financial, and logistical support. The United States would probably send only a token military force to show the flag on the Western front, just as the Russians had done. Interestingly enough, the German high command had made this same analysis.[4]

Meanwhile, a defense debate in and out of Congress ground on amid scenes of striking irrelevancy. Inertia carried the day. In mid-February, the new chairman of the House Military Affairs Committee, S. Hubert Dent of Alabama, announced that his committee "early in its hearings reached the conclusion unanimously that at least this was not an opportune time for any radical changes in the military policy of this country." The break in diplomatic relations apparently had done nothing to shake this assessment; at any rate, Dent declared that the 1917 Army Appropriations Bill would make provisions only for a regular force of 135,000 men. The bill had been drawn up, Pennsylvania's Thomas S. Crago made clear, "not as a war measure but as a great peace measure." The continuing campaign for universal military training showed a similar lack of contact with reality. The universal military training drive was powerfully strengthened, of course, by the vague feeling that full-scale war would make measures of compulsion necessary. The fact that the cau-

tious and unmartial ex-President Taft now embraced the cause emphasized the growing support for the idea. Even here, however, the sunny
attitudes of peace persisted. Universal military training, *The New York
Times* promised at the end of March, would "inflict no hardships on
anybody."[5]

The preparedness movement had been directed for too long against an
imaginary specter existing sometime in the future. Now, there was a real
enemy at hand, and many hardships were in store for the men who would
put on uniforms. America was locked into an infernal machine, its cogs
and ratchets now dragging her inexorably into the fire. In March the
Zimmermann telegram, urging that Mexico make common cause with
Germany, was published, and American merchant ships were sunk.
Prospects for peace or even an armed neutrality ebbed away. Wilson
called the newly elected Congress into special session for April 2, 1917.
At last the die was about to be cast. Along with the decision for war came
the decision for total war.[6]

*   *   *

There seemed to be no reason, in late March, for America to make a
maximum effort. Europe was far away, and the Allies, behind veils of
their own propaganda, were apparently in a secure position. A second,
and better organized, Spanish-American War was within the realms of
possibility, but America had come a long way, even since the Taft
Administration. Now the planning machinery produced by the preparedness movement and the psychological conditioning given the nation by
preparedness and the European War militated against a limited war.
Already many Americans accepted conscription and industrial mobilization as the natural handmaidens of war in this progressive era. The same
New York Times military expert who declared that America would not
seriously campaign in Europe predicted that a force of two million men
would be raised, probably by conscription, "as soon as the wheels could
be put in motion." In February, Baker had made plans for an initial
reliance on volunteering. He told Taft at the time that "great suspicion
[would be] aroused if compulsory military service were suggested at the
outset and before any opportunity to volunteer were given." But eventu-

ally the War Department planned to back up this volunteer force with men brought in by the draft. At least a million-man army was in the works from the beginning.[7]

As it happened, the volunteer system was not even attempted. It has been suggested that this was largely due to the eruption of Theodore Roosevelt onto the scene with plans to raise a volunteer division for service on the Western Front. Such a super Rough Riders unit as the colonel envisaged might well be popular enough to strip the regular armed forces of their best officers and men. The intrusion of political influence and amateurism onto the defense scene was the last thing that the professionals wanted. At any rate, the administration decided to slam the lid on the voluntary system. On March 24, the Advisory Council of the Council of National Defense recommended the enactment of Selective Service to the Cabinet, and Baker informed Wilson at the end of March that the Army would be "raised and maintained exclusively by selective draft."[8]

Selective service was not the universal military training for which preparedness enthusiasts still argued. Rather, it was a temporary and carefully tailored wartime expedient. The universal training propaganda had paved the way for its adoption, however, and once accepted by Congress, the draft, coupled with the resources of American industry, allowed the creation of a mass army of almost any size. Such a tool would suggest its own uses. *The New York Times* expert had rather weakly explained that the vast army to be created would be used for "home defense" and "domestic police" against pro-German insurrections. Domestic police did not prove to be so taxing an operation. There were better alternatives. Even before the outbreak of war, voices were demanding the dispatch of half a million men to France or even Russia. The existence of a mass army would almost drag America into full-scale intervention in Europe by its own weight. The nature of the war to come also helped. On April 2, in his war message to Congress, the most beautiful call to battle in American history, President Woodrow Wilson announced that America was fighting not just for her neutral rights but to "make the world safe for democracy." In such a lofty cause, it seemed only natural that Wilson called for the use of the nation's whole might. If unprepared, America had already braced herself to providing the force. God helping, we could do no other.[9]

13

Conclusion

The preparedness enthusiasts will drill for their country, will sacrifice time and money for their country, will die bravely for their country. But they will not think for their country. They regard that as pacifism.

—Walter Lippmann

At first glance, the United States seemed to offer a classic example of unpreparedness when she entered World War I. The country was able to field immediately only a small Regular Army and a small National Guard which, by lucky accident, had received some recent training on the Mexican Border. The Army which went to war was an obsolete one, organized on pre-1914 lines and underequipped. It had neither tanks nor gasmasks. There were only seven hundred and forty-two field pieces and forty-three heavier guns in the country, with an inadequate supply of ammunition. The Army possessed less than two thousand machine guns, and they were mostly out-of-date. The air arm consisted of hopeful plans and some handfuls of ill-assorted flying machines. Outside General Wood's door on Governor's Island, Plattsburgers drilled weekends using broomsticks for guns. The Navy was in a similar plight. Most of its ships were inneed of repair at the outbreak of war, and 90 percent of them were not fully manned; the Navy also lacked any experience in the antisub-marine warfare which was to be its main task.[1]

The head as well as the body of this military machine was weak. There were grave deficiencies in staffwork and planning. The Army General Staff in Washington had been cut back to a virtual skeleton by the National Defense Act of 1916, and what remained was not always effective. The War College Division, it developed, had never thought to supply itself with essential information about the elementals of logistics for large bodies of troops. The aged chief of staff fell asleep at one meeting with Cabinet officials, "Mars and Morpheus in one," as the secretary of the interior noted. The chief of staff for the American Expeditionary Force's supply services in World War I would later write: "The fourteen years . . . during which the General Staff had been in existence had not been spent in making plans for war, the purpose for which it was created, but in squabbling over the control of the routine peace-time administration and supply of the Regular Army and in at-tempts to place the blame for unpreparedness on Congress." In the end, the staff officer went on, "the whole General Staff and War Department organization, generally, fell like a house of cards and a new organization had to be created during the process of the war."[2]

Nonetheless, within a relatively short time, the United States was able to mobilize and arm vast forces. The nation's unpreparedness was not as great as it seemed. Leonard Wood had once written: "Modern war gives no time for preparation. Its approach is that of the avalanche and not of the glacier." Fortunately for America, this was only partly true. The theory had seemed to fit the conditions of Continental Europe, where heavily armed nations, separated only by lines on a map, were jammed together in mutual suspicion and rivalry. But the idea that wars would be won and lost by the forces immediately on hand had been disproved by the events of 1914. World War I was a war of industrial mobilization and attrition. When the United States entered the conflict in 1917, the country was doubly sheltered behind oceans which were more secure ramparts than the Army ever admitted, and behind the Allies. America did have enough time to summon up her armies. Since this was a coalition war, the Allies made up immediate deficiencies in field equipment. With a vast industrial base and a mighty manpower pool, the United States was able to perform prodigiously. By the end of 1918, the country had created an army of four million men and had deployed half of them overseas.[3]

If the preparedness movement had not created a force in being which could immediately participate in World War I, it had created, almost accidentally, the necessary preconditions for a full-scale war effort. As Walter Millis has pointed out, without the preparedness movement "it would have been psychologically as well as physically impossible for us to have gone in, when we did go in, as deeply as we did." A mass army was now acceptable. The incessant propaganda for universal military training had conditioned the public to accept conscription. The General Staff had already drawn up plans to train men under universal service in batches of 500,000 dispersed among sixteen localized training divisions. These plans were readily adapted to fit the needs of a national army raised by the draft. The Plattsburg Movement provided the necessary framework to recruit and train the vast number of reserve officers which the huge wartime force needed. At least a rudimentary effort had already been begun to coordinate the nation's industry with defense. Over a two-year period, preparedness had steeled America to meet the demands of total war.[4]

*   *   *

Doubtless it all could have been done in a better fashion. Certainly criticism has not been lacking. Years later, General of the Armies John J. Pershing would write musingly, "Let us suppose that, instead of adhering to the erroneous theory that neutrality forbade any move toward preparation, we had taken the precaution in the spring of 1916 to organize and equip an army of half a million combatant troops, together with the requisite number of supply troops for such a force." The resulting forty combat divisions, Pershing calculated, would have allowed America to intervene decisively in Europe in 1917. The commander of the AEF felt that such a force might even have deterred Germany from its decision to commence unrestricted submarine warfare and thus invite American intervention.[5]

This assessment ignores the realities of the times. There was about as much chance for the United States to create a 500,000-man field force in

1916 as there was for Congress to make Mohammedanism the state religion. A forty-division mobile army would have necessitated thousands of support troops. Such an army would never have been approved by Congress, and if created it could never have been recruited without a peacetime conscription for which the nation was not ready. Moreover, the purpose of such a formidable force in being could only have been participation, directly or indirectly, in the world war. In 1916, the United States was not prepared to accept the foreign policy which such a defense policy would imply. Very few influential people were willing to talk in such terms in the spring of 1916, and the members of the General Staff were not among them. Instead, Wilson spoke vaguely of defending the Monroe Doctrine, and the Army planned to defend the United States. The most alarmist Republicans, without administration support, only asked for a total regular force of 250,000 men, not quite enough to overwhelm the German army. The hard fact is that preparedness was proposed largely as a long-range, peacetime proposition, directed at various bugaboos that might threaten the United States after the end of the world war. Inevitably, this threw a subtle distortion into all military planning. The preparedness movement was aimed at the wrong war.

Indeed, one of the most disturbing aspects of the prewar defense movement was its lack of connection between power and policy. Military reforms were useful and necessary, but the reform movement functioned in a vacuum. It was Walter Lippmann who noted that "a nation which followed General Wood would be as defenseless as one which followed Mr. Bryan. The only difference between them is that Mr. Bryan wants a policy without armament and General Wood wants armament without a policy." Unrestrained by realistic goals, preparedness tended to become an absolute, an end, rather than a means. This trend was furthered by the lack of articulation between military and naval policy, which led to demands for both a huge army and a huge navy. Thus, military technicians called upon the United States to copy Germany, regardless of America's own special needs. Amid the tensions of world war, politicians bawled hoarsely for defense, urging the nation to defer to its generals. The urban upper middle class which had supported a good part of the earlier Progressive movement was now alarmed at the course of events, leaped aboard the defense bandwagon, and sought to hide some of its deeper insecurities over America's relative position in the world under khaki. The whole defense movement took shape in a realm apart from America's foreign policy. Preparedness was more the product of a Schumpeterian atavism than of a reasoned assessment of the country's national security requirements.[6]

Such weaknesses played into the hands of the opponents of preparedness, who questioned the need for defense when attack from abroad seemed so implausible. The accident of events passed these men by, and America did enter upon a war, so it is perhaps easy to dismiss them as shortsighted and irresponsible. But their points in the actual defense debate were by no means ill-taken. The fight over preparedness was hardly a Manichaean struggle between the forces of light and darkness. Men on both sides were intelligent, patriotic, and honest—as well as otherwise. Much of the effective resistance to extreme measures of preparedness came from rural congressmen who were not without shrewdness. Less impressionable than many preparedness advocates, these men were skeptical as to the likelihood of a physical attack on the country. They doubted that a large army could be raised in a free and unmilitaristic America, and they rejected conscription. Working out of a Jeffersonian tradition, these men emphatically did not see the barracks door as the gateway to a better America. They instinctively rejected imperialism or interventionism, and they nurtured an underlying suspicion of where a vast military apparatus might drag the United States. Their position was at least consistent, and it furnished a base from which to launch a powerful critique.

Preparedness might have evolved along more rational lines. It would have been possible for the United States to create an emergency force to meet any crisis created by the world war, and to have deferred permanent Army reform until later. The fact that these courses of action got inseparably mixed up helped to confuse the whole issue. But powerful forces on both sides might have opposed such a fusion of defense and foreign policy. At any rate, two necessary ingredients were lacking: presidential leadership and a clear understanding of the problem. Wilson, who had lofty ideas on international policy, never thought through their necessary relationship to the nation's armed might. While the administration finally endorsed preparedness, it was always abstractly. At any rate, the President never attempted to create a credible deterrent, or to gear force levels to policies. A man of peace, Wilson was always a little aloof from the military, and he scorned saber-rattling. Perhaps too, he feared that raising an emergency force might create the very emergency it was designed to prevent. The congressional debates largely took their cue from the demands of the General Staff, which was more concerned with Emory Upton than with Kaiser Wilhelm II. Any opportunity for linking power with policy was missed. Still, even a more rational peacetime preparedness would probably have made only a marginal difference. It is doubtful whether anything which could have been done within the limits of political possibility in 1916 would have kept the United States out of war in 1917. The full efforts of the country could be called forth only by the actual experience of war, not by the anticipations of peacetime.

*   *   *

America's participation in World War I fulfilled and destroyed the preparedness movement. By the end of the war, the United States had created the greatest army in its history and stood arrayed in mighty panoply. Ironically, however, in its quest for efficiency the military engine had brushed aside many of the early leaders in the preparedness fight. This was a war for professionals. Theodore Roosevelt was not allowed to raise the volunteer division of cavalry he had set his heart on. Leonard Wood, that imperfectly adjusted bearing in the military machine, was relegated to an obscure training command in South Carolina, a victim of politics and Pershing. The military revolution had devoured a few of its own children.

In the end, the preparedness movement was a military revolution which failed. Thermidor came with the end of the war. An ambitious program of postwar military legislation was quickly stifled in Congress. America was now in the mood for normalcy and retrenchment, not for heroics; enough men had now been exposed to Army life to quench most of the enthusiasm for universal military training. After Warren Harding's election, the great Navy planned in 1916 and delayed by the prosaic needs of the war was largely canceled at the Washington Conference. The postwar world seemed to hold no threats for George Babbitt. The Army reforms of 1916 were retained as part of the basic defense structure, but the structure itself was small. The strength of the Regular Army in 1929 stood at 130,000 men. The United States had largely rejected the theory of the preparedness movement. It would not arm itself in time of peace to await an indefinite enemy, a specter of a dragon.[7]

The preparedness movement which would begin before the next world war would have a more lasting effect. But then, the dragons would be real.

Notes

[1]Walter Millis, *Arms and Men: A Study in American Military History* (New York: G. P. Putnam's Sons, 1956), p. 214.
[2]Milwaukee *Free Press*, June 10, 1916, p. 2.

CHAPTER 1

[1]Hermann Hagedorn, *Leonard Wood: A Biography* (2 vols., New York: Harper, 1931), II, pp. 146-47. For a discussion of America's prewar security posture, see Richard W. Leopold, "The Emergence of America as a World Power: Some Second Thoughts," in John Braeman, Robert H. Bremner, Everett Walters, eds., *Change and Continuity in Twentieth Century America* (Columbus: Ohio State University Press, 1965), pp. 3-34.
[2]For Army statistics, see *War Department Annual Reports, 1914* (Washington, D.C.: Government Printing Office [GPO], 1915), passim. George Kibbe Turner, "Why We Have No Army," *McClure's Magazine* 37 (April 1912): 667.
[3]"Report of the Secretary of War," *War Department Annual Reports, 1913* (Washington, D.C.: GPO, 1914), p. 13. On the military legacy of the American Revolution, see Russell F. Weigley, *Towards an American Army: Military Thought from Washington to Marshall* (New York: Columbia University Press, 1962), pp. 7-8, 10-14.
[4]There are a number of good studies on the evolution of American defense policy. See especially Walter Millis, *Arms and Men: A Study in American Military History* (New York: G. P. Putnam's Sons, 1956), Russell F. Weigley, *History of the United States Army* (New York: MacMillan, 1967), and Harold and

Margaret Sprout, *The Rise of American Naval Power* (Princeton: Princeton University Press, 1939).

[5]W. W. Wotherspoon, "What Is the Matter with Our Army," *Senate Documents 38* (Document 621, 62d Congress, 2d Session, Washington, D.C.: GPO, 1912), pp. 9-16. Wotherspoon calculated that the United States government had to spend $1,470 a year for every soldier it obtained. Imperial Germany was able to field a regular army of 800,000 backed by a huge trained reserve on an annual military budget less than double that of the United States. See J. Scott Keltie, ed., *The Statesman's Year Book, 1914* (London: MacMillan & Co., 1914), pp. 412, 903. Congressman A. P. Gardner knowledgeably discusses the background of the Army rank and file in *Congressional Record*, 64th Congress, 2d Session (Washington, D.C.: GPO, 1917), p. 3376. Also, *Congressional Record*, 64th Congress, 1st Session (Washington, D.C.: GPO, 1916), pp. 4471, 4669. On civil rights legislation for soldiers, see Kirk H. Porter and Donald Bruce Johnson, *National Party Platforms*, 1840-1960 (Urbana: University of Illinois Press, 1961), p. 175.

[6]Hunter Liggett, "What Is the Matter with Our Army," *Senate Documents 38* (Document 621, 62d Congress, 2d Session, Washington, D.C.: GPO, 1912), p. 22.

[7]For one analysis of the military mind before World War I, see Samuel P. Huntington, *The Soldier and the State: The Theory and Politics of Civil-Military Relations* (Cambridge: Belknap Press, 1957), pp. 263-4.

[8]The best general account of the Army during the period before 1914 is in Weigley, *History of the United States Army*, pp. 313-41.

[9]Barton C. Hacker, "The War Department and the General Staff, 1898-1917" (M. A. thesis, University of Chicago, 1962), pp. 42-5.

[10]Hagedorn, *Leonard Wood*, passim.

[11]Elting E. Morison, *Turmoil and Tradition: A Study of the Life and Times of Henry L. Stimson* (New York: Atheneum, 1966), pp. 117-45.

[12]For a general discussion of these problems, see Henry L. Stimson, et al., "What Is the Matter with Our Army," *Senate Documents 38* (Document 621, 62d Congress, 21st Session, Washington, D.C.: GPO, 1912); Jack C. Lane, "Leonard Wood and the Shaping of American Defense Policy, 1900-1920" (Ph.D. dissertation, University of Georgia, 1963), p. 75; Otto L. Nelson, *National Security and the General Staff* (Washington, D.C.: Infantry Journal Press, 1956), p. 168.

[13]Wood to George T. Langhorn, June 11, 1914, Leonard Wood MSS, Box 79.

[14]John M. Palmer, *America in Arms* (New Haven: Yale University Press, 1941), p. 152.

[15]U.S. War Department, *Report of the Secretary of War in Response to House Resolution 707* (61st Congress, 2d Session, Washington, D.C.: GPO, 1910), p. 9.

[16]Morison, *Turmoil and Tradition*, p. 150; *The Nation* 94 (January 25, 1912): 78; Mabel E. Deutrich, *Struggle for Supremacy: The Career of General Fred C. Ainsworth* (Washington, D.C.: 1962), pp. 111-22.

[17]*The Nation* 94 (January 25, 1912): 78; Stimson, "Diary," p. 65, Henry L. Stimson MSS, Vol. 2; Deutrich, *Struggle for Supremacy*, pp. 111-22.

[18]*The Nation* 94 (January 4, 1912): 6 (June 20, 1912): 603; Stimson, "Memorandum of Sequence of Events," March 30, 1912, Henry L. Stimson MSS, Box 8.

[19]*Congressional Record*, 62d Congress, 2d Session, p. 7902; William Howard Taft, *Veto of the Army Appropriation Bill* (62d Congress, 2d Session, Washington, D.C.: GPO, 1912); Stimson, "Diary," pp. 96-100, Henry L. Stimson MSS, Vol. 2; Stimson to Taft, August 24, 1912, William Howard Taft MSS, Presidential Series II, Box 42; Frederic L. Huidekoper, *The Military Unpreparedness of the United States* (New York: MacMillan, 1915), pp. 398-403.

[20]Stimson to Winfred T. Denison, July 17, 1912, Henry L. Stimson MSS, Box 9; Morison, *Turmoil and Tradition*, pp. 189-90.

[21]*Congressional Record*, 62d Congress, 2d Session, p. 8083; Palmer, *America in Arms*, pp. 142-46; Stimson, "Diary," p. 116, Henry L. Stimson MSS, Vol. 2.

[22]"Report of the Chief of Staff, Appendix F: Report on the Organization of the Land Forces of the United States," *War Department Annual Reports, 1912* (Washington, D.C.: GPO, 1913), p. 371.

[23]"Report on the Organization of the Land Forces of the United States," p. 332.

[24]Leonard Wood to Taft, September 7, 1912, William Howard Taft MSS, Presidential Series II, Box 42; Stimson "Diary," pp. 117-18, Henry L. Stimson MSS, Vol. 2.

[25]Wood to Stimson, June 28, 1913, Leonard Wood MSS, Box 71; Scott to J. F. McGee, June 16, 1915, Hugh Scott MSS, Box 18; Martha Derthick, *The National Guard in Politics* (Cambridge: Harvard University Press, 1963), p. 31.

[26]Frederick L. Huidekoper, "Is the United States Prepared for War?", *The North American Review* (February, March 1906): 161-78; 391-407. On the Army League, see the extensive correspondence between Wood and Huidekoper in early 1913, Leonard Wood MSS, Box 71.

[27]John Garry Clifford, *The Citizen Soldiers: The Plattsburg Training Camp Movement, 1913-1920* (Lexington: University Press of Kentucky, 1972), pp. 1-29.

[28]Wood to Henry L. Stimson, September 19, 1913, Leonard Wood MSS, Box 71; Hagedorn, *Wood*, II, p. 146.

[29]Wood to Frederick Funston, July 9, 1913, Leonard Wood MSS, Box 73.

CHAPTER 2

[1]*The New York Times*, September 24, 1914, p. 10; October 2, 1914, p. 10; Spokane *Spokesman-Review*, August 13, 1914, p. 4; *The Nation* 99 (October 8, 1914): 420.

[2]Ellery Sedgwick to Leonard Wood, October 16, 1914, Leonard Wood MSS, Box 75; "Our Military Needs," *The New York Times*, October 19, 1914, p. 8.

[3]*The New York Times*, August 7, 1914, p. 3; October 16, 1914, p. 5; *Congressional Record*, 63d Congress, 2d Session, pp. 16745-47.

[4]*The New York Times*, October 31, 1914, p. 4. One of the "plans" was certainly merely the unauthorized doodlings of one Baron Von Edelsheim, a lieutenant of Guard Uhlans in the Imperial German Army who had broached such a scheme in 1901. See Alfred Vagts, "Hopes and Fears of an American-German War, 1870-1915," Part II, *Political Science Quarterly* 55 (March 1940): 63-65. McGrath to Cecil Spring-Rice, Theodore Roosevelt MSS, Outgoing Correspondence, Box 91; Theodore Roosevelt, "The International Posse Comitatus," Part II, *New York Sunday Times*, November 8, 1914, V, p. 10; "Preparation Without Militarism," *New York Sunday Times*, November 15, 1914, V, p. 5.

[5]Breckinridge, "Diary," June 16, 1915, Henry S. Breckinridge MSS.

[6]See Robert Osgood, *Ideals and Self-Interest in American Foreign Relations* (Chicago: The University of Chicago Press, 1953), p. 201.

[7]Franklin D. Roosevelt to Eleanor Roosevelt, August 5, 1914, in Elliot Roosevelt, ed., *F.D.R.: His Personal Letters* (4 vols., New York: Duell, Sloan & Pierce, 1947-50), II, p. 243; Bradley Fiske, "Diary," September 29, 1914, November 9, 1914, October 30, 1914, November 3, 1914, Bradley Fiske MSS.

[8]*The New York Times*, November 27, 1914, p. 10; Frederick L. Paxson, *American Democracy and the World War: Pre-War Years* (Boston: Houghton-Mifflin Co., 1936), p. 201; "This Is Not Militarism," *The New York Times*, December 8, 1914, p. 10.

[9]*The New York Times*, December 2, 1914, p. 1; *Washington Post*, December 2, 1914, p. 6; Cleveland *Plain Dealer*, December 8, 1914, p. 1.

[10]*The New York Times*, December 8, 1914, p. 1; Charles Seymour, ed., *The Intimate Papers of Colonel House* (4 vols., Boston and New York: Houghton-Mifflin Co., 1926-1928), I, pp. 298-99.

[11]Woodrow Wilson to Edward M. House, December 9, 1914, Wilson MSS,

Series II, Box 111; Seymour, *House*, I, p. 299; House to Wilson, December 11, 1914, Wilson MSS, Series II, Box 111; *The New York Times*, December 2, 1914, p. 3.

[12]*The New Republic* 1 (December 5, 1914): 5; Taft to Gus Karges, December 6, 1914; Taft to Robert L. O'Brien, December 8, 1914, William Howard Taft MSS, Series VIII, Box 24; William Henry Harbaugh, "Wilson, Roosevelt, and Interventionism," (Ph.D. dissertation, Northwestern University, 1954), p. 41; Osgood, *Ideals and Self-Interest*, p. 201; W. D. Foulke to Roosevelt, December 7, 1914, Theodore Roosevelt MSS, Incoming Correspondence, Box 278.

[13]James Kerney, *The Political Education of Woodrow Wilson* (New York: The Century Co., 1926), p. 352; William G. McAdoo, *Crowded Years* (Boston and New York: Houghton-Mifflin Co., 1931), p. 340; "America Unready," *The Literary Digest* 50 (June 5, 1915): 1314-15; Oswald Garrison Villard, *Fighting Years: Memoirs of a Liberal Editor* (New York: Harcourt, Brace & Co., 1939), p. 287; James C. Hemphill, "Mr. Wilson's Cabinet," *North American Review* 202 (July 1915): 115; Breckinridge, "Diary," June 16, 1915, Henry S. Breckenridge MSS; Wood, "Diary," September 2, 1914, Leonard Wood MSS, Vol. 9; "Report of the Secretary of War; Report of the Chief of Staff," *War Department Annual Reports, 1914* (Washington, D.C.: GPO, 1914), passim; *Congressional Record*, 63d Congress, 3d Session, p. 4418.

[14]Henry Cabot Lodge to Roosevelt, December 11, 1914, Theodore Roosevelt MSS, Incoming Correspondence, Box 278; Oswald Garrison Villard to Joseph Tumulty, December 11, 1914, Wilson MSS, Series VI, Folder 1935; *The New York Times*, November 23, 1914, p. 16; November 24, 1916, p. 5; Wilson to Lindley M. Garrison, December 21, 1914, Wilson MSS, Series II, Box 112; Garrison to Wood, December 16, 1914, Leonard Wood MSS, Box 74.

[15]Lindley M. Garrison, as interviewed by Gregory Mason, "America Unready," *The Outlook* 58 (December 30, 1914): 997-99.

[16]*The New York Times*, December 16, 1914, p. 1; "Nation-Wide Press Poll on Army and Navy Increase," *Literary Digest* 50 (January 23, 1915): 137, 166. In the poll, 272 editors out of about 400 found the nation's defenses inadequate. Also, 240 of the editors wanted a larger army, and 285 wanted a larger navy. Wood to Henry T. Allen, January 7, 1915, Leonard Wood MSS, Box 84; *New York Sunday Times*, January 31, 1915, IV, p. 5.

[17]Francis Vinton Greene to Charles Francis Adams, undated, Hugh Scott MSS, Box 17; *The New York Times*, July 8, 1915, p. 15; F. V. Greene to Stimson, January 21, 1915; Stimson to F. V. Greene, January 28, 1915, Henry L. Stimson MSS, Box 121.

[18]W. C. Church to Stimson, January 5, 1915, Henry L. Stimson MSS, Box 120; Stimson to S. Stanwood Menken, February 4, 1915, Henry L. Stimson

MSS, Box 122; *The New York Times*, January 11, 1915, p. 6; February 15, 1915, p. 6. Professional advisers insured that the league would support defense by dreadnoughts and a mobile army, and not just call for coast defense guns and submarines. The league did need professional advice; the first league membership certificates were engraved, without apparent irony, with pictures of an obsolescent coast defense gun and an outdated battleship. See certificate in Henry L. Stimson MSS, Box 122.

[19]Harbaugh has a very sane treatment of this in "Wilson, Roosevelt, and Interventionism," pp. 38, 113. See also the account of the public polls showing a 3-2 majority against a bigger army and navy in "Nation-Wide Press Poll," *The Literary Digest*: 168.

[20]Wood, "Diary," December 23, 1914, Leonard Wood MSS, Vol. 9; *The Outlook* 59 (April 14, 1915): 850.

[21]*The New York Times*, January 5, 1915, p. 7; January 6, 1915, p. 11; January 7, 1915, p. 5; E. David Cronon, ed., *The Cabinet Diaries of Josephus Daniels* (Lincoln: University of Nebraska Press, 1963), p. 91.

[22]William Crozier to Stimson, March 3, 1915, Henry L. Stimson MSS, Box 123; *Congressional Record*, 63d Congress, 3d Session, pp. 2062-68, 2232; *The New Republic* 1 (January 30, 1915): 3; *The New York Times*, January 23, 1915, p. 8.

[23]George Chamberlain to Garrison, January 26, 1915, File 2237877, National Archives, Army Adjutant General's Office, Record Group 94.

[24]Wood to L. S. Rowe, February 11, 1915, Leonard Wood MSS, Box 83; Breckinridge, "Diary," February 4, 1915, Henry S. Breckinridge MSS.

[25]*Congressional Record*, 63d Congress, 3d Session, p. 102; U.S. Congress, House Committee on Naval Affairs, *Hearings on the Naval Appropriations Bill* (63d Congress, 3d Session, Washington, D.C.: GPO, 1915), pp. 1059-93; *The New York Times*, December 17, 1914, p. 9.

[26]*The New York Times*, February 19, 1915, p. 8; January 15, 1915, p. 2; *Congressional Record*, 63d Congress, 3d Session, pp. 4322-3; 4415-25.

[27]Richard Parker to Wood, March 4, 1915, Leonard Wood MSS, Box 84; *The New York Times*, April 12, 1915, p. 8; *Congressional Record*, 63d Congress, 3d Session, pp. 4321-22.

[28]"Will the Close of the War Find America Unprepared to Defend Itself?", *Current Opinion* 58 (April 1915): 224; Thomas Nelson Page to Wilson, April 19, 1915, Wilson MSS, Series II, Box 119.

[29]Arthur S. Link, *Wilson: The Struggle for Neutrality, 1914-1915* (Princeton: Princeton University Press, 1960), p. 591; Fiske, "Diary," March 10, 15, 16, 17, Bradley Fiske MSS.

[30]Link, *Wilson: The Struggle for Neutrality*, pp. 368-455.

[31]*New York Sunday Times*, May 16, 1915, II, p. 1; House to Wilson, May 11, 1915, Wilson MSS, Series II, Box 120; Frank Freidel, *Franklin D. Roosevelt; The Apprenticeship* (Boston: Little Brown & Co., 1952), p. 251; Taft to Wilson, May 10, 1915, William Howard Taft MSS, Series VIII, Vol. 31; James W. Gerard to Wilson, June 8, 1915, Wilson MSS, Series II, Box 121.

[32]Roosevelt to Henry T. Allen, July 10, 1915, Theodore Roosevelt MSS, Outgoing Correspondence, Box 93; Herbert W. Hobbs, *Leonard Wood, Administrator, Soldier, and Citizen* (New York: G. P. Putnam's Sons, 1920), p. 154; Armin Rappaport, *The Navy League of the United States* (Detroit: Wayne State University Press, 1962), pp. 49-50; *The New York Times*, May 12, 1915, p. 1; June 12, 1915, p. 1.

[33]White to Charles M. Hargger, May 15, 1915, William Allen White MSS, Letter Press Book 13; *New York Sunday Times*, June 6, 1915, II, p. 3; "Preparedness for What," *The New Republic* 3 (June 26, 1915): 188.

[34]House, "Diary," July 10, 1915, Edward M. House MSS, Vol. 7; House to Wilson, July 14, 1915, quoted in Seymour, *House*, II, p. 19.

[35]Wood, "Diary," July 3, 1915, Leonard Wood MSS, Vol. 9; Joseph P. Tumulty, *Woodrow Wilson as I Knew Him* (Garden City: Doubleday, Page & Co., 1921), pp. 240-41.

[36]*The New York Times*, June 28, 1915, p. 8; Osgood, *Ideals and Self-Interest*, p. 164; George Herring, "Lindley M. Garrison and the Preparedness Movement" (M.A. thesis, University of Virginia, 1961), p. 30. For examples of particularly scathing attacks on Daniels, see *Life* 65 (May 1915), with its series of cartoons showing Daniels in a dress and wig demolishing the Navy. Link, *Wilson: The Struggle for Neutrality*, p. 592.

[37]Wilson to Daniels, Wilson to Garrison, July 21, 1915, Wilson MSS, Series VI, File 1935; Link, *Wilson: The Struggle for Neutrality*, p. 446; *The New York Times*, July 24, 1915, p. 1.

[38]*The New York Times*, July 22, 1915, pp. 1, 5; July 24, 1915, p. 1; "Preparedness for What?," *The New Republic*: 188.

CHAPTER 3

[1]Enclosure, Tilden Blodgett to Root, February 24, 1915, Elihu Root MSS, Box 129.

[2]File 2239236(B), National Archives, Army Adjutant General's Office, Record Group 94; Leonard Wood to Scott (Personal and Confidential), January 28, 1915, Hugh Scott MSS, Box 17; *The New York Times*, February 2, 1915, p. 7; File 8911-3, April 27, 1915, National Archives, Army War College Division,

Record Group 165; Enclosure, Tasker Bliss to Scott, July 8, 1915, Hugh Scott MSS, Box 19; W. W. Wotherspoon to Wood, August 24, 1914, Leonard Wood MSS, Box 74.

[3]Copy General Order No. 10, February 23, 1915, Hugh Scott MSS, Box 17; Scott to J. A. Ryan, May 25, 1915, Hugh Scott MSS, Box 18; Johnson Hagood to Wood, May 13, 1915, Leonard Wood MSS, Box 85.

[4]Garrison to M. M. Macomb; Bliss to M. M. Macomb, March 11, 1915, File 9053-1, National Archives, Army War College Division, Record Group 165.

[5]Garrison to Macomb, Bliss to Macomb, March 11, 1915, File 9053-1; Bliss to Macomb, March 17, 1915, File 9053-3, National Archives, Army War College Division, Record Group 165.

[6]Quoted in Macomb to Army War College Division Officers, April 23, 1915, File 9053-18, National Archives, Army War College Division, Record Group 165.

[7]Macomb to Secretary, General Staff, April 9, 1915, File 9053-3; C. Crawford to Secretary, General Staff, April 20, 1915, File 9053-8, National Archives, Army War College Division, Record Group 165; Garrison to Scott, April 21, 1915; Scott to Frank R. McCoy, April 30, 1915, Hugh Scott MSS, Box 18.

[8]Scott to Wood, March 1, 1915, Leonard Wood MSS, Box 82; George Marvin, "Scott, U. S. A.," *The World's Work* 29 (February 1915): 422-29; *The Nation* 101 (Auguat 12, 1915): 197; Taft to W. Gordon McCabe, September 2, 1916, William Howard Taft MSS, Series VIII, Vol. 51.

[9]Frederick M. Palmer, *Bliss, Peacemaker* (New York: Dodd, Mead & Co., 1934), p. 1; John M. Palmer, *America in Arms* (New Haven: Yale University Press, 1941), p. 299; "War Chiefs of the Army," *The World's Work* 30 (October 1915): 669.

[10]Daniel R. Beaver, *Newton D. Baker and the American War Effort, 1917-1919* (Lincoln: University of Nebraska Press, 1966), p. 12; David A. Lockmiller, *Enoch H. Crowder; Soldier, Lawyer, and Statesman* (University of Missouri Studies, Vol. 27, Columbia: University of Missouri Press, 1955), passim.

[11]Scott to Garrison, May 13, 1915, Hugh Scott MSS, Box 18; Bliss to Garrison (Confidential), May 19, 1915, File 9053-10; Macomb to Scott, April 1915, File 8938-2, National Archives, Army War College Division, Record Group 165; Scott to H. D. Slater, May 26, 1915, Hugh Scott MSS, Box 18.

[12]Wood to Tasker Bliss, August 18, 1915, Leonard Wood MSS, Box 80; George Van Horn Moseley to Wood, September 3, 1916, Leonard Wood MSS, Box 86; Bliss to Macomb, May 26, 1915, File 9053—; Scott to Macomb, June 16, 1915, File 9053-33; Macomb to Scott, June 18, 1915, File 9053-34, National Archives, Army War College Division, Record Group 165.

[13]"Epitome of Military Policy," July 10, 1915, File 9053-49, National Archives, Army War College Division, Record Group 165.

[14]"Study on Subject No. 1," May 26, 1915, File 9053-22; "Epitome of Military Policy," July 10, 1915, File 9053-49, National Archives, Army War College Division, Record Group 165.

[15]"Report of the Secretary of War," Appendix C, *War Department Annual Reports,* 1915 (Washington, D.C.: GPO, 1916), pp. 129-30; William Y. Smith, "The Search for National Security Planning Machinery, 1900-1947" (Ph.D. dissertation: Harvard University, 1960), p. 84.

[16]Study No. 7, May 1915, File 9053-22; Memorandum for Chief of Staff on Report of Captain Nolan, June 30, 1915, File 9053-40, National Archives, Army War College Division, Record Group 165.

[17]Macomb to Scott, May 8, 1915, File 9053-18; Study No. 7, May 1915, File 9053-22; Memorandum for Chief of Staff on Report of Captain Nolan, June 30, 1915, File 9053-40, National Archives, Army War College Division, Record Group 165; "Report of the Secretary of War," Appendix C, *War Department Annual Reports*, 1915, p. 117.

[18]Alfred Vagts, *Landing Operations* (Harrisburg: Military Service Publishing Co., 1946), pp. 506, 526; Macomb to Scott, June 21, 1915, File 9053-38, National Archives, Army War College Division, Record Group 165.

[19]Wood, "Diary," July 10, 1915, Leonard Wood MSS, Box 9; Wotherspoon to Wood, August 24, 1914, Leonard Wood MSS, Box 74.

[20]Memoranda by W. H. Johnston, June 17, 1915, File 9053-38; August 14, 1915, File 9053-71; Vote at Meeting of War College Division, June 29, 1915, File 9053-46, National Archives, Army War College Division, Record Group 165.

[21]Garrison to Wilson, September 17, 1915, Wilson MSS, Series II, Box 124; Garrison to Macomb, August 2, 1915, File 9053-49; Crowder to the Adjutant General, May 1, 1915, File 9053-10, National Archives, Army War College Division, Record Group 165.

[22]Macomb to Scott, File 9053-49, National Archives, Army War College Division, Record Group 165.

[23]Scott to Macomb, May 4, 1915, File 9053-36; Macomb to Scott, June 21, 1915, File 9053-38, National Archives, Army War College Division, Record Group 165; "Report of the Secretary of War," Appendix C, *War Department Annual Reports, 1915*, p. 35.

[24]Crowder to the Adjutant General, May 1, 1915, File 9053-10; Crowder to Garrison, July 31, 1915, File 9053—; unsigned memorandum, July 1, 1915, File 9053-115, National Archives, Army War College Division, Record Group 165.

[25]Crowder to Garrison, July 31, 1915, File 9053—; Condensed Outline of

Military Policy Recommended by Secretary of War, August 21, 1915, File 9053-75, National Archives, Army War College Division, Record Group 165.

[26]Macomb to Scott, September 4, 1915, File 9053-84, National Archives, Army War College Division, Record Group 165; "Report of the Secretary of War," *War Department Annual Reports, 1915*, p. 32.

[27]W. H. Johnston to Wood, November 24, 1915, Leonard Wood MSS, Box 90; Garrison to Wilson, September 17, 1915, Wilson MSS, Series II, Box 124.

[28]"Report of the Secretary of War," *War Department Annual Reports, 1915*, p. 35.

[29]Frederick M. Palmer, *Newton D. Baker; America at War* (2 vols., New York: Dodd, Mead & Co., 1931), I, pp. 40-41; Macomb to Bliss, August 24, 1915, File 6966-152, National Archives, Army War College Division, Record Group 165; F. C. Marshall to Secretary, War College Division, Leonard Wood MSS, Box 78.

CHAPTER 4

[1]Wood to Edward Carpenter, June 10, 1915, Leonard Wood MSS, Box 81; George Van Horn Moseley, "One Soldier's Journey," p. 148, George Van Horn Moseley MSS, Box 1A; Wood to E. S. Ferguson, July 10, 1915, Leonard Wood MSS, Box 80; Villard to Wilson, December 16, 1914, Wilson MSS, Series II, Box 111.

[2]Wood to E. St. J. Strachey, July 8, 1916, Leonard Wood MSS, Box 90; Peyton C. March, *The Nation at War* (New York: Doubleday, Doran, 1932), p. 58; Hermann Hagedorn, *Leonard Wood: A Biography* (2 vols., New York: Harpers, 1931), II, p. 117; Jack C. Lane, "Leonard Wood and the Shaping of American Defense Policy, 1900-1920" (Ph.D. dissertation, University of Georgia, 1963), p. 105; *The Nation* 100 (March 18, 1915): 293; Scott to Wood, November 17, 1914, Leonard Wood MSS, Box 75.

[3]Lane, "Wood," pp. 110-11; Wood to Frank McCoy, January 14, 1915, Leonard Wood MSS, Box 80; Wood to Roosevelt, December 30, 1914, Theodore Roosevelt MSS, Incoming Correspondence, Box 280; Wood to James Parker (Confidential and Personal), Leonard Wood MSS, Box 84; Wood to Scott, February 5, 1915, Scott MSS, Box 17.

[4]Arthur Hoffman to Wood, February 6, 1915; Wood to Adjutant General, March, 1915, Leonard Wood MSS, Box 85; *The New York Times*, March 1, 1915, pp. 1, 4.

[5]Scott to Wood, March 1, 1915, Leonard Wood MSS, Box 82; Wood to Scott, March 2, 1915, Hugh Scott MSS, Box 17; *The New York Times*, March 2, 1915,

p. 8; "Will the Close of War Find America Unprepared to Defend Herself?," *Current Opinion* 58 (April 1915): 227; A. M. White to Stimson, December 14, 1915, Henry L. Stimson MSS, Box 140; Frederick L. Paxson, *American Democracy and the World War: Pre-War Years 1913-1917* (Boston: Houghton-Mifflin Co., 1936), p. 289; Garrison to Wood, March 11, 1915, Leonard Wood MSS, Box 82.

[6]Wood, "Diary," March 16, 1915, Leonard Wood MSS, Box 9; Barclay Parsons to Wood, May 3, 1915, Leonard Wood MSS, Box 84; Bishop Greer to Wilson, March 2, 1915, Leonard Wood MSS, Box 83.

[7]Wood to M. M. Macomb, October 28, 1915; November 26, 1915, Leonard Wood MSS, Box 89; Ralph Barton Perry, *The Plattsburg Movement* (New York: E. P. Dutton Co., 1921), pp. 8-9.

[8]A. Lawrence Lowell to Wood, December 1, 1916; Constant Cordier to Wood, February 9, 1916, Leonard Wood MSS, Box 89; Wood to Walter Trumbull, December 24, 1914, Leonard Wood MSS, Box 75; Arthur T. Hadley to Wood, January 28, 1916, Leonard Wood MSS, Box 89; Scott to Wood, October 18, 1915, Hugh Scott MSS, Box 20.

[9]John Garry Clifford, *The Citizen Soldiers; The Plattsburg Training Camp Movement, 1913-1920* (Lexington: The University Press of Kentucky, 1972), pp. 1-24; Francis Russell, *The Great Interlude* (New York: McGraw-Hill, 1964), p. 10; Perry, *The Plattsburg Movement*, pp. 14-17; Drinker to Wood, December 18, 1914; Wood to Drinker, December 21, 1914, Leonard Wood MSS, Box 79.

[10]Clifford, *The Citizen Soldiers*, pp. 25-29; Perry, *The Plattsburg Movement*, p. 17; H. B. Hutchins to Wood, July 10, 1915, Leonard Wood MSS, Box 78; Roger Pierce to Wood, February 6, 1915, March 16, 1915, Leonard Wood MSS, Box 84.

[11]Scott to Henry S. Howland, April 5, 1915, Hugh Scott MSS, Box 18; *The New York Times*, May 25, 1915, p. 14; J. G. Harbord to Wood, May 11, 1915, Leonard Wood MSS, Box 85; Perry, *The Plattsburg Movement*, p. 20.

[12]Unsigned to Wood, May 13, 1915, Leonard Wood MSS, Box 83; Roosevelt to Wood, May 24, 1915, Leonard Wood MSS, Box 84; Scott to J. J. Slocum, June 17, 1915, Hugh Scott MSS, Box 18.

[13]Wood, "Diary," June 3, 1915, Leonard Wood MSS, Box 9; George E. Downey to Garrison, June 5, 1915; Wood to Garrison, June 26, 1915, Leonard Wood MSS, Box 82.

[14]Grenville Clark to Roosevelt, November 19, 1914, Theodore Roosevelt MSS, Incoming Correspondence, Box 277; Martin Mayer, *Emory Buckner* (New York: Harper & Row, 1968), pp. 100-01; H. S. Howland to Scott, February 5, 1915, Hugh Scott MSS, Box 17; Scott to H. S. Howland, April 5, 1915, Hugh Scott MSS, Box 18.

[15]For this whole episode, John Garry Clifford's *The Citizen Soldiers* is authoritative and indispensable. Pp. 54-91 deal with the Plattsburg Camp. See also "The Business Men's Training Camp at Plattsburg," *The Scientific American* 113 (August 28, 1915): 182; Perry, *The Plattsburg Movement*, pp. 26-27; *The New York Times*, May 11, 1915, p. 4; Russell, *The Great Interlude*, pp. 10-11; Wood to Drinker, July 16, 1915, Leonard Wood MSS, Box 80.

[16]Russell, *The Great Interlude*, pp. 10-11; Edwin R. Lewinson, *John Purroy Mitchell; The Boy Mayor of New York* (New York: Astra Books, 1965), p. 192; Perry, *The Plattsburg Movement*, pp. 26-30; Wood to B. H. Hulbert, Leonard Wood MSS, Box 85; *The New York Times*, June 30, 1915, p. 6.

[17]Russell, *The Great Interlude*, p. 12; "The Business Men's Camp," *The Scientific American*: 183; Drinker to Wood, August 10, 1915, Leonard Wood MSS, Box 80; Perry, *The Plattsburg Movement*, pp. 31, 38.

[18]Perry, *The Plattsburg Movement*, p. 42; Russell, *The Great Interlude*, pp. 9, 13-19; Richard Harding Davis, "The Plattsburg Idea," *Collier's* 56 (October 9, 1915): 7-8; *New York Sunday Times*, August 15, 1915, VI, p. 1.

[19]"A Plattsburg 'Rookie' Speaks," *American Review of Reviews* 53 (February 1916): 225; C. H. Brent to Wood, August 19, 1916, Leonard Wood MSS, Box 86.

[20]John O'Hara, *From the Terrace* (New York: Random House, 1958), p. 177; Perry, *The Plattsburg Movement*, pp. 56-57; "The Plattsburg Idea," *The New Republic* 4 (October 9, 1915): 247.

[21]Perry, *The Plattsburg Movement*, p. 56, passim.

[22]Wood to Samuel Gompers, September 20, 1915, Leonard Wood MSS, Box 82; Wood to Frank R. McCoy, September 26, 1916, Leonard Wood MSS, Box 91; Wood to William M. Ingraham, May 12, 1916, Leonard Wood MSS, Box 89; Ralph M. Easley to Wood, March 16, 1916, Leonard Wood MSS, Box 92. A further idea of the social composition of the Plattsburgers can be gathered from the fact that almost half the men at the two 1915 businessman's camps were graduates of Harvard, Yale, or Princeton. Perry, *The Plattsburg Movement*, p. 38.

[23]Wood to Edward M. House, August 12, 1915, Leonard Wood MSS, Box 83; Dudley Field Malone to Wilson, August 5, 1915, August 16, 1915; Wilson to Malone, August 19, 1915, Wilson MSS, Series II, Box 123; Russell, *The Great Interlude*, p. 16; Drinker to Wood, August 17, 1915, Leonard Wood MSS, Box 80.

[24]Russell, *The Great Interlude*, pp. 16-18.

[25]Drinker to Roosevelt, Theodore Roosevelt MSS, Incoming Correspondence, Box 288; Scott to Wood, September 1, 1915, Hugh Scott MSS, Box 20; E. B. Johns to Wood, August 30, 1915, Leonard Wood MSS, Box 85; Perry, *The*

Plattsburg Movement, pp. 45-46; "The Ex-Presidential War on the War Department," *Literary Digest* 51 (September 11, 1915): 514; *The New York Times*, August 26, 1915, p. 8.

²⁶Clifford, *The Citizen Soldiers*, pp. 92-117; also, Russell, *The Great Interlude*, p. 20; Grenville Clark to Wood, September 19, 1915; Wood to Clark, September 30, 1915, Leonard Wood MSS, Box 89; Wood, "Diary," September 29, 1915, Leonard Wood MSS, Vol. 9; Perry, *The Plattsburg Movement*, pp. 61, 66-67; Clark to Garrison, November 8, 1915, File 2338727, National Archives, Army Adjutant General's Office, Record Group 94.

²⁷Clark to Garrison, November 8, 1915, File 2338727, National Archives, Army Adjutant General's Office, Record Group 94; Clark to Roosevelt, November 30, 1915, Theodore Roosevelt MSS, Incoming Correspondence, Box 291.

²⁸Clark to Garrison, November 8, 1915; War Department Special Orders 265, November 13, 1915; Proceedings of the Board, January 10, 1916, File 2338727, National Archives, Army Adjutant General's Office, Record Group 94; Perry, *The Plattsburg Movement*, pp. 80-81; DeLancey K. Jay to Wood, November 13, 1915; Wood to Jay, November 15, 1915, Leonard Wood MSS, Box 90.

²⁹Frank Freidel, *Franklin D. Roosevelt: The Apprenticeship* (Boston: Little Brown and Co., 1952), p. 256; Hagedorn, *Wood*, II, p. 173; Wood to Roosevelt, September 17, 1915, Theodore Roosevelt MSS, Incoming Correspondence, Box 289.

CHAPTER 5

¹Joseph Tumulty to Wilson, August 9, 1915, Wilson MSS, Series II, Box 123.

²Tumulty to Wilson, August 9, 1915; House to Wilson, August 8, 1915, Wilson MSS, Series II, Box 123; Hay to Burleson, July 27, 1915; Burleson to Wilson, July 28, 1915, Wilson MSS, Series II, Box 122.

³Breckinridge, "Diary," August 24, 1915, Henry S. Breckinridge MSS.

⁴Garrison to Wilson, August, 1915; Wilson to Garrison, August 16, 1915, Wilson MSS, Series VI, File 1935; George C. Herring, "Lindley M. Garrison and the Preparedness Movement" (M.A. thesis, University of Virginia, 1961), pp. 47-48.

⁵Arthur S. Link, *Wilson: Confusions and Crises, 1915-1916* (Princeton: Princeton University Press, 1965), p. 19; Wilson to Garrison, August 19, 1915, Wilson MSS, Series VI, File 1935; *The New York Times*, September 2, 1915, p. 1; Wilson to Oswald Garrison Villard, September 7, 1915; Ray Stannard Baker, *Woodrow Wilson: Life and Letters* (8 vols., Garden City: Doubleday, Doran & Co., 1937), VI, p. 14; John Hays Hammond to House, September 2, 1915,

Edward M. House MSS, Drawer 9, File 31; Medill McCormick to Roosevelt, November 26, 1915, Theodore Roosevelt MSS, Incoming Correspondence, Box 291; Thomas Dixon to Wilson, September 10, 1915, Wilson MSS, Series II, Box 124.

⁶Herring, "Garrison," p. 48; *The New York Times*, September 3, 1915, p. 3; House, "Diary," September 24, 1915, Edward M. House MSS, Vol. 7; *The New York Times*, October 14, 1915, p. 1; October 16, 1915, pp. 1, 4; *The Nation* 101 (October 14, 1915): 452-53.

⁷Josephus Daniels to Wilson, August 20, 1915, Wilson MSS, Series II, Box 123; W. H. Cowles to Roosevelt, October 23, 1915, Theodore Roosevelt MSS, Incoming Correspondence, Box 289; *Washington Post*, October 29, 1915, p. 6.

⁸Herring, "Garrison," pp. 59-60.

⁹William F. Sadler to Tumulty, October 23, 1915, Wilson MSS, Series VI, File 1935; Scott to R. K. Evans, November 1, 1915, Hugh Scott MSS, Box 20; Memorandum by Secretary of War, October 29, 1915, File 9053-12, National Archives, Army War College Division, Record Group 165.

¹⁰William F. Sadler to Wilson, October 30, 1915, Wilson MSS, Series II, Box 126; U.S. Congress, House Committee on Military Affairs, *Hearings on H. R. 12766: To Increase the Efficiency of the Military Establishment of the United States* (64th Congress, 1st Session, 2 vols., Washington, D.C.: GPO, 1916), II, pp. 1009-11; *Army and Navy Journal* 53 (October 30, 1915): 273; Wilson to Garrison, undated, Wilson MSS, Series VI, File 42.

¹¹Garrison to Tumulty, November 1, 1915; Wilson to Tumulty, November 1, 1915, Wilson MSS, Series VI, File 42; Hay to Wilson, November 4, 1915, File 2339367, National Archives, Army Adjutant General's Office, Record Group 94; Wilson to Hay, November 5, 1915, Wilson MSS, Series VI, File 1935.

¹²James Kerney, *The Political Education of Woodrow Wilson* (New York: The Century Co., 1926), p. 358; Henry Watterson, *History of the Manhattan Club* (New York: DeVinne Press, 1915), pp. iii, xxxiii; House, "Diary," November 5, 1915, Edward M. House MSS, Vol. 7; *The Nation* 101 (November 11, 1915): 561.

¹³Ray Stannard Baker and William E. Dodd, eds., *The Public Papers of Woodrow Wilson* (8 vols., New York and London: Harper & Bros., 1925-1927), I, pp. 384-392; *The New York Times*, November 5, 1915, pp. 1, 4.

¹⁴*The New York Times*, November 12, 1915, p. 7; New York *World*, November 5, 1915, p. 12; *The New Republic* 5 (November 13, 1915): 26.

¹⁵Link, *Wilson: Confusions and Crises*, pp. 27-8; Herring, "Garrison," pp. 67-77; Timothy G. McDonald, "Southern Democratic Congressmen and the First World War, August 1914-April 1917" (Ph.D. dissertation, University of Washington, 1962), p. 168; *Current Opinion* 59 (December 1915): 379.

[16]Herring, "Garrison," pp. 67-77; *The New York Times*, November 18, 1915, p. 4; November 22, 1915, p. 1; February 5, 1916, p. 2; December 9, 1915, p. 5; Putnam to Park Benjamin, November 30, 1915, George Haven Putnam MSS.

[17]Tasker Bliss to Barclay Parsons, November 23, 1915, Bliss MSS, Box 195; Herring, "Garrison," pp. 79-80; War Department Memoranda, File 9054-1, 9054-13, National Archives, Army War College Division, Record Group 165; *The New York Times*, December 10, 1915, p. 6; Scott to C. D. McMurdo, December 11, 1915, Hugh Scott MSS, Box 21; Bliss to E. St. J. Greble, December 10, 1915, Tasker Bliss MSS, Box 196.

[18]Wood to Frederick Huidekoper, October 19, 1915, Leonard Wood MSS, Box 85; Scott to Leonard Wood, December 1, 1915, Hugh Scott MSS, Box 21; Garrison to Hay, December 1, 1915, Tasker Bliss MSS, Box 195; Scott to E. St. J. Greble, December 8, 1915, Hugh Scott MSS, Box 21.

[19]Anson T. McCook to Garrison, File 2347935, National Archives, Army Adjutant General's Office, Record Group 94; O'Ryan to Scott, December 8, 1915, Hugh Scott MSS, Box 21; A. R. Paton to Adjutant General, November 4, 1915, National Archives, Army Adjutant General's Office, Record Group 94; George Van Horn Moseley to Roosevelt, November 8, 1915, Theodore Roosevelt MSS, Incoming Correspondence, Box 290; John T. O'Ryan, "Report of the Legislative Committee of the National Guard," Tasker Bliss MSS, Box 195; E. Rumely to Roosevelt, December, 1915, Theodore Roosevelt MSS, Incoming Correspondence, Box 292.

[20]Martha Derthick, *The National Guard in Politics* (Cambridge: Harvard University Press, 1965), pp. 36-40; O'Ryan, "Report," Tasker Bliss MSS, Box 195; *American Review of Reviews* 52 (October 1915): 404.

[21]*The New York Times*, November 12, 1915, p. 7; Garrison to Anson J. McCook, December 6, 1915, File 2347935, National Archives, Army Adjutant General's Office, Record Group 94; Garrison to Wood, December 14, 1915, Leonard Wood MSS, Box 82; Scott to W. S. Scott, January 7, 1915, Hugh Scott MSS, Box 21; *The New Republic* 5 (December 25, 1915): 183.

[22]Herring, "Garrison," p. 70; Scott to W. S. Scott, December 27, 1915, Hugh Scott MSS, Box 21; George C. Herring Jr., "James Hay and the Preparedness Controversy," *Journal of Southern History* 30 (November 1964): 394; U.S. Congress, *Hearings on H. R. 12766*, I, pp. 49, 83.

[23]Garrison to Wilson, January 12, 1916, Wilson MSS, Series II, Box 130.

[24]Garrison to Wilson, January 14, 1916; Tumulty to Wilson, January 15, 1916, Wilson MSS, Series II, Box 130; Baker, *Wilson: Life and Letters*, VI, pp. 33-34.

[25]Garrison to Chamberlain, January 29, 1916, File 2356168, National Archives, Army Adjutant General's Office, Record Group 94.

[26]*The New York Times*, January 23, 1916, p. 5; Herring, "Garrison," pp. 97-98; Taft to Gus Karges, January 11, 1916, William Howard Taft MSS, Series VIII, Box 42; *The Searchlight on Congress* 1 (February 1, 1916): 7; Tumulty to Wilson, January 17, 1916, Wilson MSS, Series II, Box 130; Bliss to W. G. Haan, January 19, 1916, Tasker Bliss MSS, Box 197.

[27]Link, *Wilson: Confusions and Crises*, p. 45; *The New York Times*, January 28, 1916, p. 1; January 29, 1916, p. 1; *Congressional Record*, 64th Congress, 1st Session, p. 1511.

[28]Link, *Wilson: Confusions and Crises*, pp. 48-49; David Lawrence, *The True Story of Woodrow Wilson* (New York: George H. Doran Co., 1924), pp. 158-72; *Current Opinion* 60 (March 1916): 149 A-B; *World's Work* 31 (April 1916): 610-11; Anne W. Lane and Louise H. Wall, eds., *Letters of Franklin K. Lane, Personal and Political* (Boston and New York: Houghton-Mifflin Co., 1922), p. 201.

[29]William Henry Harbaugh, "Wilson, Roosevelt, and Interventionism" (Ph.D. dissertation, Northwestern University, 1954), pp. 138-140; Arthur S. Link, "The Middle West and the Coming of World War I," *The Ohio State Archaelogical and Historical Quarterly* 62 (April 1953): 109-21; U.S. Congress, *Hearings on H. R. 12766*, II, pp. 980-1117. For the effect of Wilson's speeches on one member of Congress, see Representative Percy E. Quin's remarks, *Congressional Record*, 64th Congress, 1st Session, pp. 2479-81.

[30]Hay to Wilson, February 5, 1916; (Confidential), February 8, 1916, Wilson MSS, Series II, Box 131.

[31]Herring, "Garrison," p. 111; "A Costly Resignation," *The New Republic* 6 (February 19, 1916): 56-57; *The New York Times*, February 10, 1916, p. 1; February 11, 1916, p. 1.

[32]Roy Watson Curry, "Woodrow Wilson and Philippine Policy," *Mississippi Valley Historical Review* 61 (December 1954): 435-52; Baker, *Wilson: Life and Letters*, VI, p. 36; Garrison to Wilson, February 9, 1916; Wilson to Garrison, February 10, 1916, quoted in David F. Houston, *Eight Years with Wilson's Cabinet, 1913-1920* (2 vols., Garden City: Doubleday, Page & Co., 1926), I, pp. 174-76.

[33]Houston, *Eight Years*, I, pp. 177-78; Moseley, "One Soldier's Journey," p. 126, George Van Horn Moseley MSS, Container 1A; New York *World*, February 11, 1916, p. 2; Scott to Garrison, February 11, 1916, Hugh Scott MSS, Box 21.

CHAPTER 6

[1]William Allen White to Roosevelt, October 28, 1915, Theodore Roosevelt

MSS, Incoming Correspondence, Box 290; *The New York Times*, November 10, 1915, p. 4.

[2]U.S. Congress, *Report of House Special Committee to Investigate the National Security League* (65th Congress, 3d Session, Washington, D.C.: GPO, 1918), p. 1803; Simeon Strunsky, "Armaments and Caste," *Annals of the American Academy of Political and Social Science* 66 (July 1916): 240. (Strunsky is particularly acute in describing some of the social pressures behind the preparedness drive.) William Howard Taft to Mabel Boardman, April 4, 1916, Taft MSS, Series VIII, Letterbook 40; Frederick L. Palmer, *Our Gallant Madness* (Garden City: Doubleday, Doran, 1937), pp. 37-8.

[3]W. L. Stoddard, "For a Citizen Army," *The New Republic* 5 (September 4, 1915): 125; Herbert L. Quick, "The Average American and the Army," *The Saturday Evening Post* 188 (March 4, 1916): 6-8, 73-77; *The New York Times*, July 21, 1915, p. 3; *New York Sunday Times*, May 30, 1915, V, pp. 6-7; *Congressional Record*, 64th Congress, 1st Session, pp. 4568, 325.

[4]"Truth About Preparedness," American Union Against Militarism MSS, Box 1; Strunsky, "Armaments and Caste," : 241; "The Press on Preparedness," *The World's Work* 31 (November 1915): 26-31. (Of 261 representative newspapers polled, only six opposed increased appropriations for defense.) U.S. Congress, *National Security League Report*, p. 1613.

[5]Hudson Maxim, *Defenseless America* (New York: Hearst International Library, 1915), pp. vii-viii, 80, 107; Allan L. Benson, *Inviting War to America* (New York: B. W. Huebsch, 1916), p. 67; *American Review of Reviews* 51 (May 1915): 628; *The New Republic* 3 (June 5, 1915): 128-29; Frederick L. Huidekoper, *The Military Unpreparedness of the United States* (New York: MacMillan Co., 1915). For a partial listing of titles, see John P. Finnegan, "The Preparedness Movement in Wisconsin" (M.A. thesis, University of Wisconsin, 1961), pp. 165-67.

[6]"The United States, An Undefended Treasure Land," *The Scientific American* 112 (February 6-20, 1915): 118-20, 158-59, 178-79; A. A. Hopkins to W. P. Evans, undated, Leonard Wood MSS, Box 81; Bradley Fiske, "The Mastery of the World," *North American Review* 202 (October 1915): 517-26; Leonard Wood, "Heat Up the Melting Pot," *The Independent* 87 (July 3, 1915): 15; Eric Fisher Wood, "The Writing on the Wall," *The Century* 91 (November 1915): 33-34; Spokane *Spokesman-Review*, April 16, 1916, p. 6; *Milwaukee Sunday Journal*, November 28, 1915, Supplement, p. 1; "America Once More Invaded," *Literary Digest* 51 (December 25, 1915): 1512; "Get Ready Number," *Life* 67 (February 10, 1916).

[7]Armin Rappaport, *The Navy League of the United States* (Detroit: Wayne State University Press, 1962), pp. 47-8; C. S. Thompson to William Allen

White, December 9, 1915, White MSS, Personal File, Box 42; Charles Larisch to Roosevelt, November 27, 1915, Theodore Roosevelt MSS, Incoming Correspondence, Box 291; Copy of *Electra*, Wilson MSS, Series VI, File 1935; Charles M. Johnson to Newton D. Baker, July 10, 1916, File 2433851, National Archives, Army Adjutant General's Office, Record Group 94.

[8]Spokane *Spokesman-Review*, January 9, 1916, IV, p. 1; Leonard Wood to J. Stuart Blackton, August 25, 1915, Leonard Wood MSS, Box 81; Blackton to Theodore Roosevelt, May 24, 1915, Theodore Roosevelt MSS, Incoming Correspondence, Box 287; *The New York Times*, August 7, 1915, p. 12; Blackton to Roosevelt, June 2, 1916, Theodore Roosevelt MSS, Incoming Correspondence, Box 303; *The Independent* 86 (June 12, 1916): 428; (June 5, 1916): 373.

[9]U.S. Navy League, *Report of the Secretary, Navy League Convention* (April 1916), pp. 1-5; T. E. Ripley to Stimson, November 11, 1915, Henry L. Stimson MSS, Box 139; U.S. Congress, *National Security League Hearings*, pp. 2045, 578, 399, 400; Taft to William A. Obenchain, May 28, 1916, William Howard Taft MSS, Series VIII, Letterbook 49; Annie L. Diggs to White, October 22, 1915, William Allen White MSS, Personal File, Box 42.

[10]U.S. Congress, *National Security League Hearings*, pp. 1799, 378-87, 272-79, 285; H. M. Allen, "Joseph Choate, An Appreciation," *The Outlook* 115 (January 3, 1917): 20-21.

[11]U.S. Congress, *National Security League Hearings*, pp. 135-36, 1017; Putnam to F. W. Hobbs, November 12, 1915, George Haven Putnam MSS; Harold T. Pulsifer, "The Security League Conference," *The Outlook* 111 (December 8, 1915): 853; Jacob M. Dickinson to Wood, Leonard Wood MSS, Box 87; D. S. Stanley to Wood, November 11, 1916, Leonard Wood MSS, Box 92; Finnegan, "The Preparedness Movement in Wisconsin," p. 4; *The New York Times*, July 23, 1915, p. 3; July 28, 1915, p. 3.

[12]Edwin R. Lewinson, *John Purroy Mitchel; The Boy Mayor of New York* (New York: Astra Books, 1965), p. 194; *The New York Times*, February 16, 1916, p. 5; C. S. Thompson to Stimson, August 14, 1915, Henry L. Stimson MSS, Box 133.

[13]*The New York Times*, September 1, 1915, p. 3; February 14, 1916, p. 2; Proudfoot's Commercial Agency to Pinchot, September 22, 1915, Amos Pinchot MSS, Box 22; Putnam to Alexander M. White, December 29, 1915; Putnam to William H. Hobbs, October 1, 1915, George Haven Putnam MSS.

[14]Evan Hollister to Henry Wise Wood, December 20, 1915, Theodore Roosevelt MSS, Incoming Correspondence, Box 292; American Defense Bulletin No. 1, Theodore Roosevelt MSS, Incoming Correspondence, Box 296; Putnam to William H. Hobbs, October 1, 1915, George Haven Putnam MSS; Truman H. Newberry to Roosevelt, Theodore Roosevelt MSS, Incoming Corre-

spondence, Box 291; Proudfoot's Commercial Agency to Pinchot, September 22, 1915, Amos Pinchot MSS, Box 22; New York *World*, January 27, 1916, p. 2; George Baker to Trustees, American Defense Society, February 11, 1916, Theodore Roosevelt MSS, Incoming Correspondence, Box 296; Philip Roosevelt to Roosevelt, Theodore Roosevelt MSS, Incoming Correspondence, Box 296.

[15]*Congressional Record*, 64th Congress, 1st Session, p. 5019; Philip Roosevelt to Roosevelt, November 28, 1916, Theodore Roosevelt MSS, Incoming Correspondence, Box 314; *The New York Times*, August 27, 1915, p. 9; *Flying* 4 (July 1915): 583; Virgil Jordan, "How You Can Help Prepare," *Everybody's Magazine* 33 (September 1915): 270; Henry Wise Wood to Roosevelt, December 9, 1915, Theodore Roosevelt MSS, Incoming Correspondence, Box 291; *The New York Times*, December 23, 1915, p. 1.

[16]Putnam to Stanwood Menken, December 23, 1915, George Haven Putnam MSS; Menken to Roosevelt, January 7, 1916, Theodore Roosevelt MSS, Incoming Correspondence, Box 293; *The New York Times*, March 25, 1916, p. 8.

[17]Wood to J. O. Skinner, March 13, 1916, Leonard Wood MSS, Box 86; Taft to Dallas Boudeman, November 15, 1915, William Howard Taft MSS, Series VIII, Letterbook 38; George Hewitt Myers to Wood, February 23, 1916, Leonard Wood MSS, Box 86; National Security League Executive Committee Minutes, March 15, 1916, Henry L. Stimson MSS, Box 146; *Army and Navy Journal* 54 (May 6, 1916): 1153.

[18]S.B.M. Young to John T. Pratt, April 12, 1916, Leonard Wood MSS, Box 90; Wood, "Diary," February 25, 1916, Leonard Wood MSS, Volume 9; *The New York Times*, March 4, 1916, p. 12.

[19]T. Robins to Roosevelt, April 4, 1916, Theodore Roosevelt MSS, Incoming Correspondence, Box 298; Roger C. Hoyt to Roosevelt, April 17, 1916, Theodore Roosevelt MSS, Incoming Correspondence, Box 299; *The Outlook* 113 (May 3, 1916); Editor of *Evening Mail* to Wilson, November 7, 1915, Wilson MSS, Series VI, File 1935; New York *Call*, December 26, 1915, p. 1; *The Scientific American* 114 (January 1, 1916): 15; Benjamin H. Dibblee to Roosevelt, May 10, 1916, Theodore Roosevelt MSS, Incoming Correspondence, Box 300; Memorandum, File 8933-222; -253, National Archives, Army War College Division, Record Group 165.

[20]*The Scientific American* 114 (April 22, 1916): 429; Spokane *Spokesman-Review*, April 9, 1916, p. 4; "Our Wingless Army," *The Literary Digest* 52 (June 17, 1916): 1769; *The New York Times*, October 29, 1916, p. 21; *The Outlook* 112 (February 23, 1916): 411; 114 (December 13, 1916): 792.

[21]"Women Who Are Sick of Pacifism," *Everybody's Magazine* 24 (May 1916): 653-54; *The New York Times*, August 3, 1915, p. 9; Mrs. William A.

Alexander to Wood, November 4, 1915, Leonard Wood MSS, Box 84; New York *Call*, December 19, 1915, p. 3; *The New York Times*, October 10, 1915, p. 3; *The Masses* 8 (July 1916): 13.

[22]"Daughters Who Were Raised to be Soldiers," *Leslie's Weekly* 122 (May 25, 1916): 547; *Washington Post*, June 11, 1916, p. 20; *The New York Times*, March 10, 1916, p. 7; April 15, 1916, p. 13; June 13, 1916, p. 11.

[23]Frederick L. Long to Wood, Leonard Wood MSS, Box 87; *The New York Times*, October 12, 1915, p. 5; John Garry Clifford, *The Citizen Soldiers: The Plattsburg Training Camp Movement, 1913-1920* (Lexington: University Press of Kentucky, 1972), pp. 186-90.

[24]New York *World*, April 16, 1916, p. 5; *Chicago Tribune*, April 20, 1916, p. 1.

[25]"A Huge Parade for Preparedness," *The Literary Digest* 52 (May 1916): 1518; *The New York Times*, April 2, 1916, p. 16; October 13, 1916, p. 5; October 16, 1916, p. 1.

[26]*Army and Navy Journal* 54 (June 10, 1916): 1315; *The New York Times*, June 4, 1916, p. 1.

[27]John O'Hara, *From the Terrace* (New York: Random House, 1958), p. 177; *The Literary Digest* 52 (March 18, 1916): 751.

CHAPTER 7

[1]Walter Lippmann, "Integrated America," *The New Republic* 6 (February 19, 1916): 63; "The Issue of 1916," *The New Republic* 7 (June 3, 1916): 107.

[2]Henry Osborne Taylor, "The Pathos of America," *The Atlantic Monthly* 117 (February 1916): 250-51; William Churchill to Scott, December 23, 1916, Hugh Scott MSS, Box 26; Roy Howard to Pinchot, May 24, 1916, Amos Pinchot MSS, Box 24; Samuel Gompers to Wood, October 6, 1915, Leonard Wood MSS, Box 82; Herbert Croly, "The Effect on American Institutions of a Powerful Military and Naval Establishment," *Annals of the American Academy of Political and Social Science* 66 (July 1916): 162.

[3]"Mobilizing American Industries for Defense," *The Outlook* 112 (April 26, 1916): 949; Stimson to Philip Roosevelt, December 17, 1915, Henry L. Stimson MSS, Box 140; *The New York Times*, May 20, 1916, p. 4; April 9, 1916, p. 6.

[4]Frederick M. Davenport, "The Pre-Nomination Campaign; The Making of the Nation," *The Outlook* 112 (April 26, 1916): 955; Croly, "The Effect on American Institutions": 157; Stimson to George A. Slater, March 20, 1916, Henry L. Stimson MSS, Box 146.

[5]"The Growing Strain on American Neutrality," *Current Opinion* 59 (De-

cember 1915): 375; House, "Diary," October 2, 1915, Edward M. House MSS, Vol. 7; *The New York Times*, April 21, 1916, p. 10.

[6]Memorandum of Conversation between Rumely and Stoddard, Theodore Roosevelt MSS, Incoming Correspondence, Box 312.

[7]*Everybody's Magazine* 34 (February 1916): 267; U.S. War Department, "Army War College Session 1914-1915," Part V, Vol. 57, pp. 138-39.

[8]Scott to W. S. Edgerly, January 24, 1916, Hugh Scott MSS, Box 21; Spokane *Spokesman-Review*, January 12, 1916, p. 4; Memorandum, January 15, 1915, File 8222-2, National Archives, Army War College Division, Record Group 165; Wood to J.S.L. Strachey, February 25, 1916, Leonard Wood MSS, Box 90; Ellery Sedgwick to Wood, October 16, 1914, Leonard Wood MSS, Box 75; "The Newer Nationalism," *The New Republic* 5 (January 29, 1916): 379.

[9]Roosevelt to E. A. Van Valkenberg, September 5, 1916, Theodore Roosevelt MSS, Outgoing Correspondence, Letterbook 96; Richard T. Ely, "Progressivism, True and False—An Outline," *Review of Reviews* 51 (February 1915): 210-11; Will Culbertson to Roosevelt, April 20, 1916, Theodore Roosevelt MSS, Incoming Correspondence, Box 299; Ellery Sedgwick to Wood, October 16, 1914, Leonard Wood MSS, Box 75; Frederick Palmer, "The War's Lesson to Us," *Collier's* 57 (March 18, 1916): 6; "Exhibit No. 7, Note on Economic Value of Military Training," U.S. Chamber of Commerce, Theodore Roosevelt MSS, Incoming Correspondence, Box 297; Julius Rosenwald to Roosevelt, May 2, 1916, Theodore Roosevelt MSS, Incoming Correspondence, Box 300.

[10]E. C. Rumely to Roosevelt, September 28, 1915, Theodore Roosevelt MSS, Incoming Correspondence, Box 289; Ralph Barton Perry, "The Vigil of Arms," *The New Republic* 8 (May 27, 1916): 82; Borah to E. H. Hasbrouck, June 17, 1916, William E. Borah MSS, Box 178; American Union Against Militarism Bulletin 2, May 27, 1916, Amos Pinchot MSS, File 15.

[11]Wood to John P. Finley, March 30, 1916, Leonard Wood MSS, Box 92; Palmer, "The War's Lesson": 6; *Army and Navy Journal* 54 (May 27, 1916): 1251; Spokane *Spokesman-Review*, January 11, 1916, p. 4; Perry, "The Vigil of Arms": 83; *Chicago Tribune*, April 24, 1916, p. 8.

[12]Ralph Barton Perry, *The Free Man and the Soldier* (New York: Charles Scribner's Sons, 1916), p. 22; *The Survey* 36 (March 25, 1916): 758; S.B.M. Young to John T. Pratt, April 12, 1916, Leonard Wood MSS, Box 90; John O'Ryan to Stimson, December 16, 1915, Henry L. Stimson MSS, Box 140; *The New York Times*, May 20, 1916, p. 1.

[13]Memorandum for the Adjutant General, February 18, 1916, File 9317-1, National Archives, Army War College Division, Record Group 165.

[14]Chamberlain to Wood, January 6, 1916; March 23, 1916, Leonard Wood MSS, Box 89; Memorandum for the Adjutant General, January 29, 1916, File

2354988, National Archives, Army Adjutant General's Office, Record Group 94; S.B.M. Young to John T. Pratt, April 22, 1916, Leonard Wood MSS, Box 86; Wood to John T. Pratt, June 22, 1916, Leonard Wood MSS, Box 91.

[15]*The New York Times*, September 30, 1915, p. 5; *Bulletin of the Public Affairs Information Service, 2nd Annual Compilation* (New York: H. W. Wilson Co., 1916), p. 168; "Military Folly in New York," *The New Republic* 7 (July 29, 1916): 318; *Everybody's Magazine* 36 (February 1917): 250; *The Independent* 85 (February 21, 1916): 253.

[16]Lane to Frederick J. Lane, July 21, 1915, quoted in Anne W. Lane and Louise H. Wall, eds., *Letters of Franklin K. Lane: Personal and Political* (Boston and New York: Houghton-Mifflin Co., 1922), pp. 177-78; Taft to Gus Karger, January 3, 1916, William Howard Taft MSS, Series VIII, Letterbook 42; *Army and Navy Journal* 54 (June 10, 1916): 1231.

[17]Croly, "The Effect on American Institutions": 168; W. T. Colyer, "The Military Mind," *The Independent* 89 (January 1, 1917): 22.

[18]F. G. Alexander to Roosevelt, January 14, 1916, Theodore Roosevelt MSS, Incoming Correspondence, Box 294; Wood to Harry F. Porter, May 26, 1916, Leonard Wood MSS, Box 91; George Perkins to Roosevelt, June, 1916, Theodore Roosevelt MSS, Incoming Correspondence, Box 304; Newton D. Baker, "Our Military Situation," *The Outlook* 113 (July 5, 1916): 551.

[19]Fiske, "Diary," July 5, 1915, Bradley Fiske MSS; *The New York Times*, July 13, 1915, p. 1; July 16, 1915, p. 1; "The Navy's Science Board," *The Literary Digest* 51 (September 25, 1915): 652-53; Fiske, "Diary," July 25, October 10, 1915, Bradley Fiske MSS; *The New Republic* 3 (July 27, 1915): 267.

[20]Lloyd N. Scott, *The Naval Consulting Board of the United States* (Washington, D.C.: GPO, 1936), pp. 40; 26-7.

[21]"Mobilizing American Industries," *The Outlook*: 947; Martin J. Gillis to Garrison, August 27, 1915, Lindley M. Garrison MSS; Gillis to Joseph E. Davies, September 23, 1915; Joseph E. Davies to Tumulty, Wilson MSS, Series VI, File 1935.

[22]Scott, *The Naval Consulting Board*, pp. 28-32; Howard E. Coffin, "Organizing Industry for National Defense," *World's Work* 32 (May 1916): 25; *The Scientific American* 114 (May 27, 1916): 567.

[23]Coffin, "Organizing Industry": 28; Thomas Robins, "America's Industrial Organization for National Defense," *The Scientific American* 115 (July 8, 1916): 40.

[24]Wood, "Diary," May 27, 1915, Leonard Wood MSS, Vol. 9; Wood to Charles R. Crane, March 4, 1916; Wood to E. C. Converse, February 2, 1916, Leonard Wood MSS, Box 89; Scott, *The Naval Consulting Board*, pp. 40-41;

George E. Hale to House, July 21, 1916; House to Wilson, July 6, 1916, Wilson MSS, Series II, Box 138.

[25]Wood, "Diary," June 3, 1915, Leonard Wood MSS, Vol. 9; House, "Diary," April 3, 1916, Edward M. House MSS, Vol. 8; Bernard Baruch to House, April 24, 1916, Wilson MSS, Series II, Box 133; Baker to Baruch, May 9, 1916, Newton D. Baker MSS, Box 1.

[26]Newton D. Baker to Wilson, April 7, 1916 (Confidential), File 2638801, Enclosure 143, National Archives, Army Adjutant General's Office, Record Group 94.

[27]House, "Diary," May 3, 1916, Edward M. House MSS, Vol. 9; Grosvenor B. Clarkson, *Industrial America in the World War* (Boston and New York: Houghton-Mifflin Co., 1923), p. 16; William Y. Smith, "The Search for National Security Planning Machinery, 1900-1917" (Ph.D. dissertation, Harvard University, 1961), p. 101.

[28]"The Medical Reserve Corps, United States Army," *The Scientific American, Supplement* 80 (October 9, 1915): 2075; Franklin H. Martin, *Digest of Proceedings of Council of National Defense During the World War* (73d Congress, 2d Session, Senate Document 193, Washington, D.C.: GPO, 1943), pp. 32, 34, 45-6; *The New York Times*, June 27, 1916, p. 4; Wood to Hugh Scott, July 14, 1915, Leonard Wood MSS, Box 80.

[29]"Plans for a Big American Navy," *The Literary Digest* 51 (October 16, 1915): 826-27; Roosevelt to William Hard, January 11, 1916, Theodore Roosevelt MSS, Outgoing Correspondence, Box 93; *The New York Times*, July 14, 1915, p. 4.

[30]Newton Baker to Wilson, April 7, 1916 (Confidential), File 2638801, Enclosure 143, National Archives, Army Adjutant General's Office, Record Group 94; Cleveland *Plain Dealer*, May 31, 1916, p. 10.

CHAPTER 8

[1]*Detroit Free Press*, April 20, 1916, p. 1; *Commercial and Financial Chronicle* 101 (December 11, 1915): 1922; *Congressional Record*, 64th Congress, 1st Session, p. 426; Oswald Garrison Villard, "Preparedness Is Militarism," *Annals of the American Academy of Political and Social Science* 66 (July 1916): 218.

[2]Hudson Maxim, ed., *Leading Opinions for and Against National Defense* (New York: Hearst International Library, 1916), pp. 65-71; *Congressional Record*, 64th Congress, 1st Session, p. 273; *Detroit Free Press*, December 2,

1914, p. 4; Bailey to D. A. Wilcox, March 28, 1916, Warren Worth Bailey MSS, Box 5; *Johnstown Democrat*, December 23, 1915, p. 8.

[3]Oswald Garrison Villard, "Our Drift into Militarism," *The Nation* 103 (August 3, 1916), Supplement: 3; Pinchot to Roy W. Howard, May 23, 1916, Amos Pinchot MSS, General Correspondence, Box 24; *Congressional Record*, 64th Congress, 2d Session, p. 3450; William Hard to Theodore Roosevelt, April 19, 1916, Theodore Roosevelt MSS, Incoming Correspondence, Box 299.

[4]*Congressional Record*, 64th Congress, 1st Session, p. 424; Villard, "Preparedness Is Militarism": 217; "Paper Soldiers," *The Saturday Evening Post* 188 (April 22, 1916): 26; *Commercial and Financial Chronicle* 101 (December 11, 1915): 1922.

[5]U.S. Congress, House Committee on Military Affairs, *Hearings on H. R. 12766, To Increase the Efficiency of the Military Establishment of the United States* (2 vols., 64th Congress, 1st Session, Washington, D.C.: GPO, 1916), II, p. 1235.

[6]Arthur Capper, "The West and Preparedness," *The Independent* 85 (January 10, 1916): 49; William Hirth to David Houston, February 17, 1916, Wilson, MSS, Series II, Box 131; William Hard, "What About Bryan?," *Everybody's Magazine* 34 (April 1916): 458-59; *Milwaukee Journal*, August 18, 1916, p. 16; Arthur C. Pound to George Perkins, April 18, 1916, Perkins MSS, General Files, Box 27; Herbert Quick, "The Average American and the Army," *The Saturday Evening Post* 188 (March 4, 1916): 6; *Congressional Record*, 64th Congress, 1st Session, p. 8969.

[7]*New York Sunday Times*, December 6, 1915, IV, p. 1; *New York Call*, January 19, 1916, p. 2; *The New York Times*, January 19, 1916, p. 6; Ralph Easley to Henry L. Stimson, May 18, 1916, Henry L. Stimson MSS, Box 149; "Labor's Dread of Preparedness," *Literary Digest* 52 (April 8, 1916): 957; *Army and Navy Journal* 54 (November 25, 1916): 397.

[8]Carl Wittke, *German Americans and the World War* (Columbus: Ohio State Archaeological and Historical Society, 1936), pp. 91, 96; Philip Roosevelt to Theodore Roosevelt, January 25, 1916, Theodore Roosevelt MSS, Incoming Correspondence, Box 296; William J. Nichols to Wood, December 29, 1915, Leonard Wood MSS, Box 90; John P. Finnegan, "The Preparedness Movement in Wisconsin, 1914-1917" (M.A. thesis, University of Wisconsin, 1961), pp. 107-13; Theodore Roosevelt to Hugo Munsterberg, January 19, 1916, Theodore Roosevelt MSS, Outgoing Correspondence, Box 93; Amos Pinchot to John Brisbane Walker, August 12, 1915, Amos Pinchot MSS, General Correspondence, Box 21.

[9]Finnegan, "The Preparedness Movement in Wisconsin," pp. 115-16.

[10]David A. Shannon, *The Socialist Party of America* (New York: MacMillan

Co., 1955), p. 89; Joshua Wanhope, "The Riddle of the Socialist Universe," *New York Call*, December 8, 1915, p. 6; *New York Call*, December 6, 1915, p. 6.

[11]Shannon, *The Socialist Party*, p. 89; *New York Call*, December 5, 1915, II, p. 8; January 8, 1916, p. 6.

[12]Shannon, *The Socialist Party*, p. 91; Wanhope, "Riddle of the Socialist Universe," p. 6; Upton Sinclair, "Democratic Defense: A Practical Program for Socialists," Theodore Roosevelt MSS, Incoming Correspondence, Box 296; Finnegan, "The Preparedness Movement in Wisconsin," p. 117.

[13]Timothy G. McDonald, "Southern Democratic Congressmen and the First World War, August 1914-April 1917" (Ph.D. dissertation, University of Washington, 1962), pp. 192-4; Bailey to N. H. Dole, December 11, 1915, Warren Worth Bailey MSS, Box 5; *The New York Times*, January 6, 1916, p. 3; February 15, 1916, p. 2.

[14]*Congressional Record*, 64th Congress, 1st Session, p. 322; *The New York Times*, September 9, 1915, p. 12; *Congressional Record*, 64th Congress, 1st Session, p. 1; *The Survey* 36 (April 22, 1916): 95.

[15]*New York Call*, December 6, 1915, p. 1; *Congressional Record*, 64th Congress, 1st Session, p. 6214.

[16]William Hard, "What About Bryan?": 466.

[17]Merle Curti, *Peace or War* (New York: W. W. Norton Co., 1936), p. 231; "Leaders Toward World Peace," *Everybody's Magazine* 33 (October 1915): 385-96; L. Hollingsworth Wood to William Allen White, May 7, 1915, William Allen White MSS, Personal File, Box 42; Donald Johnson, *The Challenge to American Freedom* (Lexington: University of Kentucky Press, 1963), pp. 1-5; *The New York Times*, December 10, 1914; December 19, 1914, p. 4.

[18]Curti, *Peace or War*, p. 237; A. A. Ekirch, *The Civilian and the Military* (New York: Oxford University Press, 1956), p. 162; *The New York Times*, September 20, 1915, p. 1; Henry L. Stimson, "Diary," February 13, 1916, Stimson MSS, Vol. 3.

[19]Samuel Crowther, "The Nourishment of the Pacifists," *The Forum* 56 (July 1916): 12-14; Johnson, *Challenge to American Freedom*, p. 5; *The New York Times*, July 10, 1915, p. 12.

[20]Minutes, November 29, 1915, American Union Against Militarism Files, Box 1.

[21]Minutes, January 3, 1916, AUAM Files, Box 1; *The Survey* 35 (January 6, 1916): 370-71; Johnson, *Challenge to American Freedom*, p. 5; *The New York Times*, February 25, 1916, p. 10; Minutes, AUAM Files, Box 1; AUAM Memorandum, "Suggestions for Reorganization," Amos Pinchot MSS, General Correspondence, Box 24; Crystal Eastman to Pinchot, undated, Amos Pinchot MSS, General Correspondence, Box 26; AUAM Bulletin, June 7, 1916,

Amos Pinchot MSS, General Correspondence, Box 15; Hallinan to Crystal Eastman, October 10, 1916, Amos Pinchot MSS, General Correspondence, Box 24.

[22]Crystal Eastman to Pinchot, March 30, 1916; May 27, 1916, Amos Pinchot MSS, General Correspondence, Box 24; Charles T. Hallinan, "The New Army Law," *The Survey* 36 (June 17, 1916): 309.

[23]U.S. Congress, Senate Military Affairs Committee, *Universal Military Training, Hearings Before Subcommittee* (64th Congress, 2d Session, Washington, D.C.: GPO, 1917), p. 774; *The Survey* 36 (April 1, 1916): 37; (April 22, 1916): 95-96; AUAM Files, Box 1; Oswald Garrison Villard to David Lawrence, April 18, 1916, Oswald Garrison Villard MSS.

[24]Villard to Lawrence, April 20, 1916, Oswald Garrison Villard MSS; *The New York Times*, April 17, 1916, p. 20; Minutes, April 24, 1916, AUAM File 1; *Literary Digest* 52 (April 29, 1916): 1256-57; John Reed to Amos Pinchot, July 14, 1916, Amos Pinchot MSS, General Correspondence, Box 26; Herbert W. Hobbs, *Leonard Wood: Administrator, Soldier, and Citizen* (New York: G. P. Putnam's Sons, 1920), pp. 179-80.

[25]Gilson Gardner to Pinchot, April 1, 1916, Amos Pinchot MSS, General Correspondence, Box 24; Allan Benson, *Inviting War to America* (New York: B. W. Huebsch, 1916), p. 69; *The New York Times*, January 21, 1916, p. 4; Lillian D. Wald to Wilson, April 21, 1916, Wilson MSS, Series VI, File 1935.

[26]Minutes, May 2, 1916, AUAM File 1; Max Eastman, *Enjoyment of Living* (New York: Harper & Bros., 1948), p. 546; *Commercial and Financial Chronicle* 102 (May 13, 1916): 1771.

[27]*Commercial and Financial Chronicle* 102 (May 13, 1916): 1771; James Kerney, *The Political Education of Woodrow Wilson* (New York: The Century Co., 1926), pp. 364-66.

[28]Villard to David Lawrence, May 9, 1916, Oswald Garrison Villard MSS.

[29]AUAM Enclosure, undated, Amos Pinchot MSS, General Correspondence, Box 15.

[30]Frank J. Gentsch to William Gordon, January 31, 1916, Wilson MSS, Series VI, File 1935; Bailey to Jesse F. Orton, April 4, 1916, Warren Worth Bailey MSS, Box 8; F. B. Kavanagh to Joseph Tumulty, February 8, 1916, Wilson MSS, Series VI, File 1935; Rupert Hughes, "The Case of Our National Guard," *Collier's* 57 (May 20, 1916): 7.

[31]Fred Keating to Bailey, August 21, 1915, Warren Worth Bailey MSS, Box 9; Charles Johnson Post, "The Army as a Social Service," *The Survey* 36 (May 20, 1916): 201-02; Finnegan, "The Preparedness Movement in Wisconsin," p. 27; Herbert Quick, "The Average American and the Army": 73; *The New York Times*, January 17, 1916, p. 3; Miles Poindexter to S. M. DeGolier, April 12,

1916, Theodore Roosevelt MSS, Incoming Correspondence, Box 278; *Congressional Record*, 64th Congress, 1st Session, pp. 6292, 4310.

[32]Fred Keating to Bailey, August 21, 1915, Warren Worth Bailey MSS, Box 9; *Congressional Record*, 64th Congress, 1st Session, p. 272; Thomas Robins, "America's Industrial Organization for National Defense," *The Scientific American* 115 (July 8, 1916): 40; John Spargo, "Sidelights on Preparedness," *New York Sunday Call* January 23, 1916, II, p. 16.

[33]Bailey to F. P. Dawson, February 29, 1916, Warren Worth Bailey MSS, Box 5; Charles T. Hallinan, "The New Army Law": 309.

CHAPTER 9

[1]Ray Stannard Baker, *Woodrow Wilson, Life and Letters* (8 vols., Garden City: Doubleday, 1927-1939) VI, p. 37; House to H. C. Wallace, March 10, 1916, Wilson MSS, Series II, Box 132; *Army and Navy Journal* 53 (February 19, 1916): 784; "Newton D. Baker, the Mayor-Idealist of Cleveland," *Current Opinion* 60 (April 1916): 246; Frederick Palmer, *Newton D. Baker; America at War* (2 vols., New York: Dodd Mead & Co., 1931), I, pp. 7-10; Daniel R. Beaver, *Newton D. Baker and the American War Effort, 1917-1919* (Lincoln: University of Nebraska Press, 1966), pp. 4, 13; Scott to Frank R. McCoy, April 10, 1916, Hugh Scott MSS, Box 22.

[2]*Current Opinion* 60 (March 1916): 151; *Congressional Record*, 64th Congress, 1st Session, p. 2535; *The New York Times*, February 13, 1916, pp. 1-2; February 14, 1916, p. 1; February 15, 1916, p. 17.

[3]*Current Opinion* 60 (March 1916): 152; Martha Derthick, *The National Guard in Politics* (Cambridge: Harvard University Press, 1965), p. 37; Memorandum by Gregory, February 24, 1916, Wilson MSS, Series II, Box 132; Wilson to Burleson, undated, Albert Burleson MSS, Box 17; Hay, "Woodrow Wilson and Preparedness," James Hay MSS; *Congressional Record*, 64th Congress, 1st Session, pp. 2630-31, 5516; Crowder to Stimson, March 12, 1916; March 14, 1916, Henry L. Stimson MSS, Box 145.

[4]William Johnston to Wood, March 28, 1916, Leonard Wood MSS, Box 90; Memorandum for the Chief of Staff, March 25, 1916, File 9054-46, National Archives, Army War College Division, Record Group 165.

[5]House, "Diary," March 15, 1916, Edward M. House MSS, Vol. 8; Bliss to Scott, March 13, 1916, Tasker Bliss MSS, Box 198; Scott to Baker, March 13, 1916, Hugh Scott MSS, Box 22; Bliss to Scott, March 24, 1916, Tasker Bliss

MSS, Box 199; Macomb to Scott, March 13, 1916, Hugh Scott MSS, Box 22; Scott to Baker, May 1, 1916, Tasker Bliss MSS, Box 200.

[6]*Congressional Record*, 64th Congress, 1st Session, p. 4097; *Chicago Tribune*, March 16, 1916, p. 2; *The New York Times*, March 23, 1916, p. 4.

[7]*The New York Times*, March 18, 1916, p. 1; *Congressional Record*, 64th Congress, 1st Session, pp. 4340-48, 4474, 4621; Frederick Huidekoper to Wood, March 21, 1916, Leonard Wood MSS, Box 88; *Chicago Tribune*, March 17, 1916, p. 6.

[8]William H. Johnston to Wood, March 17, 1916, Leonard Wood MSS, Box 90; Douglas MacArthur to Wood, March 20, 1916, Leonard Wood MSS, Box 93; *Congressional Record*, 64th Congress, 1st Session, pp. 4403-4, 4420, 4490.

[9]*Chicago Tribune*, March 19, 1916, p. 8; *Congressional Record*, 64th Congress, 1st Session, pp. 4490, 4481, 4474, 4307.

[10]Memorandum for the Chief of Staff, December 29, 1915, December 9, 1915, File 9282-4, National Archives, Army War College Division, Record Group 165; Memorandum by Secretary of War, December 4, 1915, File 2347446, National Archives, Army Adjutant General's Office, Record Group 94; *Congressional Record*, 64th Congress, 1st Session, pp. 4577, 4561, 4699.

[11]*Congressional Record*, 64th Congress, 1st Session, p. 4309; Hay, "Woodrow Wilson and Preparedness," James Hay MSS; *Congressional Record*, 64th Congress, 1st Session, pp. 4648-49; *The New York Times*, March 24, 1916, p. 4; AUAM Memorandum, undated, Amos Pinchot MMS, File 15; Wilson to Amos Pinchot, August 11, 16, 1916, Wilson MSS, Series VI, File 3016.

[12]Timothy G. McDonald, "Southern Democratic Congressmen and the First World War, August 1914-April 1917" (Ph.D. dissertation, University of Washington, 1962), p. 187; *Army and Navy Journal* 54 (March 25, 1916): 964; *Congressional Record*, 64th Congress, 1st Session, pp. 4729, 4731; William Johnston to Wood, March 28, 1916, Leonard Wood MSS, Box 90; *Congressional Record*, 64th Congress, 1st Session, p. 4357.

[13]*Congressional Record*, 64th Congress, 1st Session, p. 4007; U.S. Congress, Senate Military Affairs Committee, *Universal Military Training, Hearings Before Subcommittee* (64th Congress, 2d Session, Washington D.C.: GPO, 1917), p. 782; *The New York Times*, March 8, 1916, p. 10; George Van Horn Moseley to W. T. Ransom, May 1, 1916, George Van Horn Moseley MSS, Box 39; *Congressional Record*, 64th Congress, 1st Session, p. 3520.

[14]Crowder to Stimson, February 23, 1916, Henry L. Stimson MSS, Box 144; March 3, 1916, Henry L. Stimson MSS, Box 145; *Congressional Record* 64th Congress, 1st Session, p. 5075.

[15]Ralph Barton Perry, *The Plattsburg Movement* (New York: E. P. Dutton & Co., 1921), pp. 77-97; Grenville Clark to Borah, March 18, 1916, William E.

Borah MSS, Box 178; Grenville Clark to Stimson, March 17, 1916, Henry L. Stimson MSS, Box 145.

[16]Gardner L. Harding, "Hay Foot! Straw Foot!," *Everybody's Magazine* 35 (July 1916): 2-3; Boyd Van Benthuysen to Borah, April 14, 1916, William E. Borah MSS, Box 178; *Congressional Record*, 64th Congress, 1st Session, p. 4623; William H. Riker, *Soldiers of the State* (Washington, D.C.: Public Affairs Press, 1957), p. 78; Scott to Frank R. McCoy, April 10, 1916, Hugh Scott MSS, Box 22; Borah to Gardner L. Harding, May 9, 1916, William E. Borah MSS, Box 178; *Congressional Record*, 64th Congress, 1st Session, p. 6201.

[17]Henry Cabot Lodge to Roosevelt, April 11, 1916, Theodore Roosevelt MSS, Incoming Correspondence, Box 298; William A. Green to Wood, March 21, 1916, Leonard Wood MSS, Box 88; *Army and Navy Journal* 54 (April 29, 1916): 1115; John F. O'Ryan to Wilbur F. Sadler, May 1, 1916, Wilson MSS, Series VI, File 3016; Leonard Wood to Adjutant General, March 15, 1916, File 2380120, National Archives, Army Adjutant General's Office, Record Group 94; Stimson to Crowder, March 31, 1916, Henry L. Stimson MSS, Box 146; *Congressional Record*, 64th Congress, 1st Session, p. 5530.

[18]House, "Diary," April 6, 1916, April 14, 1916, April 15, 1916, Edward M. House MSS, Vol. 8, May 6, 1916, House MSS, Vol. 9.

[19]*Congressional Record*, 64th Congress, 1st Session, pp. 4005, 5299, 5371.

[20]*Congressional Record*, 64th Congress, 1st Session, pp. 55160, 4284, 6011-15.

[21]*Congressional Record*, 64th Congress, 1st Session, p. 5587; Scott to Henry L. Stimson, April 6, 1916, Hugh Scott MSS, Box 22; *Congressional Record*, pp. 5367, 6217, 2683, 6332, 5365, 5156, 5705, 6293.

[22]*Congressional Record*, 64th Congress, 1st Session, pp. 6359, 6343; "Comment on Congress," *Collier's* 57 (May 6, 1916): 18; McDonald, "Southern Democratic Congressmen," pp. 191-92; *Commercial and Financial Chronicle* 102 (April 22, 1916): 1504; Memorandum for the Adjutant General, March 7, 1916, File 2371975, National Archives, Army Adjutant General's Office, Record Group 94, *Congressional Record*, 64th Congress, 1st Session, p. 6335; *The Searchlight on Congress* 1 (May 10, 1916): 1.

[23]Edward H. Brooks, "The National Defense Policies of the Wilson Administration, 1913-1917" (Ph.D. dissertation, Stanford University, 1950), pp. 198-99; Baker, *Wilson*, VI, p. 305; *The New York Times*, April 24, 1916, p. 1.

[24]New York *World*, April 21, 1916, p. 10; *Congressional Record*, 64th Congress, 1st Session, pp. 6757-62; *The New York Times*, April 22, 1916, p. 6; April 26, 1916, p. 12; *Cleveland Plain Dealer*, April 21, 1916, p. 10; *New York Call*, April 26, 1916, p. 1; Champ Clark, "What We Are Trying To Do," *The Independent* 88 (December 4, 1916): 392.

[25]*Congressional Record*, 64th Congress, 1st Session, pp. 7494, 6819.

[26]*The New York Times*, May 5, 1916, p. 6; *Congressional Record*, 64th Congress, 1st Session, p. 8400; AUAM Bulletin, undated, Amos Pinchot MSS, Box 15; *Congressional Record*, 64th Congress, 1st Session, p. 7599.

[27]New York *World*, May 10, 1916, p. 10; *The New York Times*, May 11, 1916, p. 12; *Army and Navy Journal* 54 (May 13, 1916): 1179; Tumulty to Wilson, May 12, 1916, Wilson MSS, Series II, Box 145.

[28]Baker, *Wilson*, VI, p. 305; Wilson to James Munn, May 12, 1916, Wilson MSS, Series VI, File 3016; Arthur S. Link, *Wilson: Confusions and Crises, 1915-1916* (Princeton: Princeton University Press, 1965), p. 334.

[29]*Congressional Record*, 64th Congress, 1st Session, pp. 8375-96.

[30]*Congressional Record*, 64th Congress, 1st Session, p. 8375; General Staff Memorandum, Analysis of the New Army Bill, File 2406017, National Archives, Army Adjutant General's Office, Record Group 94; Grenville Clark to Baker, May 23, 1916, File 2397465, National Archives, Army Adjutant General's Office, Record Group 94.

[31]Palmer, *Newton D. Baker*, I, pp. 65-7; Scott to Frederick Funston, November 7, 1916, Hugh Scott MSS, Box 25; *The New York Times*, May 10, 1916, p. 12; Clipping, Wilson MSS, Series VI, File 3016; Wood to Henry Cabot Lodge, July 22, 1916, Leonard Wood MSS, Box 89.

[32]William Henry Harbaugh, "Wilson, Roosevelt, and Interventionism" (Ph.D. dissertation, Northwestern University, 1954), pp. 145-46; Jack C. Lane, "Leonard Wood and the Shaping of American Defense Policy, 1900-1920" (Ph.D. dissertation, University of Georgia, 1963), p. 93; General Staff Memorandum, Analysis of the New Army Bill, File 2406017, National Archives, Army Adjutant General's Office, Record Group 94.

[33]*The New York Times*, May 10, 1916, p. 12; May 21, 1916, p. 21; New York *World*, May 5, 1916, p. 4; *Congressional Record*, 64th Congress, 1st Session, p. 8137; *New York Sunday Times*, May 28, 1916, I, p. 22; *Washington Post*, June 4, 1916, p. 9.

[34]*The New York Times*, May 24, 1916, p. 1; May 23, 1916, p. 3; *Army and Navy Journal* 54 (May 27, 1916): 1257; AUAM Bulletin, May 27, 1916, Amos Pinchot MSS, Box 15.

CHAPTER 10

[1]Henry L. Stimson to Mary Rinehard, May 19, 1916, Stimson MSS, Box 149.

[2]Hermann Hagedorn, *Leonard Wood: A Biography* (New York: Harpers, 1931), pp. 187-8; William Henry Harbaugh, "Wilson, Roosevelt, and Interven-

tionism" (Ph.D. dissertation, Northwestern University, 1954), pp. 160-62; Medill McCormack to Theodore Roosevelt, June 8, 1916, telephone conversation transcript, George Perkins MSS, Box 27; Frederick M. Davenport, "Preliminary Impressions of the Chicago Conventions," *The Outlook* 113 (June 14, 1916): 356; Harbaugh, "Wilson," pp. 168-70; William E. Leuchtenberg, "Progressivism and Imperialism; The Progressive Movement and American Foreign Policy, 1898-1916," *The Mississippi Valley Historical Review* 29 (December 1952): 496.

[3]*The New York Times*, June 15, 1916, p. 1; Edward M. House to Wilson, June 18, 1916, Wilson MSS, Series II, Box 136; Joseph Tumulty to Wilson, August 10, 1916, Wilson MSS, Series II, Box 139; Louis Wiley to Hugh Scott, June 12, 1916, Scott MSS, Box 23; Warren Harding, "Says Senator Harding— Republican," *Everybody's Magazine* 35 (September 1916): 301; *The Independent* 86 (June 26, 1916): 502.

[4]*The New York Times*, June 15, 1916, p. 1; June 13, 1916, p. 5; *Congressional Record*, 64th Congress, 1st Session, pp. 12275-6; *The New York Times*, August 30, 1916, p. 6; June 10, 1916, p. 4. The Council for National Defense was the new title given the proposed Council for Executive Information; it was not the body which the War Department had recommended in 1912 to coordinate military and naval planning with foreign policy. Such a plan had been broached in the Senate, but was quickly headed off by the Wilson Administration, which did not want outside influences meddling in foreign policy. Newton D. Baker to Wilson, July 8, 1916, Wilson MSS, Series II, Box 138; William Y. Smith, "The Search for National Security Planning Machinery, 1900-1947" (Ph.D. dissertation, Harvard University, 1960), pp. 76-7, 114.

[5]Leonard Wood to Frank McCoy, July 5, 1916, Leonard Wood MSS, Box 80; *The New York Times*, July 13, 1916, p. 1; J. C. O'Laughlin to Wood, July 15, 1916, Leonard Wood MSS, Box 88; Frank McCoy to Scott, August 3, 1916, Hugh Scott MSS, Box 24. Enrollment in the Plattsburg camps, which Wood had done so much to encourage, greatly expanded, and for the first time military training was offered to boys of high school age. Ralph Barton Perry, *The Plattsburg Movement* (New York: E. P. Dutton & Co., 1921), pp. 109-10, 116-8.

[6]New York *World*, April 25, 1916, p. 8; Harold and Margaret Sprout, *The Rise of American Naval Power, 1776-1916* (Princeton: Princeton University Press, 1939), pp. 332-3; *Congressional Record*, 64th Congress, 1st Session, p. 6028.

[7]Sprout, *American Naval Power*, pp. 332-3; AUAM Bulletin, May 24, 1916, Amos Pinchot MSS, Box 15.

[8]Sprout, *American Naval Power*, pp. 335-9; Arthur S. Link, *Wilson: Confusions and Crises, 1915-1916* (Princeton: Princeton University Press, 1965), p. 337; House to Wilson, May 17, 1916, Wilson MSS, Series II, Box 135.

[9]*Congressional Record*, 64th Congress, 1st Session, p. 12697; AUAM Bulletin 55, August 10, 1916, Amos Pinchot MSS, Box 15; Warren Worth Bailey to F. C. Dole, August 8, 1916, Bailey MSS, Box 5; Arthur S. Link, *Wilson: Campaigns for Progressivism and Peace, 1916-1917* (Princeton: Princeton University Press, 1965), pp. 62-3.

[10]*The Scientific American* 115 (November 25, 1916): 472; Burton Vance to Roosevelt, June 20, 1916, Theodore Roosevelt MSS, Incoming Correspondence, Box 304; Ben Lindsay to Roosevelt, August 1, 1916, Theodore Roosevelt MSS, Incoming Correspondence, Box 305; L. R. Wilfley to Roosevelt, October 16, 1916, Theodore Roosevelt MSS, Incoming Correspondence, Box 312; H. V. O'Brien to William Lee, September 26, 1916, Leonard Wood MSS, Box 92; *New York Sunday Times*, August 13, 1916, I, p. 7; Henry Wise Wood to Roosevelt, October 31, 1916, Theodore Roosevelt MSS, Incoming Correspondence, Box 313.

[11]Harbaugh, "Wilson," p. 232; *Army and Navy Journal* 54 (November 18, 1916): 357; *The New York Times*, November 13, 1916, p. 6; June 5, 1916, p. 5; June 27, 1916, p. 10.

[12]*The New York Times*, May 10, 1916, p. 1; *Washington Post*, October 4, 1915, p. 3; *World's Work* 32 (September 1916): 529-30; A. Fleming Jones to Dr. Haussmann, May 27, 1916, George Van Horn Moseley MSS, Box 39, Scrapbook; *The New York Times*, May 23, 1916, p. 3.

[13]M. M. Macomb to Scott, March 13, 1916, Hugh Scott MSS, Box 22; *The New York Times*, June 19, 1916, p. 1; June 22, 1916, p. 1.

[14]John F. O'Ryan, "The Role of the National Guard," *North American Review* 202 (September 1915): 365-7; U.S. War Department, *Report on the Mobilization of the Organized Militia and National Guard of the United States, 1916* (Washington, D.C.: GPO, 1916), p. 31; Wood to Adjutant General, December 8, 1916, Leonard Wood MSS, Box 88; Rupert Hughes, "The Case of Our National Guard," *Collier's* 57 (May 20, 1916): 7. Coast defense units were not called up.

[15]*The New York Times*, June 22, 1916, p. 6, 3; June 24, 1916, p. 2; June 26, 1916, p. 3.

[16]U.S. Congress, Senate Military Affairs Committee, *Universal Military Training, Hearings before Subcommittee* (64th Congress, 2d Session, Washington, D.C.: GPO, 1917), p. 89; War Department, *National Guard Mobilization Report*, pp. 54, 79; Wood to Adjutant General, December 8, 1916, Leonard Wood MSS, Box 88.

[17]Senate, *Universal Military Training Hearings*, pp. 1079-80; 1022-3; Wood to Adjutant General, December 8, 1916, Leonard Wood MSS, Box 88; "Mobilizing the National Guard, A Lesson in Preparedness," *Current Opinion*

59 (July 1916): 76; Wood to Frank McCoy, July 5, 1916, Leonard Wood MSS, Box 80; Wood to R. L. Bullard, August 31, 1916, Leonard Wood MSS, Box 86.

[18]*The New York Times*, June 24, 1916, p. 7; Scott to U. S. Stewart, June 28, 1916, Hugh Scott MSS, Box 23; Senate, *Universal Military Training Hearings*, p. 904; War Department, *National Guard Mobilization Report*, pp. 53, 104; Chester T. Crowell, "Somewhere in Texas," *The Independent* 87 (August 21, 1916): 271; *The New York Times*, July 4, 1916, p. 4; Scott to James R. Garfield, July 28, 1916, Hugh Scott MSS, Box 24; *The New York Times*, July 18, 1916, p. 4; Wood to Frank McCoy, July 5, 1916, quoted in Hagedorn, *Wood*, p. 191.

[19]*The New York Times*, June 28, 1916, p. 10; Baker to Stimson, June 27, 1916, Newton D. Baker MSS, Letterbooks; Scott to Louis Wiley, July 1, 1916; Scott to James R. Garfield, July 10, 1916, Hugh Scott MSS, Box 24.

[20]Speech to National Education Association, Leonard Wood MSS, Box 90; War Department, *National Guard Mobilization Report*, pp. 95-96; Henry L. Stimson, "Some Reflections Upon Our Military Experiment of 1916," *National Service* 1 (April 1917): 156.

[21]Rupert Hughes, "The Crisis in the National Guard," *Collier's* 58 (December 9, 1916): 34; Frederick Funston to Scott, November 29, 1916, Hugh Scott MSS, Box 25; Thurman Arnold, *Fights Fair and Foul* (New York: Harcourt, Brace & World, 1965), pp. 24-25; War Department, *National Guard Mobilization Report*, p. 97; Bliss to Scott, July 24, 1916; Scott to Frederick Funston, July 29, 1916, Hugh Scott MSS, Box 24.

[22]War Department, *National Guard Mobilization Report*, p. 97; "Report of the Chief of Staff," *War Department Annual Reports, 1916* (Washington, D.C.: GPO, 1916), p. 162; Tumulty to Baker, July 28, 1916, File 2638801, Incl. 140, National Archives, Army Adjutant General's Office, Record Group 94; Senate, *Universal Military Training Hearings* pp. 1143, 986, 769; Wood to Jeffrey Montague, July 4, 1916, Leonard Wood MSS, Box 93; Halstead Dorey to Wood, July 7, 1916, Leonard Wood MSS, Box 87.

[23]*Congressional Record*, 64th Congress, 1st Session, pp. 9970-1; Baker to Wilson, July 7, 1916, Wilson MSS, Series II, Box 138; *Congressional Record*, 64th Congress, 1st Session, pp. 11601, 11620, 11643-4.

[24]*The Outlook* 113 (August 9, 1916): 815; *The New York Times*, March 31, 1916, p. 10; Scott to Robert R. McCormick, March 17, 1916, Hugh Scott MSS, Box 22; *The New York Times*, July 26, 1916, p. 1; Baker to Wilson, October 2, 1916, File 2638801, Incl. 153, National Archives, Army Adjutant General's Office, Record Group 94; Frank McCoy to Wood, July 19, 1916, Leonard Wood MSS, Box 89.

[25]"What Mexico Did for the Militia," *The Literary Digest* 53 (December 16, 1916): 1586; Hughes, "The Crisis in the National Guard," 5-6; Report of the

Executive Committee on the Mayor's Committee on National Defense, *The Mobilization of the National Guard, 1916* (New York, 1917), p. 15; *The Nation* 103 (December 14, 1916): 554; M. C. Rorty to Leonard Wood, September 29, 1916, Leonard Wood MSS, Box 92.

CHAPTER 11

[1] Baker to Wilson, December 23, 1916, Wilson MSS, Series II, Box 144; Scott to Robert Leonard, December 11, 1916, Hugh Scott MSS, Box 26; *The New York Times*, September 10, 1916, p. 16; *The New Republic* 9 (November 25, 1916): 79; *American Review of Reviews* 55 (January 1917): 21.

[2] Rupert Hughes, "The Crisis in the National Guard," *Collier's*, 55 (December 9, 1916): 5; Scott to J. Franklin Bell, July 24, 1916, Hugh Scott MSS, Box 24; *Congressional Record*, 64th Congress, 2d Session, p. 3514; *The New York Times*, August 1, 1916, p. 6; Report of the Mayor's Committee on National Defense, *The Mobilization of the National Guard, 1916* (New York, 1917), p. 19; U.S. Congress, Senate Committee on Military Affairs, *Universal Military Training, Hearings before Subcommittee* (64th Congress, 2d Session, Washington D.C.: GPO, 1917), p. 143.

[3] Senate, *Universal Military Training Hearings*, pp. 549, 128, 752, 401; Baker to Wilson, December 9, 1916, Wilson MSS, Series II, Box 143; "Comment on Congress," *Collier's* 58 (January 20, 1917): 7.

[4] Memorandum for Chief of Staff, December 9, 1916, File 9832-1 National Archives, Army War College Division, Record Group 165.

[5] *The New York Times*, December 19, 1916, p. 1.

[6] New York *World*, December 19, 1916, p. 8; *The New Republic* 9 (December 23, 1916): 199-200; Scott to D. M. Barringer, February 21, 1916, Hugh Scott MSS, Box 21.

[7] House, "Diary," November 15, 1916; November 17, 1916, Edward M. House MSS, Vol. 9; Memorandum for Chief of Staff, December 9, 1916, File 9832-1, National Archives, Army War College Division, Record Group 165.

[8] Scott to R. M. Thomas, August 7, 1916, Hugh Scott MSS, Box 24; *Everybody's Magazine* 36 (January 1917): 121; Senate, *Universal Military Training Hearings*, pp. 718-21; *The Survey* 36 (July 15, 1916): 418; Senate, *Universal Military Training Hearings*, pp. 271, 891-92; Frank L. Martin, *Digest of Proceedings of Council of National Defense During the World War* (73d Congress, 2d Session, Senate Document 193, Washington, D.C.: GPO, 1943), pp. 58-9; Douglas MacArthur to Wood, November 23, 1916, Leonard Wood MSS, Box 91; Scott to U. S. Stewart, January 27, 1916, Hugh Scott MSS, Box

87; "To Make All Our Boys Soldiers," *The Literary Digest* 54 (January 6, 1917): 4; Senate, *Universal Military Training Hearings*, p. 717; V. M. McClatchy to Scott, December 21, 1916, Hugh Scott MSS, Box 26.

⁹Chase C. Mooney and Martha E. Layman, "Some Phases of the Compulsory Training Movement, 1914-1920," *Mississippi Valley Historical Review* 38 (March 1952): 646; "American Virility in Convention Assembled," *The Outlook* 115 (February 7, 1917): 227; S.B.M. Young to Roosevelt, November 13, 1916, Theodore Roosevelt MSS, Incoming Correspondence, Box 313; *Army and Navy Journal* 54 (November 11, 1916): 326.

¹⁰John T. Pratt to Wood, May 4, 1916, Leonard Wood MSS, Box 91; W. D. Washburn to Tumulty, December 19, 1916, Wilson MSS, Series VI, File 1935; illegible to Roosevelt, July 22, 1916, George Perkins MSS, Box 27; *Everybody's Magazine* 33 (November 1915): 634; H. H. Gross to Wood, September 28, 1916, Leonard Wood MSS, Box 92; Moseley, "War Notes," October 22, 1916, George Van Horn Moseley MSS, Box 1; *Universal Military Training League* prospectus, Theodore Roosevelt MSS, Incoming Correspondence, Box 306.

¹¹Moseley to H. H. Gross, June 6, 1916, George Van Horne Moseley MSS, Box 39, Scrapbook; Senate, *Universal Military Training Hearings*, p. 304; Moseley to George Chamberlain, June 19, 1916, quoted in Senate *Universal Military Training Hearings*, pp. 312-3.

¹²H. H. Gross to Moseley, July 13, 1916; John T. Pratt to Moseley, November 27, 1916, George Van Horn Moseley MSS, Box 39, Scrapbook; Edward Harding to Newton D. Baker, January 22, 1917, File 9317-19, National Archives, Army War College Division, Record Group 165; Henry L. Stimson to Scott, December 16, 1916, Hugh Scott MSS, Box 26; *The New York Times*, February 11, 1917, p. 5.

¹³Hugh L. Scott, *Some Memories of a Soldier* (New York: The Century Co., 1928), pp. 557-8; Memorandum for Chief of Staff, February 14, 1917, File 9876-20, (National Archives, Army War College Division, Record Group 165); Scott to Louis Wiley, November 17, 1916, Hugh Scott MSS, Box 25; C. W. Kennedy to Army War College Division, December 12, 1916, File 9876-1, National Archives, Army War College Division, Record Group 165.

¹⁴Scott to Frank McGee, January 24, 1917, Hugh Scott MSS, Box 27; Moseley to Newton D. Baker, December 4, 1916, George Van Horn Moseley MSS, Box 39; Scott to James F. McKinely, January 8, 1917, Hugh Scott MSS, Box 27; Bliss to Scott, January 24, 1917, File 9876-8, National Archives, Army War College Division, Record Group 165; "A National Army," January 27, 1917, File 9876-9, National Archives, Army War College Division, Record Group 165.

¹⁵"A National Army," File 9876-9; William H. Johnston to Secretary, Gen-

eral Staff Corps, January 31, 1917, File 9876-15; Joseph E. Kuhn to Scott, April 6, 1917, File 9317-25; February 1, 1917, File 9876-15; Bliss to Chief of Staff, January 31, 1917, File 9876-13, National Archives, Army War College Division, Record Group 165; *The New York Times*, February 15, 1917, p. 10.

[16]A. C. Shallenberger to Bryan, December 28, 1916, William Jennings Bryan MSS, Box 31; Wood, "Diary," January 20, 1917, Leonard Wood MSS, Vol. 9; Newton D. Baker to Wilson, January 26, 1917, File 2638801, Incl. 71, National Archives, Army Adjutant General's Office, Record Group 94; Moseley to John T. Pratt, October 20, 1916, George Van Horn Moseley MSS, Box 39, Scrapbook.

[17]Baker to Wilson, November 19, 1916, Wilson MSS, Series II, Box 142; Daniel R. Beaver, *Newton D. Baker and the American War Effort, 1917-1919* (Lincoln: University of Nebraska Press, 1966), p. 25; Baker to D. C. Westenhaver, December 15, 1916, Newton D. Baker MSS, Letterbooks; Baker to Wilson, January 26, 1917, File 2638801, Incl. 71, National Archives, Army Adjutant General's Office, Record Group 94.

[18]*The New York Times*, January 26, 1917, p. 1.

[19]"The Warrior at the Lathe," *The Scientific American* 115 (July 15, 1916): 56; Bliss to the Chief of Staff, January 31, 1917, File 9876-13, National Archives, Army War College Division, Record Group 165; Baker to A. R. Horr, June 26, 1916; Baker to D. C. Westenhaver, December 15, 1916, Newton D. Baker MSS, Letterbooks.

CHAPTER 12

[1]Wood, "Diary," February 3, 2, 1917, Leonard Wood MSS, Vol. 9; Arthur S. Link, *Wilson: Campaigns for Progressivism and Peace* (Princeton: Princeton University Press, 1965), p. 289; Edward H. Brooks, "The National Defense Policies of the Wilson Administration, 1913-1917" (Ph.D. dissertation, Stanford University, 1950), p. 234.

[2]*The New York Times*, February 5, 1917, p. 3; February 6, 1917, p. 8.

[3]Baker to Wilson, December 26, 1916, File 2638801, Incl. 70, National Archives, Army Adjutant General's Office, Record Group 94; Franklin K. Lane to George W. Lane, February 16, 1917, Anne W. Lane and Louise H. Wall, eds., *Letters of Franklin K. Lane—Personal and Political* (Boston and New York: Houghton-Mifflin Co., 1922), p. 236; Baker to Wood, February 3, 1917, quoted in Daniel R. Beaver, *Newton D. Baker and the American War Effort, 1917-1919* (Lincoln: University of Nebraska Press, 1966), p. 236; Brooke, "Wilson Defense Policies," p. 225; Beaver, *Baker*, pp. 23-4.

[4]Frederick Palmer, *Newton D. Baker; America at War* (2 vols., New York: Dodd, Mead & Co., 1931), I, p. 62; *The New York Times*, February 11, 1917, p. 5; February 9, 1917, p. 1; February 11, 1917, III, p. 7.

[5]*Congressional Record*, 64th Congress, 2d Session, February 15, 1917, p. 3370; February 16, 1917, p. 3436; *The New York Times*, March 30, 1917, p. 10.

[6]Link, *Wilson, Campaigns*, pp. 290-431.

[7]*The New York Times*, February 11, 1917, III, p. 7; Beaver, *Baker*, p. 27.

[8]Beaver, *Baker*, p. 30.

[9]*The New York Times*, February 11, 1917, II, p. 7; March 23, 1917, p. 1; Ray Stannard Baker and William E. Dodd, eds., *The Public Papers of Woodrow Wilson* (8 vols., New York and London: Harper and Bros., 1925-1927), V, pp. 6-16.

CHAPTER 13

[1]*The New York Times*, March 22, 1917, p. 1; March 18, 1917, I, p. 20; Joseph C. Bernardo and Eugene H. Bacon, *American Military Policy; Its Development Since 1775* (Harrisburg: Military Service Publishing Co., 1955), p. 352; Edward M. Coffman, *The War to End All Wars: The American Military Experience in World War I* (New York: Oxford University Press, 1968), p. 18; Harvey A. DeWeerd, *President Wilson Fights His War: World War I and the American Intervention* (New York: MacMillan Co., 1968), p. 206.

[2]Otto L. Nelson, *National Security and the General Staff* (Washington, D.C.: Infantry Journal Press, 1946), p. 182; Benedict Crowell and Robert F. Wilson, *The Giant Hand* (New Haven: Yale University Press, 1921), p. xvii; Franklin K. Lane to George W. Lane, February 16, 1917, in Anne W. Lane and Louise H. Wall, eds., *Letters of Franklin K. Lane—Personal and Political* (Boston and New York: Houghton-Mifflin Co., 1922), p. 236; Johnson Hagood, *The Services of Supply* (Boston: Houghton-Mifflin Co., 1927), pp. 22-3, 27.

[3]Russell F. Weigley, *History of the United States Army* (New York: MacMillan Co., 1967), pp. 352-3; Hermann Hagedorn, *Leonard Wood: A Biography* (2 vols., New York: Harpers, 1931), II, pp. 152-3; Walter Millis, *Arms and Men: A Study in American Military History* (New York: G. P. Putnam's Sons, 1956), p. 237.

[4]Millis, *Arms and Men*, p. 233.

[5]John J. Pershing, *My Experiences in the World War* (2 vols., New York: Frederick A. Stokes Co., 1931), I, pp. 8-9.

[6]*The New Republic* 7 (June 10, 1916): 152-53. As one historian has noted, "between 1914 and 1917, the advocates of preparedness did more than anyone

else to confuse and cloud the American mind regarding the nation's relations to the war in Europe.'' Jack C. Lane, ''Leonard Wood and the Shaping of American Defense Policy'' (Ph.D. dissertation, University of Georgia, 1963), p. 133. In this connection, it is interesting to note that it was precisely the leading advocates of preparedness—men like Roosevelt, Lodge, Garrison, Brandegee, and Gardner—who fought against the concept of collective security and renounced American collaboration with other powers. As Congressman A. P. Gardner put it: ''I am an American. I want no internationalism. I want no conglomerate flag of all nations, with a yellow streak down the middle. I know what the Star Spangled Banner stands for.'' William Henry Harbaugh, ''Wilson, Roosevelt, and Internationalism'' (Ph.D. dissertation, Northwestern University, 1954), p. 274.

[7]Chase C. Mooney and Martha E. Layman, ''Some Phases of the Compulsory Training Movement, 1914-1920,'' *Mississippi Valley Historical Review* 38 (March 1952): 650-56; Millis, *Arms and Men*, pp. 240-48.

Bibliographical Essay

There is relatively little in the way of secondary literature bearing on the preparedness movement. As a result, the present study has been written largely from unpublished manuscripts, government documents, and the pages of contemporary newspapers and periodicals.

MANUSCRIPTS

The following manuscript collections held by the Library of Congress were consulted in the preparation of this book: the Newton D. Baker MSS, the Tasker H. Bliss MSS, the William E. Borah MSS, the Henry S. Breckinridge Diaries, the William Jennings Bryan MSS, the Albert S. Burleson MSS, the William E. Dodd MSS, the Bradley Fiske Diaries, the James Hay MSS, the Charles Evans Hughes MSS, the George Van Horn Moseley MSS, the Amos Pinchot MSS, the Gifford Pinchot MSS, the Theodore Roosevelt MSS, the Elihu Root MSS, the Hugh Scott MSS, the William Howard Taft MSS, the William Allen White MSS, the Woodrow Wilson MSS, and the Leonard Wood MSS. In addition, use was made of the Edward M. House MSS at Yale University, the Oswald Garrison Villard MSS at Harvard University, the George Haven Putnam and George Perkins MSS at Columbia University, the Warren Worth Bailey MSS at Princeton University, and the files of the American Union Against Militarism at Swarthmore College. The Army Adjutant General's file, Record Group 94, and the Army War College Division File, Record Group 165, at the National Archives, proved particularly valuable. In addition, there was a small amount of useful material in the records of the Army War College sessions, 1914-1915, held by the Office of Military History, Department of the Army.

235

NEWSPAPERS

The New York Times, with its invaluable index and comprehensive coverage, remains the most useful tool. Selective use was made of the New York *World*, *Washington Post*, *Chicago Tribune*, *Cleveland Plain Dealer*, *Detroit Free Press*, Los Angeles *Times*, *San Francisco Chronicle*, and Spokane *Spokesman-Review*. The *New York Call* provided a radical editorial viewpoint, while the *Commercial and Financial Chronicle* demonstrated that even some conservatives could be dubious about military preparations. The *Army and Navy Journal*, a partisan and not-too-reliable trade paper, could be used only with caution for statements of fact.

PERIODICAL LITERATURE

The preparedness movement generated an enormous amount of periodical literature between 1914 and 1917, much of it repetitious and of little value. Some of the most astute observers in the country, however, wrote serious studies of the preparedness movement and analyzed its deeper meaning. Among the best articles on these lines are John Dewey, "Universal Service As Education," *The New Republic* 6 (April 22, 29, 1916), Herbert Croly, "The Effect on American Institutions of a Powerful Military and Naval Establishment," *Annals of the American Academy of Political and Social Science* 66 (July 1916), and Walter Lippmann, "The Issue of 1916," *The New Republic* 7 (June 3, 1916), "Integrated America," *The New Republic* 6 (February 19, 1916). Simeon Strunsky, "Armaments and Caste," *Annals of the American Academy of Political and Social Science* 66 (July 1916), is particularly perceptive. Richard T. Ely, "Progressivism, True and False—An Outline," *Review of Reviews* 51 (February 1915), comes to a different conclusion.

A number of other contemporary articles seem particularly worthwhile. Augustus P. Gardner, "Happy-Go-Lucky Army Laws," *National Service* 1 (April 1917), presents a remarkably fair-minded evaluation of his old opponent James Hay. Rupert Hughes' two articles, "The Case of Our National Guard," *Collier's* 57 (May 20, 1916), and "The Crisis in the National Guard," *Collier's* 58 (December 9, 1916), show graphically the change in public opinion brought about by the Mexican border mobilization. Oswald Garrison Villard, "Preparedness Is Militarism," *Annals of the American Academy of Political and Social Science* 66 (July 1916), states the extreme pacifist case. Charles T. Hallinan, "The New Army Law," *The Survey* 36 (June 17, 1916), demonstrates that parts of the peace movement were capable of sophisticated analysis.

Representative pro-preparedness propaganda includes Bradley A. Fiske, "The Mastery of the World," *North American Review* 202 (October 1915), Eric Fisher Wood, "The Writing on the Wall," *The Century Magazine* 91 (November 1915), Leonard Wood, "Why We Have No Army," *McClure's Magazine* 37 (April 1912), and "Heat up the Melting Pot," *The Independent* 87 (July 3, 1916).

Other articles which proved useful enough to cite were H. M. Allen, "Joseph H. Choate: An Appreciation," *The Outlook* 115 (June 3, 1917), Newton D. Baker, "Our Military Situation," *The Outlook* 113 (July 5, 1916), Arthur Capper, "The West and Preparedness," *The Independent* 85 (January 10, 1916), Howard E. Coffin, "Organizing Industry for National Defense," *World's Work* 32 (May 1916), W. T. Colyer, "The Military Mind," *The Independent* 89 (January 1, 1917), Chester Crowell, "Somewhere in Texas," *The Independent* 87 (August 2, 1916), Samuel Crowther, "The Nourishment of the Pacifists," *The Forum* 56 (July 1916), Frederick M. Davenport, "Preliminary Impressions of the Chicago Conventions," *The Outlook* 113 (June 14, 1916), "The Pre-Nomination Campaign," *The Outlook* 112 (April 26, 1916), Lindley M. Garrison, as interviewed by Gregory Mason, "America Unready," *The Outlook* 58 (December 30, 1914), William Hard, "What About Bryan," *Everybody's Magazine* 34 (April 1916), Gardner L. Harding, "Hay Foot! Straw Foot!," *Everybody's Magazine* 35 (July 1916), Warren G. Harding, "Says Senator Harding—Republican," *Everybody's Magazine* 35 (September 1916), James C. Hemphill, "Mr. Wilson's Cabinet," *North American Review* 202 (July 1915), Virgil Jordan, "How You Can Help Prepare," *Everybody's Magazine* 33 (September 1915), George Marvin, "Scott, U.S.A.," *World's Work* 29 (February 1915), John F. O'Ryan, "The Role of the National Guard," *North American Review* 202 (September 1915), Frederick Palmer, "The War's Lesson to Us," *Collier's* 57 (March 18, 1916), Ralph Barton Perry, "The Vigil of Arms," *The New Republic* 7 (May 27, 1916), Charles Johnson Post, "The Army as A Social Service," *The Survey* 36 (May 20, 1916), Harold T. Pulsifer, "The Security League Conference," *The Outlook* 111 (December 8, 1915), Herbert Quick, "The Average American and the Army," *The Saturday Evening Post* (March 4, 1916), Thomas Robins, "America's Industrial Organization for National Defense," *Scientific American* 115 (July 8, 1919), Henry L. Stimson, "Some Reflections Upon Our Military Experience of 1916," *National Service* 1 (April 1917), Henry Osborne Taylor, "The Pathos of America," *The Atlantic Monthly* 117 (February 1916), and Oswald Garrison Villard, "Our Drift Into Militarism," *The Nation* 103 (August 3, 1916), Supplement.

Contemporary scholars have added to this literature. George C. Herring, Jr., "James Hay and the Preparedness Controversy, 1915-1916," *Journal of Southern History* 30 (November 1964), gives a sympathetic appraisal of one of the controversial figures in the preparedness movement. Chase C. Mooney and Martha E. Layman, "Some Phases of the Compulsory Training Movement, 1914-1920," *Mississippi Valley Historical Review* 38 (March 1952) is especially useful for its account of the post World War I aftermath of preparedness. Alfred Vagts, "Hopes and Fears of an American-German War," II, *Political Science Quarterly* 55 (March 1940), is invaluable. Richard W. Leopold, "The Emergence of America as a World Power; Some Second Thoughts," in John Braeman, Robert H. Bremmer, Everitt Walters, eds., *Change and Continuity in Twentieth Century America* (Columbus: Ohio State University Press, 1965), is a provocative reappraisal. Also useful were Roy Watson Curry, "Woodrow Wilson and Philippine Policy," *Mississippi Valley Historical Review* 41 (December 1954), John P. Finnegan, "Preparedness in Wisconsin: The National Guard on the Mexican Border," *The Wisconsin Magazine of History* (Spring 1964), Fred Greene, "The Military View of American National Policy, 1904-1940," *American Historical Review* 66 (January 1961), Charles Hirschfield, "Nationalist Progressivism and World War I," *Mid-America* 45 (July 1963), Arthur S. Link, "The Middle West and the Coming of World War I," *The Ohio State Archaelogical and Historical Quarterly* 62 (April 1953), William E. Leuchtenberg, "Progressivism and Imperialism: The Progressive Movement and American Foreign Policy, 1898-1916," *Mississippi Valley Historical Review* 39 (December 1952), Ernest R. May, "The Development of Political-Military Consultation in the United States," *Political Science Quarterly* 3 (July 1939), and Daniel M. Smith, "National Interest and American Intervention, 1917: An Historiographical Appraisal," *The Journal of American History*, 52 (June 1965).

GOVERNMENT DOCUMENTS

The U.S. War Department, *War Department Annual Reports* (Washington, D.C.: GPO, 1911-1917) served as an admirable place to begin this study. The War Department's *Report on Mobilization of the Organized Militia and National Guard of the United States, 1916* (Washington, D.C.: GPO, 1916) is a devastating indictment of the militia system in operation. It can be supplemented by the Report of the Executive Committee of the Mayor's Committee on National Defense, *The Mobilization of the National Guard, 1916* (New York, 1917). Three congressional hearings proved particularly useful in developing informative testimony: House Committee on Military Affairs, *Hearings on H. R. 12766, To Increase the Efficiency of the Military Establishment of the United States* (2 vols., 64th Congress, 1st Session, Washington, D.C.: GPO, 1916), House Committee on Naval Affairs, *Hearings on the Naval Appropriations Bill* (63d

Congress 3d Session, Washington D.C.: GPO, 1915), and Senate Committee on Military Affairs, *Universal Military Training, Hearings before Subcommittee* (64th Congress, 2d Session, Washington, D.C.: GPO, 1917). The debates in the *Congressional Record*, 64th Congress, 1st and 2d Sessions, were more enlightening than one might have expected. Use was also made of the following War Department documents: *Mobile Army of the United States: Letter From the Secretary of War in Response to House Resolution No. 343* (62d Congress, 2d Session, Reprinted from House Document No. 490, Washington, D.C.: GPO, 1912); *Report of the Secretary of War on House Resolution 707* (61st Congress, 2d Session, Washington, D.C.: GPO, 1910); *Report on the Organization of the Land Forces of the United States* (Washington D.C.: GPO, 1912); *Study on the Cost of the Army of the United States as Compared with the Cost of the Armies of Other Nations* (WCD-9053-120, Washington, D.C.: GPO, 1916); *Study on Educational Institutions Giving Military Training as a Source For a Supply of Officers for a National Army* (WCD-9053-121, Washington, D.C.: GPO, 1916). Other congressional documents used included House Committee on Military Affairs, *Militia Pay Bill: Views of the Minority* (62d Congress, 3d Session, Report 1117, pt. 2, Washington, D.C.: GPO, 1912); House Committee on Military Affairs, *Relief of the Adjutant General* (62d Congress, 2d Session, Report No. 508, Washington, D.C.: GPO, 1912); House Special Committee to Investigate the National Security League, *Hearings* (65th Congress, 3d Session, Washington, D.C.: GPO, 1918); Senate Committee on Military Affairs, *Hearings on Army Appropriations Bill, H. R. 18956* (62d Congress, 2d Session, Washington, D.C.: GPO, 1912); Henry L. Stimson, et al., "What Is the Matter with Our Army," *Senate Document* 38 (Document 621, 62d Congress, 2d Session, Washington, D.C.: GPO, 1912).

PUBLISHED LETTERS

The two most important compilations of letters for the purpose of this book were Ray Stannard Baker and William E. Dodd, eds., *The Public Papers of Woodrow Wilson* (8 vols., New York and London: Harper & Bros., 1925-1927), and Charles Seymour, ed., *The Intimate Papers of Colonel House* (Boston and New York: Houghton-Mifflin Co., 1926-1928). E. David Cronon, ed., *The Cabinet Diaries of Josephus Daniels, 1913-1921* (Lincoln: University of Nebraska Press, 1963), contains some useful material, as does Anne W. Lane and Louise W. Wall, eds., *Letters of Franklin K. Lane—Personal and Political* (Boston and New York: Houghton-Mifflin Co., 1922). Use was also made of Elliot Roosevelt, ed., *FDR: His Personal Letters* (4 vols., New York: Duell,

Sloan and Pierce, 1947-1950), and Constance Gardner, ed., *Some Letters of Augustus Peabody Gardner* (New York: Houghton-Mifflin Co., 1922).

MEMOIRS

The memoirs of the less than great during this period are the most revealing. Robert L. Bullard, *Personalities and Reminiscences of the War* (New York: Doubleday and Co., 1925) has some incisive comments, as does Johnson Hagood, *The Service of Supply* (Boston: Houghton-Mifflin Co., 1927). The books written by Cabinet members are less rewarding. Josephus Daniels, *The Wilson Era* (2 vols., Chapel Hill: University of North Carolina Press, 1944-1946) was written long after the events it describes. David F. Houston, *Eight Years with Wilson's Cabinet, 1913-1920* (2 vols., New York: Doubleday, Page & Co., 1926), is ponderous and padded, although it does contain the complete text of the exchange between Wilson and Lindley Garrison which led to the latter's resignation. There is not much on preparedness in Robert Lansing, *War Memoirs of Robert Lansing* (Indianapolis: Bobbs-Merrill, 1935), or in William Gibbs McAdoo, *Crowded Years* (Boston and New York: Houghton-Mifflin Co., 1931). Books by the principal generals are not much better. Peyton C. March, *The Nation at War* (New York: Doubleday, Doran, 1932) says little on the subject. John J. Pershing, *My Experiences in the World War* (2 vols., New York: Frederick A. Stokes Co., 1931) and Hugh L. Scott, *Some Memories of a Soldier* (New York: Appleton Century Co., 1928), fail to put the preparedness movement in context. Joseph P. Tumulty, *Woodrow Wilson as I Knew Him* (Garden City: Doubleday, Page & Co., 1921), contains some useful material on the political side of the Wilson administration, despite its adulatory tone. Oswald Garrison Villard's *Fighting Years: Memoirs of a Liberal Editor* (New York: Harcourt Brace & Co., 1930) gives a little information on the opposition to preparedness. Minor but amusing vignettes of incidents in the preparedness movement are provided by Thurman Arnold, *Fair Fights and Foul* (New York: Harcourt, Brace and World, 1965) and by Max Eastman, *Enjoyment of Living* (New York: Harper & Bros., 1948).

BIOGRAPHY

Good biographies exist of many of the major participants in the preparedness movement, but few have very much to say about the defense movement itself. Arthur S. Link, *Wilson* (5 vols., Princeton: Princeton University Press,

1947-1965) is magisterial, but Ray Stannard Baker, *Woodrow Wilson: Life and Letters* (Garden City: Doubleday, Doran & Co., 1927-1939) is still useful. James Kerney, *The Political Education of Woodrow Wilson* (New York and London: The Century Co., 1926) and David Lawrence, *The True Story of Woodrow Wilson* (New York: George H. Doran Co., 1924), contain helpful details. Theodore Roosevelt has been handsomely served in William Henry Harbaugh, *Power and Responsibility: The Life and Times of Theodore Roosevelt* (New York: Farrar, Straus and Cudahy, 1961). Howard K. Beale, *Theodore Roosevelt and the Rise of America to World Power* (Baltimore: Johns Hopkins Press, 1956), John M. Blum, *The Republican Roosevelt* (Cambridge: Harvard University Press, 1954), and Henry Pringle, *Theodore Roosevelt: A Biography* (New York: Harcourt, Brace & Co., 1931), offer different approaches. Pringle gives a sympathetic treatment to another president in *The Life and Times of William Howard Taft* (2 vols., Hamden, Conn.: Anchor Books, 1964).

At the Cabinet level, Elting E. Morison has provided a fine portrait in *Turmoil and Tradition: A Study of the Life and Times of Henry L. Stimson* (Boston: Houghton-Mifflin Co., 1960). Frederick Palmer, *Newton D. Baker, America at War* (2 vols., New York: Dodd, Mead & Co., 1931) can now be supplemented with Daniel R. Beaver, *Newton D. Baker and the American War Effort, 1917-1919* (Lincoln: University of Nebraska Press, 1966). No published biography of Lindley M. Garrison exists. E. David Cronon is at work on a multivolume biography of Josephus Daniels. Frank Freidel has given an account of the assistant secretary of the navy in *Franklin D. Roosevelt* (3 vols., Boston: Little, Brown and Co., 1952). The best biography of Leonard Wood is Hermann Hagedorn's rather hagiographical *Leonard Wood: A Biography* (2 vols., New York: Harper, 1931). There is also some information in Herbert W. Hobbs' campaign biography, *Leonard Wood: Administrator, Soldier and Citizen* (New York: G. P. Putnam's Sons, 1920). Frederick Palmer has written a sprightly journalistic study in *Bliss, Peacemaker* (New York: Dodd, Mead & Co., 1934). David A. Lockmiller's *Enoch H. Crowder: Soldier, Lawyer and Statesman* (Columbia University of Missouri Press, 1955) is less helpful on preparedness than one might have thought. Mabel E. Deutrich's *Struggle for Supremacy: The Career of General Fred C. Ainsworth* (Washington, D.C., 1962), has flaws but brings in interesting material. John A. Garraty has written a fine biography of a preparedness spokesman in Congress in *Henry Cabot Lodge* (New York: Alfred A. Knopf, 1953). Alex M. Arnett has written a less trustworthy account of a leader of the congressional opposition in *Claude Kitchin and the Wilson War Policies* (Boston: Little Brown, 1937). Belle LaFollette and Fola LaFollette, *Robert M. LaFollette* (2 vols., New York: MacMillan Co., 1953), is better than the usual family account.

Other biographies used in this study are James Scott Brown, *Robert Bacon: Life and Letters* (Garden City: Doubleday, Page & Co., 1923), which gives some revealing insights; Edwin R. Lewinson, *John Purroy Mitchel, The Boy Mayor of New York* (New York: Astra, 1965), Burton J. Hendricks, *The Life and Letters of Walter Hines Page* (3 vols., Garden City: Doubleday, Page & Co., 1922-1925), Martin Mayer, *Emory Buckner* (New York: Harper & Rowe, 1968), Stephen E. Anbrose, *Upton and the Army* (Baton Rouge: Louisiana State University Press, 1964), Elting E. Morison, *Admiral Sims and the Modern American Navy* (Boston: Houghton-Mifflin Co., 1942), Allan Nevins and Frank Ernest Hill, *Ford* (3 vols., New York: Charles Scribner's Sons, 1954-1957), and Michael Wresgin, *Oswald Garrison Villard: Pacifist at War* (Bloomington: Indiana University Press, 1965).

GENERAL WORKS AND MONOGRAPHS

The best overall survey of American defense policy is still Walter Millis, *Arms and Men: A Study in American Military History* (New York: G. P. Putnam's Sons, 1956). It is particularly valuable on the preparedness movement. Useful background material is also provided in Robert E. Osgood, *Ideals and Self-Interest in America's Foreign Relations* (Chicago: The University of Chicago Press, 1953) and in Arthur S. Link, *Woodrow Wilson and the Progressive Movement* (New York: Harper, 1954). A book that should not be neglected in this connection is John A. S. Grenville and George B. Young, *Politics, Strategy, and American Diplomacy; Studies in Foreign Policy 1873-1917* (New Haven: Yale University Press, 1966).

There are a number of useful accounts, touching upon various aspects of American military policy during the period. Russell F. Weigley, *History of the United States Army* (New York: MacMillan Co., 1967), is outstanding, as is the same author's *Towards an American Army: Military Thought from Washington to Marshall* (New York: Columbia University Press, 1962). See also Joseph C. Bernard and Eugene H. Bacon, *American Military Policy; Its Development Since 1775* (Harrisburg: Military Service Publishing Co., 1955), Stanley Ekirch, *The Civilian and the Military* (New York: Oxford University Press, 1956), William R. Kintner and George C. Reinhardt, *The Haphazard Years* (Garden City: Doubleday & Co., 1960), Samuel P. Huntington, *The Soldier and the State: The Theory and Politics of Civil-Military Relations* (Cambridge: Belknap Press, 1957), Otto L. Nelson, *National Security and the General Staff* (Washington, D.C.: Infantry Journal Press, 1946), John M. Palmer, *America in Arms* (New Haven: Yale University Press, 1941), and William H. Ricker, *Soldiers of the*

State (Washington, D.C.: Public Affairs Press, 1957). Alfred Vagts, *Landing Operations* (Harrisburg: Military Service Publishing Co., 1946) helps show the artificiality of the invasion scares of the period. Harold and Margaret Sprout, *The Rise of American Naval Power, 1776-1918* (Princeton: Princeton University Press, 1939), is still practically definitive for its subject.

Armin Rappaport, *The Navy League of the United States* (Detroit: Wayne State University Press, 1962) and Martha Derthick, *The National Guard in Politics* (Cambridge: Harvard University Press, 1963), are worthwhile monographs on two of the most powerful defense lobbies. Another lobby found its own contemporary chronicler. Ralph Barton Perry was an enthusiastic participant in the Military Training Camp Association, and his book *The Plattsburg Movement* (New York: E. P. Dutton & Co., 1921) is still a good account. Perry's book, *The Free Man and the Soldier* (New York: Charles Scribner's Sons, 1916), gives a revealing insight into the psychology behind the movement. Francis Russell, *The Great Interlude* (New York: McGraw-Hill, 1964) provides local color. *The Roster of Attendants at Federal Military Training Camps, 1913-1916* (New York: Military Training Camp Association of U. S., 1916) satisfactorily demonstrates the social background of the enrollees. John Garry Clifford has written an authoritative and scholarly monograph on this whole topic in *The Citizen Soldiers: The Plattsburg Training Camp Movement, 1913-1920* (Lexington: University of Kentucky Press, 1972).

There are a number of regrettably dull monographs on aspects of industrial mobilization in World War I which throw some light on prewar developments. These include Benedict Crowell and Robert Wilson, *The Giant Hand* (New Haven: Yale University Press, 1921), Grosvenor B. Clarkson, *Industrial America in the World War* (Boston and New York: Houghton-Mifflin Co., 1923), Frank L. Martin, *Digest of Proceedings of Council of National Defense During the World War* (73d Congress, 2d Session, Senate Document 193, Washington, D.C.: GPO, 1943), and Lloyd N. Scott, *Naval Consulting Board of the United States* (Washington, D.C.: GPO 1936).

Two excellent new histories discuss America's military condition at the outbreak of World War I: Edward M. Coffman, *The War to End All Wars: The American Military Experience in World War I* (New York: Oxford University Press, 1968), and Henry A. DeWeerd, *President Wilson Fights His War: World War I and the American Intervention* (New York: Macmillan Co., 1968). My study also made use of Frederick Palmer, *Our Gallant Madness* (Garden City: Doubleday, Doran & Co., 1937), and Gerard L. McEntee, *Military History of the World War* (New York: Charles Scribner's Sons, 1937).

Social aspects of the preparedness movement were touched on in two general surveys: Frederic L. Paxson, *American Democracy and the World War: Pre-War*

Years: 1913-1917 (Boston: Houghton-Mifflin Co., 1936) and Mark Sullivan, *Our Times: The United States, 1900-1925* (6 vols., New York: Charles Scribner's Sons, 1926-1935). Henry Watterson, *The History of the Manhattan Club* (New York, 1915), also fills in a few useful details.

On the various groups opposed to preparedness, a number of monographs were helpful. Among them were Carl Wittke, *German Americans and the World War; Ohio Historical Collections* 5 (Columbus: Ohio State Archaelogical and Historical Society, 1936), David A. Shannon, *The Socialist Party of America* (New York: MacMillan Co., 1955), Donald Johnson, *The Challenge to American Freedoms* (Lexington: University of Kentucky Press, 1963), and Merle Curti, *Peace or War* (New York: W. W. Norton Co., 1935).

The preparedness movement produced a snowstorm of print, largely repetitions. Suitable examples can be found in Hudson Maxim, ed., *Leading Opinions Both For and Against National Defense* (New York: Hearst International Library, 1916). Hudson Maxim, *Defenseless America* (New York: Hearst International Library, 1919), was a sensationalist argument for preparedness; Frederic Louis Huidekoper, *The Military Unpreparedness of the United States* (New York: Macmillan Co., 1915), was a more restrained one. The Socialist pamphleteer and presidential candidate Allan L. Beason attempted a rebuttal in *Inviting War to America* (New York: B. W. Huebsch, 1916).

UNPUBLISHED

W. W. Tinsley, "The American Preparedness Movement, 1913-1916" (Ph.D. dissertation, Stanford University, 1940), was the first monographic study of the defense movement; its usefulness is sharply limited by the fact that it was written largely from newspaper sources. William Henry Harbaugh, "Wilson, Roosevelt, and Interventionism" (Ph.D. dissertation, Northwestern University, 1954), is a model of perceptiveness and good writing. Timothy G. McDonald, "Southern Democratic Congressmen and the First World War, August 1914-April 1917: The Public Record of Their Support For or Opposition to Wilson's Policies" (Ph.D. dissertation, University of Washington, 1962) has some useful breakdowns of congressional voting. George C. Herring, Jr., "Lindley M. Garrison and the Preparedness Movement" (M.A. thesis, University of Virginia, 1961), is a helpful study. John P. Finnegan, "The Preparedness Movement in Wisconsin, 1914-1917" (M.A. thesis, University of Wisconsin, 1961), is a local analysis.

Use was also made of Edward H. Brooks, "The National Defense Policy of the Wilson Administration, 1913-1917" (Ph.D. dissertation, Stanford University,

1950), John Milton Cooper, Jr., "The Vanity of Power: American Isolationism and the First World War, 1914-1917" (Ph.D. dissertation, Columbia University, 1968), Barton C. Hacker, "The War Department and the General Staff, 1898-1917" (M.A. thesis, University of Chicago, 1962), Homer L. Ingle, "Pilgrimage to Reform: A Life of Claude Kitchin" (Ph.D. dissertation, University of Wisconsin, 1967), Jack C. Lane, "Leonard Wood and the Shaping of American Defense Policy, 1900-1920" (Ph.D. dissertation, University of Georgia, 1963), and William Y. Smith, "The Search for National Security Planning Machinery, 1900-1947" (Ph.D. dissertation, Harvard University, 1960).

Index

Abbott, Lawrence, 58
Addams, Jane, 130, 131
Aero Club, 99-100, 102
Ainsworth, Fred C., 15-16, 46, 85, 141
American College of Surgeons, 119
American Defense Society, 95, 97, 99, 101
American Federation of Labor, 125
American Institute of Engineers, 100
American League to Limit Armaments, 76, 130-131
American Legion, 59-60, 100, 101, 104, 165
American Revolution, 7
American Society of Aeronautical Engineers, 100
American Society of Civil Engineers, 60
American Union Against Militarism, 131, 132-136, 153, 157, 163
American Women's League for Self-Defense, 103
Americanism, 108, 159, 160

Anti-Enlistment League, 131
Anti-Militarism Committee, 131
Anti-Preparedness Committee, 131-134
Arabic (steamship), 76
Army, U.S.
General Staff, 4, 11, 12, 15, 16, 17, 34, 35, 36, 42-56, 57, 74, 84, 102, 113, 129, 140, 154, 155, 175, 176, 177, 180, 181, 183, 190, 191, 192, 194
Medical Reserve Corps, 119
Ordnance Corps, 120
professionalism in the, 8
reform movement, 5-56
Service Corps, 16
War College Division, 43-44, 47-50, 51, 55, 56
Army Appropriations Act (1912), 16
Army League, 20, 96, 97, 101
Army War College, 10
Association for National Service, 102, 178, 179
Automobile Club, 100

247

Bacon, Robert, 70, 101, 159, 164, 178
Bailey, Warren Worth, 123, 128, 136, 137, 163
Baker, Newton D., 106, 113, 114, 115, 118, 119, 120, 140-142, 147, 149, 161, 168, 170, 174, 180, 181, 182, 184, 185, 187, 188
Baruch, Bernard, 31, 32, 63, 118
"Battle Cry of Peace, The" (film), 96
Baxter, George, 99
Beckham, J.C.W., 152
Belgian Relief Commission, 103
Bell, J. Franklin, 174
Benedict, Crystal Eastman, 132
Benson, Allan, 127, 132
Benson, William S., 38
Berger, Victor, 127
Biddle, A. V. Drexel, 102
Blackton, J. Stuart, 96
Blease, Cole, 166
Bliss, Tasker H., 42, 45, 46, 55, 56, 82, 142, 169, 181, 182
Borah, William, 111, 162
Brandegee, Frank, 149, 150
Breckinridge, Henry S., 26, 29, 45, 53, 56, 71, 74-75, 78, 90, 111
Brent, C. H., 67
Brewster, William F., 98
Bryan, William Jennings, 26, 37, 74, 79, 90, 121, 128, 129, 135, 181, 192
Buchanan, Frank, 128, 164
Burleson, Albert S., 74, 82, 141
Butler, Nicholas Murray, 22, 27, 130

Callaway, Oscar, 129, 133, 164
Cannon, Joseph, 24, 139
Capelle, Eduard von, 184
Carnegie Endowment for International Peace, 8

Catt, Carrie Chapman, 131
Chamberlain, George, 34, 37, 42, 43, 78, 82, 86, 112-113, 145-148, 152, 156, 165, 170, 179-180, 181, 183
Chilton, William E., 76
Choate, Joseph, 92, 98
Church, W. C., 32, 58
Civil War, 7
Clark, Champ, 140, 152
Clark, Grenville, 64, 67, 70, 71, 147
Clarke Amendment, 89
Cleveland Chamber of Commerce, 116
Coast Artillery Corps, 35, 43
Coffin, Howard, 116, 117, 118
Committee of One Hundred, 64-65
Conference Committee on Preparedness, 100
Congress of Constructive Patriotism, 178
Coudert, Frederic L., 98
Council of Executive Information, 156
Council for Industrial Preparedness, 118
Council of National Defense, 18, 27, 146, 161, 185, 188
Crago, Thomas S., 186
Crampton, Henry, 117, 119
Croly, Herbert, 107, 108, 114
Crowder, Enoch, 46, 52, 54, 63, 81, 141, 146
Crowles, W. H., 77
Culbertson, Will, 110
Cummins, Albert, 128
Curtis, Charles G., 178
Curtiss Aircraft Company, 103

Daniels, Josephus, 26, 29, 33, 37, 40, 75, 76, 95, 100, 105, 115, 118, 162, 163, 185

Davenport, Frederick M., 106
Davis, "Cyclone," 164
Davis, Richard Harding, 65-66
Day, James R., 71
Debs, Eugene, 126
Defense Act (1916), 4
Defense Advisory Council, 177, 186
Defenseless America (Maxim), 94, 96
Democracy, 110-111, 188
Dent, S. Hubert, 152, 186
Derby, Lloyd, 70
Dick Act (1903), 10, 13, 174
Dixon, Thomas, 76, 96
Drinker, Henry S., 62, 65, 69, 70
DuPont, T. Coleman, 122

Eastman, Max, 132, 134
Edison, Thomas, 93, 115
Ely, Richard T., 110
Endicott Board, 44
Epitome of Military Policy, 47-48, 51

"Fall of a Nation, The" (film), 96
Fiske, Bradley A., 26, 95, 115, 186
Ford, Henry, 131-134, 135, 153
Foster, J.F.C., 147
Franz Ferdinand, Archduke, 21
Frick, Henry Clay, 102
Funston, Frederick, 142

Gallinger, Jacob, 81
Gard, Warren, 144
Gardner, A. P., 22, 24, 25, 26, 27, 28, 32, 34-36, 127, 143, 144, 156
Garrison, Lindley M., 19, 26, 29-30, 32, 33, 34, 36, 51-55, 59-60, 71, 74-78, 81-86, 89-90, 101, 109, 119, 144, 155
  resignation of, 139-141

Gary, Elbert, 102
German-Americans, 125-127, 133, 160
Ghent, W. J., 127
Gifford, Walter S., 116, 161
Gillis, Martin, 116
Godfrey, Hollis, 117, 119
Gompers, Samuel, 107, 125, 177
Gordon, William, 136
Green, Francis Vinton, 98
Green, William, 125
Greer, David, 60, 130
Gregory, Thomas W., 141
Gross, Howard H., 178

Hallinan, Charles T., 132, 133, 134
Hammond, John Hays, Jr., 102
Harding, Warren, 158, 160, 194
Hardwick, Thomas, 150, 151, 155
Harvard University, 61
Harvey, George, 58
Hausmann, J. E., 59
Hay, James, 16, 33, 47, 74-75, 77, 78, 79, 82-86, 88-89, 137, 141-145, 151-155, 164
Hay Act, 165, 166, 171, 174
Hayden, Carl, 145
"Henry Street Group," 130, 131
Hensley Resolution, 163
Herbert, Victor, 96
Hibben, J. G., 62
Higgins, Anne, 104
Hillquit, Morris, 127
Hobson, Richmond P., 37
Hoffman, Arthur S., 59, 104
Holmes, John Haynes, 131-132
Holt, Hamilton, 130
House, Edward M., 26, 28, 39, 74, 108, 118, 119, 134, 140, 149, 163, 173, 176-177

House Military Affairs Committee, 16, 33, 34, 35, 74, 82, 83, 85, 88, 89, 90, 124, 141, 143-144, 147, 165, 181, 186
Houston v. Moore, 141
Howard, Roy, 107
Hughes, Charles Evans, 159, 164, 174
Huidekoper, Frederick L., 20, 94-95

Industrial mobilization, 114-120, 161
Institute of Radio Engineers, 100
Intercollegiate Socialist Society, 127
International Order of Military Women, 104
Isolationism, 22

Jay, DeLancey, 70
Jefferson, Thomas, 128
Johnston, Gordon, 59-60
Johnston, W. H., 51, 143
Joint Army-Navy Board, 6
Jones, Wesley, 139, 149
Jordan, David Starr, 127, 136
Joy, Henry, 97
Jutland, Battle of, 162

Kahn, Julius, 143-144, 145, 152
Kahn, Otto, 181
Kean, Jefferson R., 119
Keating, Fred, 128, 136
Kelley, Mrs. Florence, 131
Kellogg, Paul, 130, 131
Kern, John, 77
Kitchin, Claude, 77, 80-81, 88, 122, 128, 140, 164
Kuhn, Joseph, 181

LaFollette, Robert, 91, 124, 128
Lane, Franklin K., 36, 113
Lansing, Robert, 40, 149

League to Enforce Peace, 97, 130
Lee, Blair, 170
Lewisohn, Alice, 132
Liggett, Hunter, 9
Lindsay, Ben, 164
Lippmann, Walter, 106-107, 189, 192
Lochner, Louis, 131
Lodge, Henry Cabot, 24, 25, 29, 30, 86, 148, 159
London, Meyer, 128, 138, 145, 152
Lowell, Abbott Lawrence, 61
Lusitania, 3, 37, 38, 40, 46, 62, 63, 64, 130, 151

MacArthur, Douglas, 143, 177
Macomb, Montgomery M., 44, 47, 56
Madero, Francisco, 19
Mahan, Alfred Thayer, 8
Malone, Dudley Field, 69
Manhattan Club, 79, 108
Mann, James, 33-34, 81, 83, 87, 143, 152, 153, 156
Marine Corps, 43
Martin, Glenn L., Aircraft Company, 103
Maryland League of National Defense, 182
Maryland State Penitentiary, 102
Maxim, Hudson, 94, 96
Maxim Munitions Corporation, 94
McAdoo, William, 120, 141
McCormick, Robert R., 93
McCumber, Porter J., 149
McKellar, Kenneth, 93
McMillen, Emerson, 103
Menken, S. Stanwood, 26-27, 97-98, 100, 101
Mexican Revolution, 13, 19, 141-142, 165-171, 174-175
Milbank, J. Hungerford, 103-104
Military training, 61-68, 72, 77,

84, 101, 102, 103-104, 109-114, 120, 146-147, 156, 160, 175-176, 177-183, 186-187, 188, 194
Military Training Camp Association, 70-71, 97, 147, 170, 178
Military Training Commission, 113
Military Unpreparedness of the United States, The (Huidekoper), 94-95
Millis, Walter, 3, 191
Mitchel, John Purroy, 97, 98, 102
Mondell, Walter, 123
Monroe Doctrine, 24, 146, 192
Morgan, J. P., 178
Morgan interests, 123
Moseley, George Van Horn, 179, 181-182
Movement for National Preparedness, 103
Myers, George Hewitt, 101

National Academy of Science, 118
National Aero Fund, 103
National Civic Federation, 27, 125
National Defense Act (1916), 155-156, 159, 160, 174, 175, 180, 185, 190
National Educational Association, 177
National Guard, 46, 48, 53, 54, 61, 77-78, 79, 82, 83-84, 86, 88, 102, 103, 129, 138, 141, 145, 147-148, 150, 155, 159, 165-172, 174-175, 177, 182, 185, 189
National Guard Association, 77-78
National Protective Society, 101
National Research Council, 118
National School Camp Association, 104
National Security League, 27, 31-32, 38, 81, 96-102, 103, 143, 178, 179
National Woman's Special Aid Society, 103
Naval Consulting Board, 115-117
Navy, U.S., 6, 7, 18, 20, 24, 26, 28, 32, 33, 39, 43, 50, 51, 76-77, 103, 114, 115-116, 122, 160, 161-163, 179, 189-190, 194
General Board, 37, 40, 77
Navy League, 20, 32, 38, 95, 96, 97, 100, 101, 103, 134, 164
New Nationalism, 17, 67, 109, 115, 120
New York Mayor's Committee on National Defense, 171, 174
Nolan, Dennis, 49, 50
Norris, George, 91
Norwich College (Vermont), 61

O'Hara, John, 67
Organized Militia, 6, 10, 13, 18, 44, 53, 74, 86
O'Ryan, John F., 83, 113, 148, 171, 173, 175

Padgett, Lemuel, 163
Page, Thomas Nelson, 36
Palmer, Frederick, 110, 111
Palmer, John M., 17
Parker, Alton B., 32, 92, 98, 99
Parker, James, 59
Parsons, Barclay, 60
Patriot Film Corporation, 96
Peace Insurance (Stockton), 94
Peary, Robert, 102
Pepper, George Wharton, 71, 112
Perkins, George, 114, 178
Perry, Ralph Barton, 111
Pershing, John J., 142, 165, 191, 194
Phelps, William Lyon, 107
Philippines, 89

Pinchot, Amos, 107, 123, 134
Plan Green, 6
Plattsburg Movement, 103, 161, 191
Plattsburg training corp, 65-72
Polk, Frank, 177
Post, Charles Johnson, 136
Pratt, John T., 178
Preparedness parades, 104-105
Princeton University, 61
Progressive Movement, 3, 9-10, 13, 16, 17, 20, 31, 109, 110, 192
Progressive party, 17, 25, 29, 99, 160, 162, 164
Putnam, George Haven, 27, 97, 100

Quakers, 132
Quick, Herbert, 136
Quin, Percy E., 121, 129

Red Cross, 100, 103, 119
Reed, James, 150
Reed, John, 133-134
Report on the Organization of the Land Forces (1912), 18-19, 34, 42, 43, 44, 47, 48
Reserve Officers Training Corps, 144
Revenue Act (1916), 137
Robins, Thomas, 101
Rogers, H. H., 32
Roosevelt, Franklin D., 26, 37, 72, 161
Roosevelt, Philip, 100
Roosevelt, Theodore, 3, 11, 17, 24-25, 26, 29, 30, 31, 38, 58, 60, 63, 64, 67, 69-70, 71, 72, 77, 80, 84, 92, 97, 99, 100-101, 107, 108-112, 114-115, 120, 126, 133, 149, 151-152, 158, 159, 160, 161, 164, 188, 194
Roosevelt, Theodore, Jr., 64

Root, Elihu, 10-11, 12, 119
Root, Elihu, Jr., 64
Rosenwald, Julius, 110
Rough Riders, 11
Russell, Charles Edward, 127

Sadler, William F., 77, 78
Sanford, Rollin B., 119
Scott, Hugh L., 45-47, 55, 56, 59, 64, 85, 90, 107, 109, 140, 142, 167, 169, 173, 175-176, 177, 180, 181
Sedgwick, Ellery, 110
Selective Service, 188
Senate Military Affairs Committee, 145, 176, 180
Sherman, Lawrence, 150
Sherrill, Charles Hitchcock, 105
Shirley, Swagar, 35, 57
Sinclair, Upton, 127
Slater Act, 113
Slocum, J. J., 63
Smith, Hoke, 149, 150, 151
Socialist party, 126-128
Society for Constructive Defense, 136
Society of the National Reserve Corps of the United States, 62
Spanish-American War, 10, 11
Statement of a Proper Military Policy, 55, 146
Stimson, Henry L., 5, 11-14, 16-18, 19, 32, 98, 107, 130, 141, 144, 148, 159, 168
Stockton, Richard, Jr., 94
Strunsky, Simeon, 92
Sussex crisis, 105, 148

Taft, William Howard, 14, 16, 17, 28, 29, 45, 69, 76, 86, 92, 101, 114, 185, 187
Taft Administration, 8, 12, 187
Tavenner, Clyde, 122, 133, 134, 137, 164

Taylor, Henry Osborne, 107
Thompson, C. S., 99
Thompson, De Lloyd, 104
Tumulty, Joseph, 39, 73-74, 76, 77, 78, 86, 153, 160

Underwood, Oscar, 33, 150
Union League, 79, 84, 159, 178
U.S. Chamber of Commerce, 92, 102, 110, 117, 177
Universal military training, *see* Military training
Universal Military Training League, 178-179, 182
Untermeyer, Samuel, 132
Upton, Emory, 54, 194

Vanderbilt, Cornelius, 98
Vandercook-Browne, Mrs. E., 103
Vardaman, James K., 128
Villa, Pancho, 141, 175
Villard, Oswald Garrison, 30, 58, 76, 121, 122, 123, 130, 131, 133, 134
Virginia Military Institute, 61
Vitagraph Company, 96

Wald, Lillian, 130, 131, 132, 134
Walker, J. Bernard, 32
Walsh, David, 113
Wanamaker, John, 98
War Department, U.S., 6, 13, 16, 30, 34, 35, 42, 43, 45-47, 53-56, 57, 58, 59-62, 65, 71, 74, 75, 79, 81-84, 88, 89, 90, 109, 120, 140, 141, 143-144, 146, 148, 149, 155, 166-171, 177, 185, 188, 190
War of 1812, 54
Warren, Senator, 152
Washington, George, 7
Watterson, Henry, 79
"We Boys" ring, 99
Weeks, John W., 119
Welsh Act, 113

White, John P., 125
White, William Allen, 92
Whitman, Charles, 98
Williams, John Sharp, 150
Wilson, Woodrow, 5, 6, 17, 19, 25, 27-28, 30, 32, 34, 36, 37, 39-41, 42, 43, 46, 52, 54-56, 59, 62, 64, 65, 69, 70, 73-81, 83, 85-90, 98, 100, 108, 114, 116, 118, 130, 132-135, 140-145, 150, 151-156, 159-165, 175, 176-177, 182, 185, 188, 192-194
Wilson Administration, 3, 4, 8, 25-26, 27, 29, 32, 33, 34, 36, 37-40, 68, 69, 71, 72, 76-78, 90, 93, 98-101, 105, 108, 113, 115, 134, 141, 156, 160-165, 177, 184-185, 187, 193-194
Wise, Stephen, 132, 133, 134, 135
Woman's Preparedness Camp (Chevy Chase, Maryland), 103
Women, preparedness movement and, 103-104
Women's Peace party, 131
Wood, Fisher, 95
Wood, Henry Wise, 100, 164
Wood, L. Hollingsworth, 130, 131, 136
Wood, Leonard, 5, 9, 11-20, 26, 30, 36, 43, 47, 51, 57-72, 82, 84, 95, 101, 109, 111, 114, 117, 118, 144, 148, 155, 158, 159, 161, 167-172, 174, 177, 179, 184, 185, 189, 190, 192, 194
Works, John D., 93, 128-129
World War I
  outbreak of, 21, 22
  U.S. participation in, 184-195
Wotherspoon, W. W., 20, 29, 43, 45, 51

Yale University, 61
Young, S.B.M., 178

Zimmermann telegram, 187

About the Author

John Patrick Finnegan received his doctorate in American history from the University of Wisconsin. He has taught at Ohio University, the University of Maryland, and, most recently, at Chicago State University.